THE NEW NATION

1800–1845

THE NEW NATION
1800-1845

REVISED EDITION

John Mayfield

THE MAKING  OF AMERICA

General Editor: David Herbert Donald

AMERICAN CENTURY SERIES

 HILL and WANG · New York

A division of Farrar, Straus, and Giroux

To my mother and father

Copyright © 1961 by Charles M. Wiltse
Copyright © 1982 by John Mayfield
Foreword copyright © 1982 by David Herbert Donald
All rights reserved
Printed in the United States of America
Published simultaneously in Canada by
McGraw-Hill Ryerson Ltd., Toronto
First edition, 1961
Revised edition, 1982
Designed by Nancy Dale Muldoon
Fourth printing, 1987
Library of Congress Cataloging in Publication Data
Mayfield, John.
The new nation, 1800–1845.
(American century series)
Bibliography: p.
Includes index.
1. United States—History—1783–1865.   I. Title.
E338.M34   1982   973   82–9325
ISBN 0–8090–7291–2   AACR2
ISBN 0–8090–0153–5 (pbk.)

Foreword

THE first half of the nineteenth century presents special difficulties to the historian of the United States. These decades do not constitute a clearly defined epoch, like the preceding age of the American Revolution or the subsequent Civil War and Reconstruction period. The years between 1800 and 1845 were, on the one hand, a time of triumphant American nationalism; they also witnessed the emergence of the most virulent sectionalism. This was an age of expansion, when the republic more than doubled in territory and the American people poured into the Mississippi Valley, across the wide Missouri, and ultimately reached the Pacific; but it was also a time of consolidation, with a disproportionate increase of population along the Eastern seaboard and the rise of large cities. These years witnessed the triumph of democracy, when the equalitarian principles of the Jeffersonians were put into practice in the age of Jackson; they also saw the rise of a Jacksonian aristocracy of wealth, when a few manufacturers, merchants, bankers, and planters amassed huge fortunes and there was greater disparity between rich and poor than ever before in American history. During these years the great humanitarian reform movement flowered, and there were strenuous efforts to improve education, elevate the status of women, better the lot of the deaf, dumb, and blind, reform the criminals, and free the slaves. At the same time American Negro slavery was becoming more firmly entrenched and slaveholders grew less willing than ever even to contemplate the end of their "peculiar institution."

It is little wonder, then, that American historians have had difficulties in dealing with an era so complex and contradictory. As a result, most of the best writing on the period—and there is much of it, unequaled in our historical literature for depth and subtlety—has focused on particular trends, on specific episodes, and on colorful individuals. There have been few attempts at synthesis.

The New Nation, 1800–1845, by John Mayfield, offers a broad overview of the whole period. Originally, Dr. Mayfield, who has taught history at the University of Kentucky, planned only a revision and updating of Charles M. Wiltse's 1961 volume of the same title in the Making of America Series. As he worked, however, it became increasingly clear that the scholarly research of the last two decades demanded not merely a reassessment of particular events during these years but a reevaluation of the period as a whole. Though he drew on Professor Wiltse's book to some extent, particularly in his narrative sections, Dr. Mayfield went on to write what is essentially a new book, and a very different interpretation of the age. Generously recognizing that fact, Professor Wiltse suggested that only Dr. Mayfield's name appear on the title page.

The New Nation is a fresh study of the Jefferson–Jackson period that reflects the author's particular interests and special qualifications. A historian sensitive to developments in American art, architecture, literature, and philosophy, he shows how changes in culture paralleled simultaneous social and economic transformations. In his previous book, *Rehearsal for Republicanism: Free Soil and the Politics of Anti-Slavery* (1980), he began tracing the connections between ideology and politics during this stage of American growth. Now in *The New Nation* he continues to give close attention to the role of ideas in history, and he takes patterns of thinking seriously—even those that to a later generation have sometimes seemed silly or superficial.

But what most distinguishes this book is John Mayfield's willingness to accept as fact that American life during the first half of the nineteenth century was characterized by crosscurrents and opposing tendencies. Unlike some earlier historians who sought to find in the age a single dominant pattern or characteristic, he views it as a time of change, contradiction, and ambivalence. As a result, he has produced the richest, most subtle, and most complex picture we have yet had of the Middle Period of American history.

Beautifully written, couched in nontechnical language, based on the most recent research, John Mayfield's *The New Nation* superbly fulfills the objective of the Making of America Series: to make the best of historical scholarship available to the general reader who is not a specialist in American history.

Harvard University   David Herbert Donald

Contents

THE JEFFERSONIAN REPUBLIC

one

1

The New Nation

IN November 1800, Abigail Adams journeyed south from Boston to join her husband in the new capital city, Washington, D.C. Nothing in the letters she had received prepared her for what she found. Washington was a mix of woods and swamp, "romantic," she thought, "but a wild wilderness at present." Alexandria, across the Potomac, was tolerable, but Georgetown to the north was "the very dirtyest Hole I ever saw." The President and the 130 federal employees in the city shivered in the autumn damp, because—although wood was plentiful—"people cannot be found to cut and cart it." The Executive Mansion was especially jarring. Only one wing had been completed, the main stairs had not been built, and laundry hung in the East Room. The outlines of a splendid home were evident, but, she concluded, "this House is built for ages to come."

Washington was a monument to expectations. On paper, Pierre Charles L'Enfant's design for a capital was imaginative and ambitious. At George Washington's request, L'Enfant had designed a federal city of balance and openness. Each branch of the government was separate, in accordance with the Constitution, and was to occupy its own enclave. Connecting these branches were broad avenues that cut diagonally across the basic gridiron arrangement of streets. The map gave an impression of constant movement and exchange. L'Enfant urged that the public buildings be built in the style of Greek or Roman temples, logical, rational, functional. He also insisted that strict codes govern private dwellings. The entire city should be brick or stone—structures of permanence.

Reality in 1800 did not conform to desire. Congress adopted L'Enfant's plan in 1791 and immediately modified it. Some of the French-born engineer's schemes were too expensive; some were inconvenient. Most surrendered to the pressure of land speculators who streamed in, throwing up wood shanties haphazardly. Construction of the public buildings was painfully slow; eight years passed before the White House was habitable, seven before Congress could deliberate in the Capitol. The splendid columns of both White House and Capitol soared gracefully from mud, for no sidewalks had been built. Cow paths served for streets. Ventilation in the House chamber was so bad that representatives called it the Oven. The Supreme Court interpreted law in the basement below. Clustered around the public edifices were boardinghouses and shops that stank of butcher's waste, and tangled woods that bred excellent partridges, foul air, and lethal mosquitoes. To one observer, the scene presented "the appearance of a considerable town, which had been destroyed by some unusual calamity."

L'Enfant's grand design remained a paper dream, because there was no central authority to implement it. The multiple pressures of speculators, strong-willed congressmen, and state interests combined to fragment the regulations on which the plan depended. L'Enfant himself was fired a few years after construction began, the victim of his own stubbornness. Thereafter, a succession of architects quarreled over the placement of every stone, until Benjamin Latrobe assumed control in 1803. Latrobe's fascination for buildings of Roman design marked the city until it was burned in 1814. Four years later Charles Bulfinch, who favored the Greek revival style, took over. Even with Bulfinch's careful attention to detail, the growth of the city was agonizingly slow. It was "the City of Magnificent Intentions," wrote Charles Dickens in 1842. "Such as it is it is likely to remain."

And yet the dream of a planned monument to republicanism persisted. Congress never stopped trying to perfect the subtle blend of sophistication and wildness that L'Enfant had desired. The city was physically large, with ample space for parks and woods, and speculation in land kept most of the city undeveloped. The fascination with classic architecture continued, as more public edifices appeared. These were surrounded by homes and shops that represented a simpler, more natively American style. Despite these incremental attempts at sophistication, the city remained primitive until the Civil

War, when the growing importance of the federal government generated new interest in L'Enfant's design.

In its intent, its design, and its unfinished chaos, Washington symbolized the new nation. The United States in 1800 was a creation of paper, a model republic. Just as L'Enfant wished to bring classical grandeur to formless woods, those who framed the Constitution hoped to impose a stable democracy on a raw wilderness. On paper, the design was a perfect construct of rationality and good sense. In reality, the republic existed as an almost ungovernable collection of diverse elements caught up in an atmosphere of rapid and unpredictable change. After a quarter century of independence, the differences among Americans remained as apparent as the common qualities that had united them against England. Differences of heritage, of culture, of occupation fragmented the new nation into regional groupings of pluralistic and diversified states. These centrifugal forces, given added strength by isolation, material abundance, and innovations constantly being introduced by science, appeared to defy all attempts at harnessing. Thus, while Americans longed for stability and predictability, they lived in a world of change that was at odds with their ideal. The result was a society of contrasts—crude and civilized, violent and peaceful, exuberant and restrained—which to some seemed almost adolescent. "The American nation," observed a Scottish visitor, "is in a sort of middle state between barbarism and refinement."

The forces of change were many. European visitors during the first half of the nineteenth century were astounded at the size of the new republic. They were also struck by its emptiness. At the beginning of the century slightly more than five million persons inhabited a land mass roughly equal to that of continental Europe—a population density of 6.41 per square mile. Almost all of this population lived east of the Appalachians. Some clustered in cities along the Atlantic seaboard or in isolated settlements bordering rivers and lakes; most lived on farms. Of the sixteen states, only Kentucky and Tennessee lay west of the mountains; neither possessed more than a few thousand English-speaking residents. Nearly one-third of the republic was unorganized territory north of the Ohio River or south of Tennessee. There the wilderness was absolute. Forests were dense, untamed, and ubiquitous; Indians, a persistent menace; solitude, a constant companion.

Yet the wilderness was receding to the pressures of population and migration. Between 1800—only two years after Thomas Malthus had warned the world about the dangers of overpopulation—and 1850, Americans multiplied at an average annual rate of 3.2 to 3.6 percent, the biological maximum. Most of the increase was native-born; immigration added the rest. Immigration and natural fertility combined to make the United States the fastest-growing nation in the world throughout the nineteenth century. Although the tide of newcomers from Europe ebbed during the Napoleonic wars, it swelled again after 1815, with each shipload of immigrants adding variety to a culture already rich in Yankees, Yorkers, Dutch, Quakers, Irish, French, and blacks. The five million Americans living in 1800 quintupled by 1850.

The dramatic growth in population increased mobility. By 1800 the mountains and dense forests no longer confined the spread of westward migration, as they had during the eighteenth century. Families and fortune seekers pushed through gaps in the Appalachians, while others hired flatboats or floated rafts down the Ohio River. Still others crossed the Great Lakes into the Old Northwest or pushed north from the Gulf into the Mississippi Territory. Whatever the means of travel, the journey was difficult and tedious. A person leaving New York for the Ohio Territory, for example, spent three days covering the first two hundred miles inland. Thereafter, his progress slowed by half. A trip from New York to New Orleans consumed four weeks; from New York to Fort Dearborn (later Chicago), six. Despite the hardships, the center of population moved steadily west. In 1790, half the population lived east of a point near Baltimore; by 1840, that point had shifted to west of the Appalachian range. "In most places there is not a single grown man or woman native to the place or, indeed, to the territory . . . " commented one traveler in 1847. "Many of them have moved a number of times, always farther west, and they will very likely do so again."

The driving force behind this restiveness was land. Over eight-tenths of the population in 1800 earned their living from the soil, as befitted the agrarian republic of Thomas Jefferson's dreams. But while most produce fed or clothed the farmer himself, land was so rich and plentiful that surpluses were generally available for the market. The nature of this commerce varied by sections. In the northeastern and central Atlantic states farmers raised grains, flax, woolens, and beef to sell in the towns and ports. Settlers on the Cumberland Plateau in Kentucky produced hemp for ropes, while Pennsylvania farmers turned their corn into whiskey. Southern planters grew rice, sugar, tobacco, and, of course, cotton. Between 1792—the last year before Eli Whitney introduced the cotton gin—and 1800, total cotton output jumped from three million to thirty-six million pounds. Even that increase was inadequate to meet demands from British textile mills, so the price of cotton and land rose accordingly. In every region, the growth of commercial agriculture created a phenomenon unknown to the Old World: land became—as well as hearth and home—a commodity to be bought and sold. Americans were speculators.

Commerce encouraged urbanization. While the center of population for the entire country moved west, that of the coastal states often moved east, as cities along the seaboard grew with the market. In New England, for example, the small farmers of the interior served the needs of maritime entrepreneurs. The latter included merchant aristocrats such as the Cabots or Crowninshields, who owned fleets of vessels that ranged the globe, or single-vessel fishermen who operated on credit or commission. Both earned profits that financed new ventures, paid wages, built warehouses and homes, and filtered down to support churches and schools. This pattern of economic and social diversification was repeated in other growing cities along the coast. Baltimore was the fastest-growing city in the nation in 1800, prospering from the tobacco trade of Virginia and Maryland. Charleston and Savannah served the lower South. And to the west was New Orleans —not yet a part of the United States in 1800, but strategically located at the gateway of a territory of almost unimaginable wealth.

The two largest and most important cities, however, were Philadelphia and New York. Until 1800, Philadelphia had been the capital of the new nation. With a coterie of scientists, artists, and philosophers, it was the intellectual capital still. Unchallenged in finance, Philadelphia was the home of almost half of all banking capital in America. The city boasted the most extensive and varied industry in the country and a substantial foreign commerce. Philadelphia was also the starting point for much of the trans-Allegheny trade. Using the Conestoga wagon, which could carry up to two tons of cargo, traders carried furniture, tools, household wares, even printing presses, to the new communities beyond the mountains in return for grain or flour or whiskey. The chief competition for the wagon was the keelboat, yet the internal trade provided more than enough business for both. Together, they helped make Philadelphia the largest city in the nation.

By 1800, Philadelphia was losing its prominence to New York, a bustling, noisy, smelly city packed into the lower tip of Manhattan. New York was many-faceted and multinational. At the lower tip was Battery Park, which Frances Trollope considered one of the most beautiful city landscapes she visited in her many travels. The spot, with its cool, perpetual breeze and splendid view, was a favorite promenade for gentlemen and ladies. At no great distance to the north, however, was the Five Points, a squalid mess of paupers and prostitutes. Much of the population was transient and cosmopolitan. British and Yankee sailors mingled with Irish and German laborers, Scotch traders, free blacks, and slaves; farmers who came into the city before dawn to market produce often spoke Dutch. Those who settled in the city permanently were businessmen or professionals who worked ten to fourteen hours a day, bent on acquiring wealth and multiplying it.

New York's commercial prominence was a result of topography. Like Philadelphia and Boston, the city was a busy port for the world shipping trade and a logical stopover for coastal sailing vessels. Like its rivals, New York serviced a large agricultural hinterland. Its initial advantage, however, was the Hudson River, which was navigable up to Albany, 150 miles inland. Commercial agriculture flourished on either side of the Hudson. From Albany, a ribbon of cultivated land ran west along the Mohawk, and to the east and north the farms of New York merged with those of Vermont and touched Quebec at the head of Lake Champlain. Two major roads, moreover, ran west from the Hudson to a point near Rochester. By 1800, there were outposts at Oswego and Niagara, and farmers were already pushing into the Genesee Valley and on to the watershed of the Allegheny. In sum, transportation and migration were comparatively easy through the state, and New York City was a natural gateway.

By 1800, the cities and the countryside were beginning to experience the first effects of the Industrial Revolution. The most visible signs of change were in New England, where individual entrepreneurs combined native inventiveness with strikingly modern techniques of production and organization to create the forerunners of the factory system. In 1790, for example, Samuel Slater evaded the laws of his native England (which forbade the emigration of textile workers) and smuggled the plans of Arkwright's power loom to America in his head. Slater's textile mill in Pawtucket, Rhode Island, was the first of its kind in the United States, and others soon appeared along the fall line from New Hampshire to Connecticut. The high-output, low-unit-cost production initiated by the textile industry spread to other, more sophisticated enterprises. In Plymouth, Connecticut, Eli Terry converted his clockmaking business to mass production. And in New Haven, Eli Whitney, whose cotton gin was being shamelessly pirated to feed the increasing demand for textile fiber, turned to the manufacture of firearms. The parts of his rifles were so precisely tooled that they were interchangeable.

The revolution was also at work in the central Atlantic states. The coal of Pennsylvania remained unmined, save for cooking and heating, but iron was smelted with charcoal from native hardwoods up and down the Schuylkill Valley and in northern New Jersey. Both states had foundries and forges to temper the metal and convert it to nails, horseshoes, guns, and tools. Some of this iron production went to the manufacture of increasingly sophisticated steam engines, which, in addition to their original use in pumping water, were now driving milling machinery and boats. Steamboats had been plying the Delaware intermittently, in fact, ever since John Fitch made his first successful run in 1787. By 1800, Oliver Evans, in Philadelphia, was developing a high-pressure engine that would greatly extend the use of steam as a motive force. In the 1780s, the same man had created a system of water-driven belts and conveyors to move grain through the milling process. By automating the operation, Evans developed a prototype of the assembly line.

AMERICANS greeted such changes with breathless optimism. To them, every improvement was a sign of progress, which they reverentially viewed as a central, perhaps even definitive, trait of American culture. Progress was evident not only in the crude steam engines, the tiny cities, the clipper ships, and the move west but in the unprecedented freedom that Americans regarded as a birthright. The republican revolution of the late eighteenth century produced a nation of individuals who were persuaded that the United States was providentially blessed. Some divine plan had apparently ordained that a great experiment in democracy would be performed on these shores. Here free men and women would break free of the restraints endured by European societies and push back the limits of improvement and innovation. Amid such prospects, Americans regarded change as boundlessly good.

The price of change, however, was instability. Americans, noted one observer, "are in haste to be all that they are yet destined to be," and they became ill-tempered and impatient when confronted with obstacles. Moreover, change was usually accomplished by competition, and competition discouraged the fraternalism necessary for a stable society. One man's success was often bought with another man's failure. Mobility only accentuated the problem. And every new inch of territory strained the fabric of American culture more, challenging the cohesiveness of its institutions and its values. In this world of permanent flux, Americans longed for stability. Alongside their faith in progress came a desperate search for unity, for without unity their march toward destiny could easily become a plunge into anarchy.

By 1800, the expansion of the new republic had far outpaced the development of its institutional ties. No national church united believers and enforced orthodoxy. No elaborate governmental bureaucracy ministered to the whole people and reminded them of their connection to the state. Apart from postmasters and soldiers, the federal government employed fewer than two thousand persons in 1800 to serve the needs of five million—all spread over a territory equal to the size of continental Europe. The military was small and not highly regarded. At a time when Napoleon could send 40,000 troops into a single battle, American soldiers and seamen numbered about 6,500. The judicial system was undermanned; judges were overworked and forced to adapt the law to a bewildering array of legal innovations. Transportation and communications were glacially slow. There was no king, no pope—not even an archbishop—no titled aristocracy, no national university. Even the authority of the gentry—whose informal demands of respect and obedience made colonial America a deferential society—was under attack. And nothing had yet emerged to replace these Old World ties of community.

Also missing were common standards and manners. The lack of restraints encouraged Americans to be volatile, competitive, ambitious, and changeable. They formed attachments one day, abandoned them the next. European visitors who came to the new nation in search of a phrase that might define the American character often returned in bewilderment. Americans were simultaneously thin-skinned and tolerant, boastful and shy, reserved and hospitable, withdrawn and gregarious. They seemed obsessed with the past and compelled not to repeat the mistakes of history; they were also enamored of the future and driven by visions of creating the richest, most civilized country on earth. They could be aggressively proud of the fluidity and rawness of their society, yet their popular literature and their misty-eyed efforts to preserve even the tiniest fragments of memorabilia revealed a sentimentality that was almost maudlin. They seemed unable to set standards of what was valuable and what was not, a confusion that gave American society a transitory, fickle quality. "Everything is for sale, provided the owner is offered a tempting price," commented a French visitor. "He will part with his house, his carriage, his horse, his dog—anything at all."

The confusion of standards was most apparent in the conflicting ways in which Americans interpreted their Revolution. All rejoiced at the death of colonialism; almost all celebrated a new, more egalitarian spirit in American culture. The most radical dimension of that spirit was the concept of self-rule, which entrusted the health of society to the individual citizen and his ability to direct his own destiny through reasoned choice. Intelligent decisions by rational men would lead, it was presumed, to a harmonious society, safeguard natural rights, and insure that the natural talents and virtue of ordinary citizens would flourish. But the concept was new and untested in 1800. Many feared that an egalitarian society, free of traditional restraints, would fly out of control. Some, such as John Adams, longed for a return to habits of deference to the "best men." "Inequalities of mind and body," he argued, "are so established by God Almighty . . . that no art or policy can ever plane them down to a level." Adams's assessment of human nature was unpopular, but the fear of an unrestrained, anarchic society persisted.

Without quite realizing it, Americans were confronted with a problem basic to all democratic societies: how to maintain a stable balance between the individual's desire for liberty and the community's need for restraints. In the new nation the problem took many forms. Americans searched for means of directing individual energies along lines that would benefit all. They needed ways of granting all men access to political power while preserving continuity and order. They longed for common goals and ideals that would encourage a spirit of brotherhood yet leave room for the innovator and the eccentric. They looked for mechanisms that would make the federal government a strong agent of all the people without infringing on the special and varied interests of the states.

During the first half of the nineteenth century, the resolution of this problem followed two intertwined paths. To satisfy the need for organizational ties, Americans began to develop new types of institutions—institutions capable of directing the energies of a free society, without being compulsory or aristocratic. The structure of these institutions was democratic and—to a point—systematic. At the same time Americans searched for some way of transcending the ideological differences inherent in a pluralistic culture. As the power of public opinion grew, there had to be some way of insuring that the people would use their influence to noble ends. In a pattern typical of emerging nations, Americans began to view their development as a nation in moral terms. This was the highest of all forms of authority, one vague enough to be used in a variety of contexts yet strong enough to command strict obedience and loyalty. Creating democratic institutions and endowing them with a moral purpose, then, became the hoped-for balance between liberty and restraint in the new nation.

Two entirely disparate events in 1801 foreshadowed the ways by which Americans attempted to realize their goals. In Kentucky, a series of revivals began that were to be known as the Second Great Awakening; the meeting at Cane Ridge was the largest, most publicized, and in time most legendary. Carefully planned and executed by ministers from both inside and outside the state, the Cane Ridge revival attracted multitudes—estimates ran as high as 25,000. For several days and nights in August, at least eighteen clergymen preached to the throng, luridly portraying the torments of hell and the glories of heaven. They exhorted sinners to repent, to set aside worldly ambitions and temptations and humble themselves before a higher authority, who would take control of their lives and give them inner peace. The response was anything but peaceful. Listeners fell, quivered, shouted, sang, barked, or laughed. Bonfires burned at night, giving the scene an aura of the very hell that was to be feared. During the course of the meeting, thousands were "saved" and returned to their farms and homes with a new resolution to live the good, Christian, moral life. Over the next four years the miracle of Cane Ridge spread, as large sections of the frontier heeded the call.

Kentucky was a natural place for such phenomena. Thinly populated, isolated by a mountain barrier from the rest of the nation, inhabited mostly by the poor and struggling, the state was an extreme example of the fragmentation that threatened American society. Life there was lonely and hard, with few comforts and fewer diversions. Settlers used what little spare time they had in cockfighting, horse racing, and cardsharping—vices that flourished in the almost utter absence of civil or religious authority. The state legislature met sporadically and deliberated ineffectually. Churches were uniformly small and lacked influence; schools, except for Transylvania College in Lexington, were virtually nonexistent.

In these surroundings, the only authority was moral and voluntary. If not for the fact that most Kentuckians were honest, upright men and women whose sense of individual and social ethics recognized the need for temperance and harmony, the state would have lapsed into anarchy. Yet these same frontier settlers were disturbed by the lack of restraints in their society, and for them the revivals were quite literally a godsend. Cane Ridge pitted divine sovereignty against chaos with no doubts as to the winner. The revivalists espoused a God who intervened in everything, bringing fortune as a reward and famine as a punishment for every human act. Under such an omnipotent, omnipresent authority, society was promised regeneration through salvation.

The most compelling aspect of this regeneration was its appeal to both the individual and the community. The Cane Ridge revival focused on the person, stripped him of his pretensions, and left him naked before God. Overwhelmed by the divine presence—which seemed to filter through the trees like smoke from the campfires—the individual could do little but submit to His demands. And each convert, upon returning home, could take comfort from the presence of others who also had been saved. This combined moral force, the revivalists promised, would be an irresistible army in the restoration of order. "It is a very comfortable thing to be in a country where religion has obtained the preeminent influence," commented one visitor to the state. "That is those that have it shows it, and those that have it not wish to be considered religious for the credit it gives in the society."

The revivals complemented other desires and needs. The remarkable success of the meetings, for example, infused new life into the clergy, who at last had evidence that even the roughest society could be rescued from perdition. These men returned to their churches with fresh determination to bring God and order to the frontier; in time, their efforts bore fruit, as churches and schools appeared throughout the state. In a more general sense, the missionary zeal of the revivals meshed well with the nation's self-appointed duty to lead the world in progress and civilization. Most of all, the revivals were conducted in a spirit of egalitarianism. Here was salvation for all, and those who defended the meetings (many did not) were careful to note that simple country folk had been quickest and most passionate in response to God's call. Unencumbered by institutions or traditions, the yeoman farmer was clearly assuming responsibility for maintaining social order through the exercise of moral authority. During the coming decades, this faith in voluntary, individual action in the name of moral regeneration would become a powerful instrument of social reform.

BUT the most important national event of 1801 was the accession of Thomas Jefferson to the Presidency. Jefferson kept his inauguration simple, partly to maintain an image of agrarian simplicity and partly to offer a contrast to the turbulent circumstances surrounding his election. Only two weeks before he took office, the selection of a Chief Executive had been in doubt; an earlier vote in the Electoral College produced a tie between Jefferson and Aaron Burr, and the contest had gone to the House of Representatives. Jefferson's ultimate and narrow victory over Burr had come only with the help of Federalists, who regarded him as the lesser of two monstrous evils. The actual transfer of power, however, had been refreshingly peaceful. "I have this morning witnessed one of the most interesting scenes, a free people can ever witness," wrote the wife of a Washington journalist. "The changes of administration, which in every government and in every age have most generally been epochs of confusion, villainy, and bloodshed, in this our happy country take place without any species of distraction, or disorder." Her optimism notwithstanding, Jefferson's enemies awaited a second revolution.

It was indeed a revolution—a quiet one—and, like other revolutions, had its theoretical and practical sides. After twelve years of Federalist rule, during which Washington and Adams had attempted to centralize and extend the power of the new government, Jefferson was prepared to redefine the limits of republican authority. In his inaugural address, he acknowledged the conflicts that attended his election and the despair those conflicts generated in the hearts of a few. "Some honest men," he noted, doubted that a government of free

men possessed the "energy to preserve itself." Such fears, he countered, were unfounded. The republic was not merely secure but was
"the strongest . . . on earth." Isolated from the violence tearing at
Europe, endowed with a rich continent, and blessed with a populace
that was superior to any other in industry and moral judgment, what
else could the new nation want to insure its happiness? "Still one thing
more, fellow-citizens—a wise and frugal Government, which shall
restrain men from injuring one another, shall leave them free to
regulate their own pursuits of industry and improvement, and shall
not take from the mouth of labor the bread it has earned. This," he
concluded, "is the sum of good government."

Jefferson believed strongly in a concept of limited government, one
that worked gently and invisibly within strict institutional boundaries.
He had returned from his extensive travels in Europe with lofty
contempt for the top-heavy bureaucracies of England and France. He
despised especially the military, which he regarded as paid mercenar-
ies for greedy aristocrats. He was suspicious of banks, which encouraged debt and robbed the laborer of his independence. And he was
particularly distrustful of aristocracies based on wealth and birth—
"artificial," he called them, "a mischievous ingredient in government"
—that hindered the free expression of the popular will. Each of these
liabilities came together in the person of Alexander Hamilton—to
Jefferson a courtesan who sought to rule through intrigue, force, and
devious schemes of governmental centralization.

But Jefferson also believed in the essential harmony of republican
society and the collective wisdom of the individuals who constituted
it. This wisdom rested on the moral perceptiveness of the common
man. "State a moral case to a ploughman and a professor," he wrote.
"The former will decide it as well, and often better, than the latter,
because he has not been led astray by artificial rules." In this explosive
statement Jefferson argued two things. First, what society needed
were persons of character, not intellect or education. There was an
underlying moral law in the universe capable of being grasped by good
men regardless of their wealth or formal training. This moral force
was most easily observed in the workings of nature, which conformed
to universal laws, was economical, even predictable. Clearly the
ploughman, surrounded by the majesty and goodness of nature, held
an advantage over the isolated professor or the frivolous aristocrat.

The second point followed the first. If virtue flowed from natural sources, then it was absurd to attempt to graft artificial distinctions of wealth and heredity onto republican government. Elites, men of power and influence, inevitably led every society, but their rise to position should be the product of industry, virtue, and native intellect —not their birth. A natural, not hereditary, aristocracy would emerge, led by the combined moral wisdom of the nation's plain republicans. Though the virtuous ploughman might occasionally be led astray, his common sense would ultimately triumph. "In general," he wrote in 1813, "they will elect the really good and wise."

Jefferson's faith in the popular will was an early justification of an entirely modern political force: public opinion. In contrast to traditions of deferential authority, public opinion was fast emerging as the surest means of making decisions that would allow maximum liberty for the individual while maintaining the social cohesion necessary for stability. This egalitarian process contained an element of risk, for the essential safeguard of rights in a democratic society was the willingness of each of its members to accept the responsibility and sacrifice inherent in self-rule. But since anyone who did not share in these responsibilities was a potential threat to those who did, it was desirable to include as many as possible in the political process. Moreover, if one really believed—as Jefferson did—that enlightened opinion rested on the innate moral perception common to all men, then the foundations of good government were secure.

To conservatives, this was nonsense. Hacking away at traditional and tested patterns of authority would produce only chaos and, eventually, a new, more despicable dictatorship. Fisher Ames of Massachusetts feared that the passions of the people, cut loose from traditional restraints, would create demagogues. "The consciousness, or the opinion, that [the people] possess the supreme power, will inspire inordinate passions; and the violent men, who are the most forward to gratify those passions, will be their favorites. What is called the government of the people is in fact too often the arbitrary power of such men."

Jefferson was sensitive to these fears, so he worked to make his Administration as efficient, as reasonable, and as restrained as possible. For this task, he was well equipped. Despite his shy manner, Jefferson was a deceptively good executive. He possessed a keen political sense, which except on rare occasions made him a model of patience and reasonableness. He was also a hard worker. In Washington he labored long after his subordinates had gone to bed; at Monticello he kept in close and frequent contact with developments in the capital. Overlaying these traits was a self-conscious determination to set precedents of simplicity and economy. His state dinners were informal but tasteful; mostly he dined alone. To argue his policies, he preferred intimate personal conferences rather than public speeches.

Circumstances favored his efforts. Jefferson entered office as the leader not only of a nation but of a party. The congressional Republicans who accompanied him to Washington were anxious for power, yet unaccustomed to using it, and they turned naturally to the President for direction. Jefferson's response belied his earlier condemnation of factionalism. He gently persuaded certain congressmen to be his spokesmen and cultivated the support of others by inviting them to breakfast or dinner. Often he helped draft legislation, sometimes writing entire bills himself. Always, however, Jefferson was careful not to let his efforts be known. He used the same approach on his Cabinet, which he relied on and developed, and which he controlled.

Jefferson's most useful tool in reconstructing the government, however, was his popular mandate. Despite his narrow victory, Jefferson interpreted his election as, at the very least, an overwhelming rejection of Federalism and a public demand to frame new policies. His approach was cautious. He did not, for example, dismantle the Bank of the United States, even though he considered the institution a threat. In 1801, he instructed his Secretary of the Treasury, Albert Gallatin, to revise federal economic policy, and a year later Gallatin produced a long, ably reasoned report, which advocated retrenchment and payment of the national debt but which left the Bank untouched. (Ten years later, Gallatin, with Madison, would urge that it be rechartered.) Jefferson accepted Gallatin's report for two reasons. First, however obnoxious the Bank might be, it was the lawful creation of a majority of Congress. To attempt to kill it before its charter expired would run against Jefferson's own ideas about majority rule. "It mortifies me to be strengthening principles which I deem radically vicious," he observed, "but this vice is entailed on us by the first error." Second, the Bank was a threat only so long as Federalists directed the course of the national government. The election of 1800 had replaced Federalist ideology and men with Republican ideology and men; a change of policies could now develop over time. "We shall be able by degrees to introduce sound principles and make them habitual," the President concluded.

He was less patient, but still cautious, about removing Federalists from positions of power. Most lower-level officeholders kept their jobs, although the military and diplomatic corps were slashed. Moreover, certain tax collectors and inspectors were fired as Jefferson's policy of retrenchment took effect. But, try as he might, Jefferson was never able to purge the judiciary of all the "midnight appointments" Adams had made in the last days of his Presidency. The thorniest of these was Jefferson's distant cousin, John Marshall, the new Chief Justice. Marshall's concept of government stressed balance, not retrenchment, and in his role as head of the Court he was determined to make the process of judicial review impervious to the blandishments of public opinion or the pressures of partisan politics. This outlook naturally pitted him against the new President. The two first clashed when Jefferson refused to allow Secretary of State Madison to issue the commission of one of Adams's appointees, a justice of the peace. Marshall allowed Jefferson's decision to stand, but used the occasion of *Marbury* v. *Madison* in 1803 to assert the power of the Supreme Court to overrule acts of Congress. In 1804 Jefferson attacked the Court directly by bringing articles of impeachment against Samuel Chase, an old and slightly addled Federalist Justice. Yet here, in the one case where Jefferson attempted to use his congressional majority to upset the constitutional balance of power, even the members of his own party balked. Jefferson met with a cold rebuff.

DESPITE occasional setbacks, Jefferson continued to extend the power of the executive in Washington. His most aggressive—and most tormented—use of his authority centered on the purchase of the Louisiana Territory. In 1800 Napoleon had seized control of Louisiana from the Spanish, who had ruled it since 1763. French imperialism was a clear threat to the commerce of the Mississippi and Ohio valleys and a potential source of war in the West. Disturbed by these prospects, the President sent first Robert R. Livingston, then James Monroe, to France with instructions to buy New Orleans and the Floridas. Napoleon, however, surprised the negotiators. Short of cash and pressured by his ongoing conflict with England, he offered the entire Louisiana Territory for $15,000,000. The bargain was quickly struck, and in July 1803 the news reached Washington.

Jefferson first balked, then agreed. The Constitution did not specifically permit such a dramatic use of executive power, and Jefferson— ever watchful of precedents—agonized over his decision. Ultimately, however, this objection paled before larger matters that in his mind involved the future of republican (and Republican) rule in the new nation. "There is on the globe one single spot," he explained to Livingston, "the possessor of which is our natural and habitual enemy. It is New Orleans, through which three-eighths of our territory must pass to market . . ." So long as Spain, weak and ineffectual, governed Louisiana, peace would prevail. French rule, however, inevitably meant war, a war that would "marry ourselves to the British fleet and nation." This Jefferson could not accept, both because he was convinced that war and standing armies were anathema to republics and because he thoroughly disliked the British. Any liaison with England would increase the British influence on the United States, and that in turn would give new life to the Federalists.

More optimistically, Jefferson regarded the Louisiana Territory as the natural extension of his agrarian republic. A free Louisiana would open the way for yeomen farmers to expand their domain. "The future inhabitants of the Atlantic and Mississippi States will be our sons," he wrote. Principles of republican nationalism would grow and flourish there. On the other hand, if the United States were constricted to the land east of the Appalachians, the mobs and commercial rabble of the cities would multiply, and republicanism would be lost.

JEFFERSON'S quiet but aggressive use of executive power did not, however, extend the authority of the federal government to the nation as a whole. While power was increasingly being centralized in Washington, it was being cut back elsewhere. Although the Bank endured, Jefferson encouraged the growth of state and local rivals, which by 1811 had the combined strength to prevent its recharter. Moreover, both the President and his Treasurer insisted that all internal taxes be abolished and the national debt reduced. Congress agreed, thus delivering a fatal blow to the far-reaching designs of Hamiltonian Federalism. As federal income shrank, plans for linking East and West through an elaborate system of canals and turnpikes were shelved. The army and navy were cut back; the diplomatic corps was trimmed. With the federal government pursuing a vigorous course of retrenchment, the purchase of Louisiana only strained the ties of national authority more. Most Americans appeared to approve this course, however, for in the election of 1804 they returned Jefferson to office with a comfortable majority.

But what of the Federalists? Jefferson's election broke their power but did not eliminate their followers or their ideals. Some, notably Timothy Pickering and his Essex Junto, responded with threats of secession and the creation of a New England confederacy. Most simply accepted the decision of 1800 and searched for ways to overcome it through constitutional means. Those means led them toward organized efforts of party competition and, gradually, to an acceptance of the people's right to rule. Thus, the revolution of 1800 began to extend to the loyal opposition.

Jefferson's election taught the Federalists that they could no longer assume that power was theirs by birthright; they must work for it. In practice, this meant organization and direct campaigning. In January 1801, a meeting at the Tontine Coffee House in Albany set up a party caucus and a series of committees to give system and structure to party efforts; later the Washington Benevolent Societies appeared as rivals to the Republicans' Tammany Hall. Party newspapers emerged, determined not only to reflect public opinion but to influence it. As more and more of these political organizations sprang up throughout the new nation, led mostly by young men, traditional Federalist concepts of authority began to decay. Federalists began to recognize that, without popular approval, it was impossible to obtain power. Power had become the gift of the people, as Jefferson's election demonstrated only too well. It was necessary therefore to organize public opinion, enlighten it, influence it, and direct it. Although the work of young Federalists went for nought—they never again elected a President or controlled Congress—their efforts helped usher in a new era of party competition. During the decades that followed, organized and structured political parties would emerge as modern replacements for the traditional, personal mechanisms of the deferential society.

THUS, by the end of Jefferson's first term, new patterns of democratic authority had begun to take form. Jefferson's domination of the federal government suggested that power in Washington was amenable to centralization if—and only if—the President himself was a capable administrator and strong party leader. Outside the federal city, however, the fluidity and egalitarianism of American society tended to fragment power into units that could be joined only by systematic means of expressing public opinion—the political party. And where institutions of authority were nonexistent—as in Kentucky—Americans turned to voluntary restraints that rested on the individual's sense of propriety and moral conduct.

But each of these forms of authority was fragile. Without a strong executive, power in Washington might revert to Congress, where it would disperse under the pressure of local interests. The organization of public opinion required party leaders to respond to contradictory demands of local, state, regional, and national interests, a delicate task that demanded foresight and self-sacrifice. And the voluntary exercise of moral restraints—even those dictated by God—depended on individual self-discipline. Institutional structures to encourage this discipline were as yet unformed. This institutional chaos was troublesome, at best, in times of peace. In war, however, it posed a mortal threat to the future of the new republic.

2

Securing
the Revolution

FROM its inception as an independent nation, the United States was deeply enmeshed in foreign affairs. The Revolution severed Americans from the economic and diplomatic protection they had enjoyed as British colonials and propelled them into a world arena of cultural and commercial rivalries, Machiavellian intrigue, and imperialistic violence. The most vexing of these rivalries was that between Britain and France. The French Revolution unleashed radical and explosive energies of reform and conquest and rekindled a conflict with England that by 1789 was centuries old. In 1792 war broke out between the two powers and with only a brief hiatus continued until 1814.

The United States was drawn irresistibly into this conflict. The French Revolution appealed to certain Americans who viewed French imperialism as a forceful—if often erratic—agent of democratic reform. Even the rise of Napoleon did not erase their conviction that England was the enemy of republicanism in the Western world. But other Americans believed that French social radicalism led to anarchy, then despotism. They saw British armies and gunboats as logical weapons in an all-out struggle to preserve civilization from chaos. During the 1790s these opposing views became focal points of partisan conflict. The passions thus excited colored elections, embittered old friends, and ultimately helped remove John Adams from the Presidency.

But the conflict was more than ideological. The United States was a commercial republic that depended heavily on the maritime trade of the North Atlantic. By 1800, American vessels were the foremost neutral carriers of goods on the high seas, serving particularly the triangular trade between the Continent, the Caribbean, and the United States. As England's involvement in naval warfare deepened, American ships proliferated to fill the gap between British demands for goods and its capacity to transport them. Similarly, trade between France and Spain and their West Indian colonies was carried in American vessels, which evaded British restrictions by calling first at an American port, unloading and paying duty, and then reexporting the goods. In addition to the cash provided by such ventures, the triangular trade furnished the United States with manufactured articles and luxuries. At a time when nine dollars could transport a ton of cargo three thousand miles across the Atlantic—but only thirty miles inland from Philadelphia—the importance of the Atlantic trade could not be overstated. Its protection, then, became a consuming interest of every President and every Congress from 1789 onward.

The territorial ambitions of the new republic were also at stake in the resolution of the European conflict. The United States was encircled on three sides by British, French, and Spanish settlements, and a decisive shift in the balance of power in Europe could seriously affect the security of the frontier. Jefferson's purchase of Louisiana was an unexpected benefit from the conflict, yet it did little to remove the threat. Britain still ruled Canada, and Spain—a French ally—still owned Florida. Moreover, American acquisition of Louisiana meant that after 1804 the United States was charged with the duty of protecting what it had bought. Given the tiny military apparatus available to the new nation, America's ability to discharge this duty was, at best, questionable.

The European conflict, then, posed serious dangers to the United States. It raised fundamental questions concerning the direction democratic authority would take in the new republic; it raised a serious —perhaps crippling—threat to the health of the American economy; it reinforced the fact that, until the United States was firmly in possession of the continent, the new nation could enjoy no real internal security from the pressures of the outside world. Within each of these problems, however, was a tempting promise. If the United States could meet the challenge to its autonomy, then the security and progress of the republic would be assured. If the shipping lanes to England and the Continent could be kept open, then—no matter how long the war lasted—the American economy would prosper. And, as the Louisiana Purchase demonstrated, skillful manipulation of the needs of any or all of the belligerents could open up the American West to peaceful and rapid settlement. Shadowing all these promises, however, was the possibility that the United States might become involved in a war that it did not want, could not fight, and probably could not win.

ALTHOUGH these problems had been an incessant plague to the Adams Administration, an uneasy peace ruled the Atlantic during the first half of Jefferson's first term. Then in 1803 war resumed; the British immediately imposed a blockade of European ports under French control. In 1805 the conflict entered a new and deadly phase. At Austerlitz, Napoleon won a stunning victory over the combined Austrian and Russian armies that gave him supremacy on land, while Lord Nelson's defeat of the French and Spanish navies at Trafalgar assured English superiority on the high seas. Shortly thereafter, Britain outlawed the reexport trade that had given American ships access to the French West Indies and sent so many warships into American waters that no merchantman could enter or leave a harbor except under British guns. The shipping lanes between England and the United States remained open, but a key source of revenue had been cut off or—if American captains so chose—transformed into a deadly game of smuggling.

Moreover, England increased its impressment of sailors on American ships. Chronically short of manpower, the British navy had developed during the 1790s the legally dubious art of stopping American vessels, searching them for English expatriates and deserters, and impressing them back into His Majesty's service. From a humanitarian perspective the practice was anathema to the United States, which traditionally depended on immigration as a source of population. From a practical standpoint, impressment robbed American ships of needed hands and exposed both crew and cargo to search and seizure. There were only two ways to protest impressment, however. Either American ships could be armed, at the risk of propelling the country into a war with the world's greatest sea power, or the Americans could negotiate. The first course was unacceptable; the second did not work.

Napoleon watched these developments with keen interest, of course. Both England and the United States were maritime powers, he reasoned, and Atlantic shipping lanes were vital to each. As long as American ships conformed to British trade restrictions, England could seal off the Continent while maintaining a steady supply of the goods and raw materials it required. But American hostility to these restrictions, and impressment, was obvious and growing. If Napoleon could turn this hostility into war, he would in effect reopen the naval conflict with England, only using American ships.

He implemented his strategy in 1806 with a decree from Berlin that closed those ports under his control to any neutral vessel that had first stopped in England. The British immediately responded with Orders in Council requiring neutral ships to obtain licenses in England before traveling into the blockaded zone. For a time American commerce suffered few ill effects, because Napoleon chose not to enforce the Berlin decree; he was waiting for an agreement with Czar Alexander that would seal off England's last continental source of grain. The agreement was reached in the summer of 1807. The Berlin decree was promptly invoked, and—when England responded with yet another proclamation that stepped up impressments and tightened the blockade—Napoleon ordered from Milan that any neutral ship complying with the new restrictions was to be confiscated forthwith.

In this game of diplomatic chess, the British committed a costly mistake. In June 1807, shortly before Napoleon's latest change of policy had become known in Washington, the frigate *Chesapeake* set sail from Norfolk bound for the Mediterranean. Its captain, James Barron, expected no action for at least several weeks; coils of rope cluttered the decks and encumbered the ship's guns. The ship was thus helpless when it was overtaken by a British man-of-war, the *Leopard*. The *Leopard* ordered the frigate to heave to and prepare for boarding; when Barron refused, the *Leopard* opened fire at point-blank range. Minutes later, with three dead and eighteen wounded, Barron struck his flag. British sailors then boarded the *Chesapeake* and removed one Englishman and three Americans who were alleged deserters from the English navy. The Englishman was later hanged, and the Americans impressed into service. Damage done, the commander of the *Leopard* graciously refused to take the *Chesapeake* as prize, nor did he accept Barron's sword.

The *Chesapeake* incident was an outrage, and war would have been a popular response. In port cities from Savannah to Boston town meetings and angry mobs assembled to protest the British action, and in Norfolk vigilantes searched the streets for British sailors. Town officials there refused to water and provision English ships. In the West, the *Chesapeake* affair fueled a growing hatred of the British alliance with the Indian tribes, particularly the Shawnee. For a time, Napoleon's own depredations of American shipping were forgotten.

But Jefferson did not want war. As a politician, he realized that his party was not single-minded in its hatred of the British; Napoleon's strategy was too obviously calculated to involve the United States in war for anyone seriously to believe that Britain was the only enemy America faced. Moreover, outside his party, there was enough Federalist resistance to conflict with England to convince the President that the country would enter a war divided and weak. New England in particular was culturally and commercially tied to the United Kingdom, and war might have the effect of rekindling the power of the Federalist opposition. Anything, then, that endangered the Republican ascendancy was to be carefully avoided.

Jefferson's major reservation against war, however, concerned its effect on republican government. Throughout his career he had argued that authority should be limited and power circumscribed. Any agency of government that interfered with, or attempted to direct, the affairs of men would certainly upset the natural harmony of interests that was the source of unity in a free society. War was an awesome vehicle for the use of power; it would undo his efforts to dismantle Federalist mechanisms of centralized authority. The army and navy would undoubtedly be expanded; the United States would inexorably raise a large standing army like those that served the monarchies of Europe. This, he believed, would provide the tools for strangling civil liberties and individual rights. Even where the direction of such armies was guarded by scrupulous men, the frightful expenses required to maintain them would lead to higher taxes and consolidation of financial resources, which Jefferson believed would encourage the creation of a moneyed aristocracy. Mostly he feared an increase in executive authority. Powerful men attracted courtiers who would attempt to use their influence for their own schemes. "The greatest mischiefs that I apprehend from the war," his friend Gallatin warned, "are the necessary increase of executive power and influence, the speculations of contractors and jobbers, and the introduction of permanent military and naval establishments." In short, once war or the threat of war had passed, there was no guarantee that the federal government would shrink in size.

Beyond that, Jefferson and his advisers assumed that their best weapon against the European powers was trade. Both belligerents, they reasoned, depended on the United States for essential raw materials, while Americans received only "luxuries" in return. To restrict or threaten to end the carrying trade, then, would bring immediate concessions. Accordingly, Jefferson had moved, months before the *Chesapeake* incident, to use trade as a peaceful means of insuring American neutrality. In 1806 he had threatened Britain with a nonimportation act that would prohibit certain articles from entering the United States unless a new agreement replacing Jay's Treaty of 1794 could be reached. To negotiate the new treaty, he had sent James Monroe and William Pinckney to London to persuade the British to give up impressment and to permit the triangular trade to reopen. The two envoys returned with a document that was little if any better than the one John Jay had negotiated a decade earlier, which also failed to end impressment or to deal effectively with the West Indian trade. Rather than submit such a farce to the Senate, Jefferson allowed the treaty to die quietly in the State Department. The attack on the *Chesapeake* only added to the frustration Jefferson already felt at his initial failure to reach a compromise.

During the autumn of 1807, the President moved more vigorously to wring concessions without resorting to war. Again he failed. The special British envoy who arrived in mid-November to discuss the *Chesapeake* was instructed not to negotiate at all until British vessels were readmitted to American waters. The same ship brought Americans the first word that England had responded to Napoleon's Berlin decree by stepping up impressments and tightening trade restrictions. The news propelled Jefferson into decisive action. Even before he had learned that Napoleon had begun confiscating ships under the terms of the Milan decree, he persuaded Congress to impose an embargo.

THE Embargo of 1807 was Jefferson's most extreme, most daring, and most fruitless attempt to use trade as a means of peaceful coercion. Unlike nonimportation—which could be used selectively and to a limited extent—the embargo prohibited the exportation of any goods whatever from the United States. Under British orders and French decrees, American ships were subject to seizure by one belligerent or the other, no matter where they went or what they carried. Jefferson determined to "protect" them by seeing that they went nowhere and carried nothing. Yet, although the embargo was total, Jefferson's real enemy remained England. Britain was the chief maritime competitor, and the principal antagonist, of American shipping. It was also the most dependent on American produce. Through an embargo, Jefferson hoped to starve England into a change of policy, and he counted on his fellow citizens to respond by doing without manufactured luxuries and uniting behind him.

In intent, the embargo was an international extension of Jefferson's policy of retrenchment. By removing American ships from the high seas, the President hoped to show that a republic could survive and prosper without resorting to the fearful centralization of power that would accompany war. Yet the act itself was an obvious and obnoxious intrusion of the federal government into the lives of American citizens. To enforce it successfully would demand constant oversight of ports and shipping lanes and total obedience from persons whose very livelihood had, with the stroke of a pen, been torn from them. During the fifteen months the embargo was in effect, neither result was forthcoming.

While the embargo did have a limited impact on Britain and France, it was most disruptive at home. For a short while American shipping lay paralyzed; then—as ingenuity responded to the challenge—it began to recover. Smuggling found new life. Ships at sea were warned wherever communication was possible, and many of them did not make home ports for the duration of the act. Instead, they piled up profits for their owners in whatever trade came to hand, for any risk was better than the certainty of rotting at the wharves in Boston or New York. Merchantmen caught in port went into the coastal trade, picked up huge cargoes for use at home, and then mysteriously disappeared to emerge in Nova Scotia or the Bahamas. In an effort to plug the leaks, Jefferson required certificates of necessity from governors in states that imported products from other states in coastal vessels. The governors, even Republican ones, replied by routinely issuing whatever certificates were requested. Despite these leaks, the embargo had a calamitous effect on the port cities of the Atlantic. Unemployment soared, and with it came bitter resentment of the President and his policies.

The major effect of the embargo was political. In New England, Federalism experienced a rebirth. Using new techniques of organization and protest, Federalists capitalized on the discontent generated by the embargo, and a few began to talk of a separate New England confederation. Fortunately for the Republicans, most local elections —ones that determined state legislatures and the choice of Presidential electors—were held in the spring of 1808, before the full severity of the restriction was felt. But although Jefferson's handpicked successor, James Madison, won handily in the fall, the Republican Party was split among those who supported the President's choice, Southern factionalists who endorsed James Monroe, and disaffected New Yorkers who rallied behind George Clinton. Not surprisingly, Federalists tripled their electoral vote of 1804. Republican hegemony was not broken, but it was badly shaken.

Another political result of the embargo was less obvious, but potentially more serious. In this, the most ambitious display of Jefferson's desire to restrain the use of executive authority, the President had created a political monster that threatened to undo the republican harmony he had worked so hard to achieve. Smuggling—and the tacit encouragement given it by the states—and the increase in partisan factionalism were all protests against the exercise of national authority. Every protest, in turn, encouraged the kind of regional and political fragmentation that worked against Jefferson's ideal of a unified, peaceful republic. Irregular and ineffective attempts to enforce the act, followed by its repeal shortly before Jefferson left office, only weakened the prestige and power of the government more. By the onset of war, the authority and prestige of the central government had badly deteriorated.

JAMES MADISON entered the White House in an atmosphere of faction and distrust that he was ill equipped to change. Madison shared his predecessor's republican philosophy, and he was determined to complete the dismantling of Federalist agencies of centralized power. Like Jefferson, he feared the effects of war on a peace-loving democracy, and he resolved to avoid conflict by diplomatic manipulation of the carrying trade. But Madison did not share Jefferson's enormous prestige, nor was he so skillful a politician. While Jefferson had succeeded in increasing the power of the Presidency, even as he reduced the influence of the federal government, Madison was unable to lead effectively either in Washington or in the country at large. In part his failure was due to his own personality; in part it sprang from the divisions that plagued his party. Madison never commanded the respect and the unity that Jefferson enjoyed, and he was hampered by rivalries within his Cabinet that forced him to direct foreign affairs by himself and in the presence of conflicting advice. The result was eight long years of frustration, uneven and often contradictory leadership, and an agonizing drift toward war.

The Cabinet problems focused on the role of Albert Gallatin. Gallatin was soft-spoken, perceptive, and often acute; he was also born in Switzerland. Although Gallatin was unquestionably the most experienced choice to head the State Department, his talents and his foreign birth provoked hostility among a core of Southern Republicans; notably, William Branch Giles of Virginia and Samuel Smith of Maryland. They doubted Gallatin's patriotism, his neutrality when dealing with France, and his loyalty to the Republican Party. They pressured Madison relentlessly to exclude him from the new Administration. Madison compromised, sending Gallatin to the Treasury and appointing Smith's incompetent brother Robert to serve at State. Robert was eventually replaced by James Monroe, but not before he had seriously weakened the effectiveness of his post. The incident illustrated what was to be a recurring problem in Madison's Presidency: he was often unable to resist political pressures from Congress, and he was handicapped by mediocre assistants.

Without a sure hand at the State Department, the diplomatic imbroglio with Britain and France worsened. Congress replaced the embargo with a nonimportation act that limited restrictions to the two warring powers, but promised to restore trade with the belligerent that lifted its blockade first. Madison foolishly allowed the new British minister, David Erskine, to convince him that Britain would reopen its shipping lanes to American vessels if the United States would restore commerce with England while enforcing the embargo against France. But Erskine had no authority to negotiate such an agreement. When London disavowed the bargain and recalled Erskine, the President was forced to revoke his decision.

Congress then proposed its own solution to the problem, but with no better success. A curious act called Macon's Bill No. 2, passed in May 1810, inverted the terms of the Nonintercourse Act. Both Britain and France were invited to abolish all restrictions on trade. Should either accept the offer before March 3, 1811, the other was to be given three months to do the same, after which time the President was empowered to invoke nonintercourse against it. Great Britain officially ignored the offer but began issuing licenses to American ships permitting them freely to enter British ports in defiance of their own government. Characteristically, Napoleon's response was more subtle. He let it be known that as of November 1, 1810, the Berlin and Milan decrees would no longer be applied to American ships. John Quincy Adams warned Madison of probable trickery, but the President was satisfied with Bonaparte's word. A proclamation was issued on November 2, 1810, imposing nonintercourse against Great Britain if the Orders in Council were not repealed in three months. At the designated time, the proclamation was validated by act of Congress. All the while, Napoleon was still seizing American ships in French waters and selling them as prizes. Madison had begun his Administration by offering, in effect, to become an ally of Great Britain against France. Within two years he was in what amounted to alliance with France against Great Britain.

THE tension on the high seas was matched by increasing hostilities on the frontier. The drive for new lands was pushing white settlements deep into Indian country in the Illinois and Indiana territories. Indians had resisted through intermittent skirmishes and scalpings for years, but organized warfare was slight until two Shawnee brothers, Tecumseh and the Prophet, brought the Western tribes together in a powerful confederacy that temporarily halted the surge of westward expansion. Western settlers had no doubt that Great Britain was equipping and supporting Tecumseh; they had seen British hands behind every Indian uprising since the Revolution. They saw safety for themselves only in driving the British from the North American continent. Southern planters, who coveted the rich river bottoms of the Mississippi Territory but who found the Creeks in their way, felt much the same way toward the Spanish in Florida.

During 1811 this expansionism found a political voice among a small group of congressmen popularly known as War Hawks. They included Henry Clay of Kentucky, John C. Calhoun, Langdon Cheves, and William Lowndes—all of South Carolina—as well as Peter B. Porter of western New York and others. Each was young, aggressive, and capable, and each was decidedly anti-British. Their demands for more decisive measures to confine British imperialism received a boost on November 7, 1811, when a force under General William Henry Harrison routed a segment of Tecumseh's braves near the point where the Tippecanoe River flows into the Wabash. Although Tecumseh was absent during the battle—and thus lived to plague the frontier more—the skirmish opened a new phase in the war for the Western territories. The War Hawks redoubled their efforts to secure the West for settlement—through negotiations if possible, through war if not.

The War Hawks, however, did not dominate Congress. Their desire for war was matched by the vocal, and visceral, opposition of Federalists in the House and Senate. Any decision for war thus rested with the President and the moderate Republicans, who constituted a majority in Congress. During 1811 Madison surveyed the deteriorating state of Anglo-American relations with mounting alarm and reluctantly concluded that the time for decisive action was fast drawing near. Despite his pacific nature and his fear of the effects of war, the President was ahead of most of his party in concluding that hostilities were inevitable. Still, he wanted a thorough debate on the subject; consequently, he called Congress into session on November 7, 1811— one month ahead of schedule.

The moderate Republicans who assembled on that date were anything but united in their determination to go to war. The situation with England had not materially changed in years, and no single outrage on American interests was sufficient to declare a state of national emergency. But the droning failure of diplomacy had brought the nation to a point of acute frustration that was best reflected in the attitudes and actions of moderate Republican congressmen. These men listened to the appeals of the War Hawks, tolerated the jibes of Federalists, and through it all suffered the confusion of mortals torn by indecision. Their speeches during the long session gave the impression of men spoiling for battle and were delivered as public encouragements to a nation badly in need of unity. They were partly directed to England, where, it was hoped, a strong display of resolve would persuade the British to make concessions. Behind the façade of belligerence, however, Congress was divided on almost every bill that would have helped prepare the country for war. Congress had already allowed the charter of the Bank of the United States to lapse, leaving the nation with no central agency to administer funds in time of crisis. Measures to expand the army were at best modest. And in January 1812, Republicans in the House helped defeat a measure that would have added ten frigates to the navy.

What finally moved the President and Congress to declare war on Britain were the failure of negotiations and the repeated insults inflicted on the national honor. As usual, impressment and commercial restrictions were the sorest wounds. Years of patient persuasion had done nothing to convince the British that the United States would not tolerate such an outrage indefinitely; nor was there any prospect of change. And nothing Napoleon did had shaken the conviction that Britain was chiefly responsible for the privations endured by American merchantmen. England ruled the seas; it was England's responsibility to rule them fairly. It had not done so, as the constant reports of seized vessels confirmed.

These insults to American honor fed other fears, whose roots lay deep in the ideology of republicanism and nationalism. Too much patience would ultimately have a corrosive effect on the autonomy of the new nation. England, Madison charged, had trampled "on rights which no independent nation can relinquish." To ignore such outrages merely invited future aggressions, which in the end would lead not only to commercial domination from abroad but, in the words of one congressman, to "despotism direct." Clearly, if the republican experiment were to succeed, it could do so only in an autonomous and independent state. Furthermore, since the United States was the only major republic in the Western world, the reputation and honor of republicanism would be sullied by submission. So long as the United States believed in its moral duty to demonstrate the vitality of democratic institutions, it must do so vigorously and—if necessary—by force.

Moreover, the unhappy position of being neither at war nor at peace had encouraged political dissent and threatened national unity. Already certain New England Federalists were calling for a separate confederation; they provided an incessant clamor of satire and ridicule against the Republican Administration. If the country wandered aimlessly down paths of fruitless negotiation with an implacable foe, the gloomy prospect of Federalist majorities in the Congress and, ultimately, a Federalist President would become reality. All the gains made in twelve years of Republican rule would be lost, and the nation would probably fall under the sway of the British anyway. "The honor of the nation and that of the party are bound up together," wrote one Republican editor, "and both will be sacrificed if war be not declared." Adding urgency to this crisis were the spring elections in Massachusetts and New York, which returned Federalist majorities to the state legislatures.

So moderates and War Hawks alike moved slowly toward a declaration of war. The opposition argued over and over again that the Berlin and Milan decrees were not revoked, and that Bonaparte—not England—was the real enemy. But when negotiations in the spring of 1812 still failed to wrest major concessions from the British, Madison and his party sadly gave in to the inevitable. On June 1 he sent a war message to Congress, which, after almost three weeks of debate, concurred. The vote followed party, not sectional, lines. While most of the Republican ballots cast against the war came from the Northeast, two-thirds of the Republican congressmen from that section, with massive support from the West and South, joined Madison in the call for war. The entire Federalist delegation, however, opposed, and twenty-two Republicans in both houses followed suit.

The declaration of war came too soon, by the length of time it took a fast ship to sail from England to America. Napoleon's power had attained its peak in the winter of 1811–12. All Europe save Russia was under his control, and Russia—as Great Britain soon learned—was all but isolated as far as commerce was concerned. The British people had already become restive when a crop failure raised the price of wheat beyond reach of workers idled by the closing of both Continental and American markets for British manufacturers. Riots were translated into political action, a new government came into power, and the Orders in Council were repealed in London, even as the Congress in Washington declared them to be a cause for war.

THE United States entered the War of 1812 badly divided. Almost every institution that could have helped prosecute the war was either nonexistent, defunct, or so torn by factionalism as to be virtually powerless. Nor did the new nation possess the unity of purpose and zeal to wage the conflict vigorously. Madison's leadership as President and commander in chief, for example, was inadequate and hampered by bickering and political infighting within his own party. The Cabinet squabbles that had plagued his Administration from the start continued, despite Monroe's assignment to the State Department. The War and Navy Departments were in especially bad shape, and changes there in early 1813 brought men of mediocre talent and less experience. Throughout the struggle, Madison was often unwilling or unable to fire incompetents—a fact that placed too much of the responsibility for directing the effort into his own hands. Yet the President was neither experienced in military conflict nor aggressive enough to risk making mistakes. He involved himself in tormented debates over the best course of action, and often did not act at all.

Part of his problem stemmed from lukewarm support—or active hostility—from other Republicans. Much of the trouble lay in the Senate, which took thirteen days to endorse the declaration of war and then did so by a margin of only 19 to 13. Thereafter, the Senate deliberated endlessly over the means of fighting England, with less than satisfactory results. Certain dissident Republicans questioned the timing of the war and the capacity of the nation to win it. Others, like the brilliant—but questionably sane—John Randolph of Roanoke, doubted the logic and morality of attempting to save a republic through violence. Still others were restive under Madison's leadership and felt that the war would be an utter disaster if he were left in command. This latter group clustered around De Witt Clinton and his uncle George of New York. The Clintons were loyal Republicans and skilled politicians who were unhappy with the limited, restrained use of authority practiced by Virginia Presidents. Their constant challenges to Madison were strong enough to give De Witt Clinton 89 electoral votes in 1812 against the President's 128—not enough to unseat him, but sufficient to demonstrate the weakness of Madison's support.

Other divisions, outside the Republican Party, also hampered the war effort. The strongest support for the conflict came from Southern and Western states, where territorial ambitions combined with wounded national pride to encourage an all-out effort to defeat the British. In the Northeast, however, enthusiasm was weak. New England merchants, for example, failed to see the logic of waging war with a major source of trade and income. The cost of British spoliations on American commerce had never equaled the profits to be made in the carrying trade, and—when war was declared—these merchants reacted bitterly and vocally. Bells tolled a steady lament in Providence at the news of war; ministers and stump speakers delivered long jeremiads against the government's failure to negotiate a peace. During the war, New England shipowners continued to trade with Great Britain, which secretly issued licenses that permitted American vessels to pass the blockade and sail for Lisbon (where the cargo would be reexported to the British Isles). These licenses quickly became a commodity in Boston, where they often brought as much as $1,000 on the public exchange. The net effect of such dealings was to place a substantial number of Americans in defiance of their own government.

Federalists naturally deplored the war. They had long been displeased with Britain's policy of impressment and commercial restrictions and had hoped for a peaceful resolution of the crisis. Yet they questioned Madison's sincerity and effectiveness as a negotiator. The President, Federalists charged, had not pursued economic sanctions vigorously enough, nor had the situation with Britain changed sufficiently to warrant an armed conflict. In their eyes, the war was simply an artifice to prop up a failing Administration and discredit the patriotism of those who argued against it. Moreover, the war seemed to be a deliberate attempt to sabotage the political and economic interests of the commercial states—states such as New York, where Federalism was experiencing a rebirth and Republicans were divided. To Federalists, then, "Madison's war" was a creation of political and sectional frustrations and not a genuine national crisis. In the fall elections of 1812, they capitalized on the discontent caused by the war and doubled their representation in the next Congress.

Even those who voiced support for the war seemed to lack the unity of purpose to fight it effectively. Congress took months to authorize new warships—most of which were not completed until after hostilities had ended. The nation thus entered the conflict with barely a score of vessels equipped to fight on the high seas; Britain had hundreds (although, mercifully, not all were sent into American waters). This lack of commitment to naval readiness originated in part in the assumption—common among Southern and Western congressmen—that the war was to be won primarily on land. But although Congress authorized an army of 75,000 men, less than half that number responded to the call for volunteers. Even if they had, the nation would have lacked the funds to equip and pay them. The government relied chiefly on loans to finance the conflict, but few in the Northeast—where most capital was concentrated—were willing to risk their fortunes in an unpopular war. The $80,000,000 in securities authorized by the Treasury were sold only at uncomfortably high interest rates.

IN these circumstances, the war got off to a dismal start. The conquest of Canada was a primary objective, yet efforts during 1812 to drive the British from the region surrounding the Great Lakes were disastrous. Major General William Hull was neatly finessed into surrender by a British force at Detroit without a fight. The garrison at Fort Dearborn, where Chicago now stands, was massacred as soon as news of the war reached the frontier. In October, Major General Stephen Van Rensselaer crossed the Niagara River to seize Queenstown, but his New York militiamen refused to move from the soil of their home state, leaving the spearhead of regulars to be captured by Canadians. A month later Major General Henry Dearborn—formerly Jefferson's Secretary of War and perhaps the most experienced officer in the army—led a substantial force to Canada by way of the traditional Lake Champlain invasion route. His men also refused to cross the border and returned without ever engaging the enemy.

1813 brought hope and a stalemate. The navy registered its sweetest victory on September 10, when ships led by Captain Oliver Hazard Perry defeated a British force at Put-in-Bay on Lake Erie. "We have met the enemy and they are ours," reported Perry, thus giving Americans supremacy on the Great Lakes and a much-needed battle cry. A month later General William Henry Harrison finally caught up with Tecumseh at the battle of the Thames, on the Ontario Peninsula northeast of Detroit. Tecumseh was killed, reportedly by Colonel Richard M. Johnson, who left Congress to lead a regiment of Kentucky riflemen. While the United States had still not taken Canada, the northwestern frontier was at last secure. Other victories that year, however, were few. American privateers captured hundreds of British merchant ships, but American warships were unable to break the tightening coastal blockade. Early in 1814 the blockade was extended to the New England coast, thus closing off the last vestiges of American commerce with Europe.

From the beginning, Madison hoped for an early peace, and when an offer from Czar Alexander to mediate between the United States and Great Britain came in March 1813, he seized upon it eagerly. The President named as negotiators John Quincy Adams, minister to Russia, James A. Bayard, Federalist senator from Delaware, and Secretary of the Treasury Albert Gallatin. Gallatin was initially rejected by the Senate because he had not formally resigned his Cabinet post, but was later confirmed. The progress of negotiations was painfully slow. Lord Castlereagh, the British Foreign Minister, rejected the Czar's offer of mediation but informed Madison in January 1814 that he would deal directly with the American commissioners. It was August of that year before the mission—now expanded to five members with the addition of Henry Clay and Jonathan Russell—arrived in Ghent to begin deliberations.

The task facing the commissioners was not made easy by the progress of the war. During 1814, American military commanders were sometimes victorious, often defeated. On the Niagara frontier, General Jacob Brown captured Fort Erie on July 4. One of his subordinates, Winfield Scott, won the battle of Chippewa the following day and a bloody engagement at Lundy's Lane three weeks later. In the South, General Andrew Jackson and his Tennessee militia crushed the Creek Indians, and on September 11 Thomas McDonough destroyed a British fleet off Plattsburgh on Lake Champlain and compelled withdrawal of British land forces there. More typical, however, were defeats. After Napoleon's abdication in April, England turned its attention to an early end to the American conflict. In August, British troops routed a force of Virginia militiamen at Bladensburg, Maryland, and swept into Washington, where they burned the Capitol, the White House, and other public buildings. Only a determined stand by the Maryland militia the following night at Fort McHenry spared Baltimore from the same fate. Yet this American victory did not rescue the Chesapeake area from British control, nor did it stop British plans for a decisive assault on New Orleans.

BY late fall 1814, the republic appeared to be in peril. The Treasury was again empty, and the new Secretary, Alexander J. Dallas of Philadelphia, could only propose the reestablishment of Hamilton's Bank of the United States to avoid bankruptcy. Monroe had assumed command of the War Department after the Bladensburg fiasco, yet there was too little time and too little money at his demand to reverse the threat of future British victories. The British fleet was patrolling Cape Cod, and land reinforcements—Wellington's veterans from Europe—were on their way. Congress was in turmoil, and Madison's leadership was at its nadir. Most discouraging, the unity of spirit and natural harmony which was supposedly the greatest asset of a republican society was in shambles. Discord and unrest reached a peak on October 5, 1814, when the Massachusetts legislature called a convention of the New England states "to lay the foundation for a radical reform in the National compact." The call was accepted, with December 15 as the date and Hartford, Connecticut, the site.

The Hartford Convention was the culmination of a long series of frustrations and disappointments that had alarmed New England

Federalists for years. To the delegates, Jefferson, Madison, and the Virginia strain of republican thought the two represented were the real enemies to the United States. Through them, the nation and the Republican Party had been encouraged to set aside the restraints and wisdom of capable, elite leadership and to follow instead the passions of the mob and the frontier. The result had been a decline in the fortunes of New England and a threat to the very existence of the republic. If the war was lost, the country would fall under the control of England; if it was to be won, an American Napoleon would have to emerge. Either outcome meant the death of republicanism. To certain radical Federalists, such as Timothy Pickering, the only escape was a separate New England confederacy, which—free from the abuse of misguided men in Washington—could negotiate a separate peace. To the moderates, led by Harrison Gray Otis, the best remedy was to restrict the influence of the common man in the formation of national policy and—particularly—to strip Southerners and Westerners of their power to direct the affairs of New England.

When the convention met, the moderates were in control. Brushing aside Pickering's plea for a new confederation, they proposed a series of constitutional amendments: these would require a two-thirds vote in both houses of Congress to admit new states, to impose commercial restrictions, or to declare war. They would abolish the ratio by which five slaves counted as three free men in apportioning representation in the House. They would confine federal officeholding to the native born, and limit the President to one term. They would also prohibit any state from furnishing two consecutive incumbents of that office. The intent throughout was unmistakable. Conservative New Englanders were determined to redefine the bases of republican authority by returning it to the hands of "the best men" and giving the North veto power over the ambitions of the South and West.

The Hartford Convention was more than a political protest. It symbolized a serious cleavage in the way Americans had come to view the development of republican authority during the long course of negotiations and war. The Jeffersonian Republicans believed in diversity, pluralism, and limited government; they relied on the innate good sense of moral citizens to provide direction and stability to the new republic. They had faith that the natural harmony of sectional, economic, and cultural interests would produce a united commonwealth.

The Hartford delegates offered a different interpretation of republicanism, which was not quite Hamiltonian but certainly not Jeffersonian. Unlike earlier Federalists, those at Hartford did *not* call for the creation of extensive, powerful national institutions of social control. They called instead for more checks and balances on the demands of ordinary citizens, with the intent of purifying the body politic of its dross elements. Those elements, they believed, had led the country into a war that was misdirected in its goals and was anarchic in its prosecution. Significantly, the delegates implicitly and explicitly identified the frontier and the South as the regions in which the true nature of republicanism had been lost. The former produced hotheads; the latter generated dreamers who had constructed their schemes with the forced labor of bondmen. The safety of the republic, then, demanded a moral rejuvenation of its citizens. During the next forty years, such hopes and fears would find new outlets in the proliferation of New England reformers.

JUST as the nation seemed most divided and most in danger of civil war, however, two events brought a sudden peace and an unexpected burst of national pride. Even as the Hartford Convention met, the British had concluded that a total victory over the United States was sure to be too long and too costly to justify the results. That fact, plus the dogged persistence of the American commissioners, persuaded them to negotiate a treaty that was signed on Christmas Eve, 1814. The treaty did little but end the fighting. It reestablished the prewar boundaries between Canada and the United States, said nothing about impressment, and left all other issues to be resolved later. But it did end the war. The American commissioners signed with relief, if not enthusiasm.

Two weeks after the treaty was signed, but before the news had reached America, Andrew Jackson won a stunning victory over British regulars at New Orleans. With a motley army of Tennessee and Kentucky militia, local volunteers, some Indians, blacks, and Gulf pirates, Jackson's small army all but exterminated their attackers while suffering few casualties. Jackson's strategy had been cunningly brilliant: hide behind bales of cotton, force the British to expose themselves, and decimate the enemy. The victory was a climactic, euphoric end to a depressing war, and it greatly enhanced the popularity of the colorful and controversial general. News of it—coming shortly before word reached Washington that a peace treaty had been

signed—made the Hartford protest appear petulant and a little imma-
ture.

The course of the war had been a near-disaster; its conclusion,
however, bore all the marks of a splendid victory. The spirit of unity
that followed the victory was essential to the development of American nationalism. For the second time in forty years, Americans had
struggled with the most powerful nation on earth and had won, even
if the Peace of Ghent was no more than an armistice. National honor
had been upheld and even enhanced by Jackson's triumph at New
Orleans. American independence had been reasserted; after so many
years spent in fear of European entanglements, the United States was
at last free of its colonial status. Most important, the republican
experiment had been preserved. "The late war," Madison told Congress, ". . . had become a necessary resort to assert the rights and
independence of the nation. It has been waged with a success which
is the natural result of the wisdom of the legislative councils, of the
patriotism of people . . ." In the swell of pride following the peace,
Americans shared a buoyant sense of confidence, of national unity.
The war, Gallatin observed, "has renewed and reinstated the national
feelings which the Revolution had given and which were daily less-
ened. The people have now more general objects of attachment with
which their pride and political opinions are connected. They are more
American; they feel and act more like a nation, and I hope that the
permanency of the Union is thereby better secured." The utter collapse of Federalism after the Hartford Convention only served to
bolster his optimism.

This burst of nationalism and the collapse of Federalism produced
two notable side effects. Despite the bungling and ineptitude by which
a Republican Administration and Congress had prosecuted the war,
the satisfactory conclusion of hostilities helped ratify Jefferson's ideal
of a limited, restricted government. Sectional and local interests—and
the inability of the central authority to restrain them—were forgotten
in the general relief that followed the Peace of Ghent, and Jeffersonian
republicanism received an important ideological sanction as a result.
The natural harmony of a republic, as envisioned by Jefferson, appeared capable of meeting any crisis, domestic or foreign, with ultimate success. After 1815, and after the disgrace heaped upon the
Hartford Federalists, Jeffersonianism and its variations dominated
American political thought for the next half century.

Without strong opposition, however, Jeffersonian republicanism was free to pursue new goals and directions. Party struggles during the first decades of the new nation had been particularly intense, because neither side accepted the presence of competing views as logical and healthy to a republic. Political enemies existed to be vanquished, not accommodated, because their continued presence presumably posed a threat to the security of the republic. Among Republicans, this misconception of the nature of party politics meant ideological rigidity, although not ideological consistency. After 1815, the removal of the Federalist threat eased the pressure to resist any and all attempts to use the federal government as an active agent of social control. New concepts of republicanism began to emerge which looked for some middle ground between the extremes of strictly limited government and aggressive Hamiltonianism.

The shift was apparent in the thinking of James Madison. The war had taught the President that weak institutional restraints were as deadly to the health of the republic as too much central control. A strong republic, he concluded, could not depend solely upon the virtue of its ideals. "Experience has taught us," Madison warned Congress, "that neither the pacific dispositions of the American people nor the pacific character of their political institutions" could protect them in times of crisis. Real independence meant national self-sufficiency, and that in turn required that natural republican unity be strengthened by institutional bonds. This was especially important in the economic realm. In 1816 Madison called for the protection and encouragement of domestic industries, better means of inland transportation, and a second United States Bank.

3

Expanding
the Republic

A T the close of the War of 1812 the United States looked forward
to an era of unprecedented stability and prosperity. Old foes
had been vanquished, threats had been removed, and in the peace that
followed Jackson's victory at New Orleans the republic seemed secure. The troubling fear of foreign conflict—which had long rumbled
through American society like a cannonball loose in a ship's hold—
was gone. So too, it was hoped, had the wrenching internal dissensions
symbolized by the Hartford Convention. Americans were at last free
to pursue their dreams in a spirit of harmony and unity, and the
republic entered the postwar era swelled with confidence and optimism.

In fact, an age of unprecedented change and increasing complexity
had begun. The newfound security and self-confidence of the nation
released pent-up energies that propelled the Union into an era of rapid
and unsettling social change. Americans were on the move—geo-
graphically, economically, politically. The acquisitive instinct grew
strong and then stronger as they demanded more: more territory,
more avenues to easy wealth, more access to political power. As
English visitors were fond of pointing out, this restless impatience
with the status quo could be interpreted as the crassest form of materialism. But, seen in a kinder light, it was simply the collective expression of a maturing, expanding young republic. Either way, Americans
began to extend themselves, both singly and as a nation, along paths
that had barely been contemplated only a generation earlier.

ONE aspect of this restlessness was territorial expansion. Nothing
captured the American imagination more than the promise of land.

Riotously beautiful, almost empty, the North American continent dazzled settlers with its promise and its unpredictability. Nature there seemed to exist only in extremes: the savages were wilder, the weather more unpredictable, the terrain more varied, than any place known to the Old World. Its vastness defied description. As late as 1800 and beyond, there were no reliable maps of the interior. A few explorers, Spanish and French mostly, had ventured outside the settled regions north of Texas and west of the Mississippi Valley, but their reports were fragmentary, often contradictory, and filled with hyperbole. Every exploration discovered something new, yet behind the newness lay centuries of unrecorded change and development. It was as if a separate universe, with its own laws of time and space, had lain fallow for eons, waiting for the touch of civilization. "Who can tell how far it extends," asked Michel-Guillaume de Crèvecoeur in 1782. "Who can tell the millions of men whom it will feed and contain?"

The frontier was a repository of dreams and fantasies. For the hard-nosed and upwardly mobile, it promised land and wealth. "There is room for every body in America," Crèvecoeur added. "Has he any particular talent or industry? He exerts it in order to procure a livelihood, and it succeeds . . . Does he want uncultivated lands? Thousands of acres present themselves, which he may purchase cheap. Whatever be his talents or inclinations, if they are moderate, he may satisfy them." The sheer size of the storehouse of resources to the west discouraged moderate inclinations, of course. Americans formed their dreams in a physical environment that seemed boundless.

The frontier appealed to other instincts. If the continent was a gigantic Cibola, full of mythical cities of gold, it was also an earthly Eden, a garden, in which man could experience a rebirth of spirit and purpose. Tilling this garden, wrote John Winthrop in the seventeenth century, produced an end "Double morall and naturall, that man might injoy the fruites of the earth & god might have his due glory from the creature." Two hundred years later the garden was still fresh, exciting the same dreams of a new beginning. Wrote Bronson Alcott in 1834: "Living on the accumulated treasures of the past in a new theatre of action, we have monopolized the best of time and space, and stand on a vantage ground to which no people have ever ascended before."

The idea that Americans possessed "the best of time and space" inspired them with a sense of mission and purpose. Quite naturally, Americans regarded themselves as the finest products of European civilization, and the continent as the finest example of God's creations. The convergence of the two was not lost on the founders or their descendants. Their experiment in republicanism was under a special charge to use its human and natural resources wisely. Americans were a chosen race, destined by God to lead the world to new heights of culture and achievement. In this unfolding of the divine plan, there might be transient conflict as competing forces of wildness and civilization struggled to reach equilibrium, but traditional notions of time and space—limitations, mostly, imposed by history and overcrowding—were no longer relevant. The American mission was to rewrite history in fresh surroundings.

This compelling sense of mission fueled the urge to acquire and settle the continent. In the early years of the republic, acquisition was largely a matter of survival, for the United States was surrounded by anti-republican forces British, French, Spanish, and Indian—whose presence threatened the new nation with a never-ending series of border wars. The obvious solution was to drive the alien elements out and secure the frontier. The War of 1812 helped solve part of the problem; thereafter, American foreign policy was mostly directed toward completing the task. In time, however, the acquisitive spirit assumed a logic of its own. If, as Americans reasoned, God had ordained that an experiment in democracy would be begun on these shores, He must also have set aside the continent for Americans and Americans alone. "It belongs of *right* to the United States to regulate the future destiny of *North America,*" argued one newspaper in 1803. "The country is *ours;* ours is the right to its rivers and to all the sources of future opulence, power and happiness, which lay scattered at our feet." Territorial expansion, then, was inevitable—a goal captured in 1845 in an obscure editor's phrase, "manifest destiny."

These were grand, perhaps grandiose, visions for a nation that had barely escaped calamity in the war with Britain and did not yet fully control what it already possessed. Although the eyes of the nation were firmly fixed on the endless prairies and mountains that stretched to the Pacific coast, its feet were still planted in the new territories east of the Mississippi River. During the first half of the nineteenth century, this gap between aspiration and reality produced a similar bifurcation in acquisition and settlement. American foreign policy became geared to the long drive west, exploring means and ways of annexing some lands and of securing first option on others. Settlement, on the other hand, was a shifting mosaic of communities and homesteads that proceeded by fits and starts. Nonetheless, American expansionism before the Civil War was astonishingly rapid. Fed by a population that doubled every twenty years, the United States grew from a basically coastal republic in 1800 to a continental empire in 1850.

ALTHOUGH the War of 1812 removed the most serious brake on American expansionism, acquisition had begun in earnest over a decade earlier. In 1800 the Spanish empire was in its last stage of decay, and the final, conclusive struggle between England and France was about to begin. For the United States, the convergence of these two events was a godsend and a challenge. The Spanish colonies to the west and south of the new republic were a sumptuous feast of land and resources that no American could ignore, and the American appetite for territory was ravenous. So was that of the British and French. Napoleon stripped Louisiana from Spain in 1800 and undoubtedly would have taken more if war had not erupted with England shortly thereafter. As it was, the conflict diverted the energies of the European powers just long enough to allow the United States to begin its own program of hemispheric domination.

The purchase of Louisiana was an unexpected windfall, the direct result of Napoleon's need to raise cash. No other single acquisition was as important to the expansion of the republic. Yet, even before the sale was proposed, Jefferson had made plans to explore and map the continent all the way to the Pacific. His eyes were on the Oregon Territory. In 1803 he persuaded Congress to finance a mission under his personal secretary, Meriwether Lewis, and a twenty-eight-year-old army lieutenant, William Clark, to find a water route to the Pacific. Lewis and Clark left in July and returned three years later. In the interim they reached the headwaters of the Missouri in Montana, wintered near the Pacific Ocean at the mouth of the Columbia, and prepared invaluable reports not only on the terrain but on the flora and fauna, and the Indian tribes, of the Pacific Northwest. While Lewis and Clark were exploring the north country, Zebulon Pike journeyed from St. Louis up the Mississippi and back, then set forth to Colorado, where in 1806 he wintered at Pueblo and unsuccessfully attempted to climb a peak he named after himself. From there he pushed south to Santa Fe and Taos, and on across the Rio Grande into Chihuahua. Other expeditions—one headed by the astronomer Thomas Freeman—looked for the headwaters of the Red River in Texas. The intent of these missions was only partly scientific. Jefferson wanted information that would open routes for commerce and—eventually—settlement.

While Jefferson looked west, others looked south. By 1800 planters and settlers in Georgia and the Mississippi Territory regarded Spanish Florida as a logical—and necessary—extension of the new republic. Spain's hold on Florida was precariously weak and grew weaker as the situation in Europe worsened. During the first decade of the nineteenth century, Americans began drifting into the colony—particularly the western neck that stretched along the valuable coastline to the Mississippi. Spain was helpless to prevent the migration, and by 1810 most of the settled areas of West Florida were American enclaves. The unsettled regions, however, were havens for marauders, runaway slaves, and, above all, the Seminole Indians. Of all southern tribes save the Cherokees, the Seminoles were the most organized, the most independent, and the most restive under foreign domination. In their capacity for devastating raids and harassment, they were unequaled. To the United States, the combined presence of Spaniards, free blacks, pirates, and Indians was an intolerable affront to the destined use of the continent, and one that could be countered only by annexation.

In a classic example of expansionism, Americans chipped away at Spanish authority in Florida. After the purchase of Louisiana, Jefferson attempted to buy the territory from Spain. The effort failed, so his successor, Madison, concluded that Florida had been part of the original bargain with Napoleon. Madison's conviction inspired American colonists in the extreme western tip of the region, lying between the Mississippi and Pearl rivers, to revolt against Spain in 1810 and to seize that area by force. Three years later, at the height of the conflict with Britain, Madison used his war powers to extend American sovereignty from the Mississippi to the Perdido—just east of Mobile Bay. But Madison was cautious about going too far. He made no attempt to annex the Florida peninsula itself.

In 1817 the United States tried again. Skirmishes with the Indians had intensified, and pirates had taken control of Amelia Island, at the mouth of the St. Marys River on the border between Georgia and

Florida. Late that year the new President, James Monroe, ordered the navy to seize Amelia Island, which it did promptly. At the same time Monroe sent Andrew Jackson to pursue a band of marauding Seminoles into Florida. If the Indians took refuge in a Spanish fort, Jackson was to ask the Secretary of War for instructions. Otherwise, he was to destroy the Seminoles wherever he found them.

Jackson accepted the assignment with his usual zeal. During the early months of 1818 he tracked the Seminoles through the swamps and woods of the neck of West Florida. In March he found them near the Spanish fort of St. Marks, which he seized to prevent the Indians from taking cover there. Once inside the captured fort, Jackson found two British subjects, one an elderly Scottish trader and another a British officer, who he wrongly concluded had directed the Indian raids. Jackson court-martialed and executed both, then moved in the wake of the fleeing Seminoles to Pensacola, where he stormed Fort Barancas.

Jackson's exploits were popular but controversial. He had placed the United States in the curious position of defending an American general who had executed British subjects at a captured Spanish fort during the course of attacking an independent Indian nation. The British and Spanish legations in Washington reacted hotly, and Secretary of War John C. Calhoun, whose direct orders Jackson had disobeyed, demanded a court of inquiry. The President was inclined to agree. But John Quincy Adams, the capable and farsighted Secretary of State, defended the errant general. Adams saw that Jackson had unintentionally enhanced American chances to purchase Florida, by demonstrating with swift and brutal efficiency the ability of the United States to take the territory by force. After heated and secret debates in the Cabinet, Adams finally convinced his colleagues that to punish or even to disavow Jackson would throw away a key bargaining advantage. The captured forts were returned to the Spanish; Jackson received not even a reprimand.

Apparently Adams's strategy worked. Jackson's exploits signaled a new aggressiveness behind American expansionism that no European power—least of all, Spain—could ignore. During the latter half of 1818, Adams intensified his efforts to buy Florida, and in February 1819 he successfully negotiated a sale. Spain agreed to sell the territory for $5,000,000 and a repudiation of American claims to Texas and California. The agreement also defined the northern boundary of

Spanish possessions in the Southwest, drawing a line at the forty-second parallel between California and the Oregon country. The treaty barely escaped defeat in the Senate, however. Some regarded the purchase as a strategic move to advance the Presidential aspirations of Adams—which in part it was. Others refused to give up Texas, doggedly maintaining that it had been included in the Louisiana Purchase. Despite these objections, and despite a three-year delay in winning approval from the Spanish, Florida was annexed. Settlers poured in, and in 1822 the region was formally organized as a territory.

ALTHOUGH Florida was a prime example of acquisition by infiltration and violence, American expansionism also followed other strategies. The United States was eager not only to root out the last vestiges of colonialism in the Western Hemisphere but to discourage any new attempts to implant European—particularly British—influence there. The first task was less a matter of strategy than of allowing the Spanish empire to crumble of its own accord. During the Napoleonic wars, Spain's hegemony over its Central and South American colonies steadily eroded, and by 1815 Argentina, Chile, and Venezuela were in open revolt. Mexico soon followed suit. As the new republics gained their independence, they naturally turned to the United States for aid and recognition—which most Americans, including several key members of Congress, were eager to grant.

The Administration was more reluctant. Monroe was cautious by nature, and Adams feared that a premature recognition of the new republics would jeopardize the delicate negotiations over Florida. Moreover, Adams preferred to wait until the postwar situation in Europe had stabilized and Britain's involvement with the South American trade had been measured. Adams's plan was to secure Florida first, while allowing others to publicize, unofficially, American support of the new republics. It was an overly cautious policy. Spain was too weak to reverse the deterioration of its empire, no matter what the United States did, and England was not inclined to offer any assistance to its historic rival, Spain. The unnecessary delay in granting recognition unfortunately opened decades of suspicion and distrust of the United States among the new republics.

Still, the threat of British intervention in South America was real. After 1815, England began steadily to improve its position there, opening markets for its manufactured goods and contracting for access to the rich mineral deposits of Mexico, Brazil, and other areas in return. As Britain's investments in South America grew, so did its desire to protect them. The situation reached an unexpected crisis in 1823, when France threatened to help restore the Spanish monarchy and indicated that it might help recoup lost Spanish colonies in the New World as well. The British Foreign Minister, George Canning, was alarmed, as were the Americans. Since neither England nor the United States stood to gain by a restoration of Spanish colonialism, Canning suggested that the two nations issue a joint declaration of policy, mutually disavowing territorial ambitions while warning against interference by others. Before notes could be exchanged, however, France repudiated any designs on the former Spanish colonies, and Canning dropped the subject.

Not so the Americans. Canning's suggestion triggered a complex reaction in the White House, the State Department, and among the various contenders for the upcoming Presidential election. Monroe and most of the Cabinet initially welcomed the proposal for a joint declaration. It would provide the United States with a powerful and well-armed ally to resist the encroachments of monarchical interests in the Western Hemisphere. Monroe was concerned not only with Spain but with Russia, which was attempting to extend its territories in Alaska and the Pacific Northwest. The President took the proposal to Jefferson and Madison—as he was accustomed to do when faced with knotty problems—and both concurred.

But Adams objected. Long years of confrontation with the foreign offices of Europe had convinced him that an Anglo-American resolution would gain nothing for the United States. France and Russia would regard such a treaty as a British declaration and would respect it—or ignore it—solely from that perspective. A unilateral statement issued directly from Washington, on the other hand, would force all colonial powers, Britain included, to an awareness that the United States was intent on establishing its own hegemony in the affairs of the Western Hemisphere. Moreover, if Adams had read Canning correctly, the British were in no mood to challenge the Americans at that time. Hence, a distinctly American document would carry few risks.

Adams was also looking ahead to the upcoming Presidential contest, as were other Cabinet members and Speaker of the House Henry

Clay. To forge ahead of his competitors, Adams needed some bold stroke by which he could extend his base of support outside his native New England. To have agreed to a joint declaration would have done his enemies no harm but would have hurt Adams. To advocate a unilateral statement, on the other hand, would offer the voters unequivocal proof of Adams's nationalism. He would be seen as a man of the times—perhaps slightly ahead of them. During long and often fiery discussions with the President and the Cabinet, Adams pressed his views. It was far better to act alone, he argued, than "to come in as a cock-boat in the wake of the British man-of-war."

Finally, Monroe agreed. In his annual message of December 1823, the President issued what was to be known (somewhat ironically, in light of Adams's role) as the Monroe Doctrine. Indirectly acknowledging the independence of the former colonies to the south, Monroe asserted that the Americas, "by the free and independent condition which they have assumed and maintain," were thenceforward closed to any future colonization by any European power, and he warned that any attempt to do so would be considered an unfriendly act toward the United States. To make the declaration reciprocal, Monroe also stated that the United States would not involve itself in European affairs—an allusion to the revolutionary movement in Greece—unless its rights were "invaded or seriously menaced." But the President carefully left open the possibility and the right of the United States to intervene and expand where needed in the Western Hemisphere.

Reactions to the Monroe Doctrine were mixed. The British, particularly Canning, regarded the message as a pretentious, somewhat irritating boast, but did nothing. Canning well knew that the United States was incapable of defending the Monroe Doctrine without a war, and that war would be costly to the new nation. England still possessed the military and economic strength to pursue a vigorous course of colonization in any part of the world, as the rapid spread of the British Empire during the nineteenth century would prove. Moreover, a treaty negotiated with the Americans in 1818 opened the vast Oregon Territory to joint settlement by both Britain and the United States. And nothing in the Monroe Doctrine prevented the English from developing their economic base in South America. In short, Canning chose not to react to the message directly simply because he did not need to.

Americans accepted the message with serene praise. The press welcomed it as an event "worthy of commemoration," but the few commemorations that occurred were curiously perfunctory and low-key, as if there was nothing especially brash about challenging the world's greatest colonial powers. For most Americans, the Monroe Doctrine was merely an affirmation of what they already assumed: that the United States was fast becoming the preeminent force in the Western Hemisphere. By 1823 the sense of mission was so deeply ingrained in the American mind that few questioned the republic's right to dictate hemispheric relationships. That the message was in fact pretentious, brash, and belligerent never occurred to a nation absorbed in fulfilling its inevitable destiny.

Its weaknesses notwithstanding, the Monroe Doctrine completed the contours of federal policy toward territorial expansion. What land the United States could buy—as in the case of the Louisiana Territory—it would purchase gladly. What it wanted but could not buy outright—as in the case of Florida—it would take, using a combination of diplomacy and military force. And the United States would protect both its acquisitions and its future options through diplomatic manipulation. For most of the nineteenth century these attitudes (they never really achieved the status of formal policy) surrounded every addition of new territory.

WHILE diplomats worked to extend the boundaries of the new republic, settlers rushed to fill its interior. During the first half of the century, most of this migration was directed toward the Old Northwest and the lower Mississippi Valley, where the United States held undisputed claim. More than a million acres were taken up by homesteaders and speculators in 1815, and thereafter each year's total exceeded that of the year before. As the lands were sold and resold, population in the territories and the Western states multiplied. Mississippi, for example, had only 31,000 inhabitants in 1810; by 1840 it had 376,000, having more than doubled its population every decade. The figures for Ohio were even more dramatic. With only 45,000 residents (about one per square mile) in 1800, it recorded over 2.5 million in 1840 (37 per square mile).

Federal land policy encouraged this increase. Before 1800 the government regarded the public lands primarily as a source of income, to be surveyed and sold in large, rectangular blocks. The intent was to raise badly needed cash while lending order and predictability to westward expansion. There were two problems to this approach: it favored the wealthy speculator over the common settler, and it ignored the natural contours of the land—which were anything but rectangular. Moreover, it did not acknowledge the rights of the squatter who might have settled the land long before any survey was made. By 1800 the system had begun to change, responding—often belatedly —to the demands of the small homesteader. In 1800 the minimum lot was reduced from 640 to 320 acres, and provisions were made for buying land on credit. In 1804 the smallest lot was reduced to 160 acres, and the price lowered to $1.64 per acre. In 1820 the acreage was halved again and the price dropped to $1.25, although credit sales were abolished. During the 1830s a series of acts gave the squatter first option on the land he had claimed—a recognition capped by a "preemption" act passed in 1841. These measures reflected a subtle but important shift in land policy: the nation now valued settlement ahead of revenue. Cheap land at low prices encouraged people to fill up the West quickly and to drive the frontier back.

It was an innovative policy and one that facilitated growth, but its effects were not always what had been intended. Although most of the actual settlers were families, much of the land still went to speculators, who took advantage of low prices to buy large lots, which they resold at high prices, usually financed at exorbitant rates by unstable frontier banks. Moreover, the settler was often a speculator himself. In the cardshark atmosphere of the West, the temptation to make a fast profit from land could ensnare even the most responsible family man. The American farmer, Alexis de Tocqueville observed, frequently bought land "in order to sell it again, and not to farm it." The result was all too often overextended credit, and cycles of boom and depression.

BUT nothing diminished the magnetic appeal of the frontier. As the settlers streamed west, the empty lands began to fill, and as the lands filled, a frontier culture began to take root. Its most distinctive feature was its desperate urge to create and maintain order. Although Western folklore is rich with tales of the solitary trailblazer—the pure individualist living free of the trappings of civilization—the dominant characteristic of the actual settler was his determination to maintain continuities with the life he had left behind. A heavy load of cultural baggage accompanied every move; the migrant took not only his plows and his dishware but also his institutions and his biases. "One should not assume any connection between the pioneer and the place that shelters him," wrote Tocqueville.

> All his surroundings are primitive and wild, but he is the product of eighteen centuries of labor and experience. He wears the clothes and talks the language of a town; he is aware of the past, and curious about the future, and ready to argue about the present; he is a very civilized man prepared for a time to face life in the forest, plunging into the wildernesses of the New World with his Bible, ax, and newspapers.

This subtle transplantation of ideas and habits made the frontier a land of surprising contrast.

Most came in groups, the most common being the family. The average settler was between the ages of twenty-five and forty-five, married, with children. Often the husband would migrate first, checking out transportation and potential homesites alone or with an elder son. Once settled, he would send for his wife and children or perhaps return East to bring them back himself. Given the crude state of transportation, the journey was invariably slow and used every available type of conveyance. A family moving to Indiana, say, from Pennsylvania might travel by wagon until it reached Pittsburgh, then either build a raft or book passage on a riverboat to navigate the Ohio as far west as Louisville, then complete the trip by wagon. The load of baggage tended to lighten during the journey. It was common for a family to begin its trek laden with furniture, tools, crockery, even books. By trip's end only the tools and most treasured items remained, the rest having been sold for needed cash or simply discarded to save weight.

There were certain patterns to these moves. Settlements along the Great Lakes, for example, contained a large portion of transplanted Yankees who had filtered west through New York or Pennsylvania and had taken passage on lake steamers to reach the frontier. Towns here tended to resemble their counterparts due east—tight, neat, and orderly. A traveler from Boston who visited the Western Reserve (that part of Ohio surrounding Cleveland) would feel at home. The lower Mississippi Valley was predictably Southern. Towns were fewer, and life was organized around the cotton culture. The middle region, extending roughly a hundred miles either side of the Ohio

River, was the most diverse. "Little Egypt"—southern Illinois—was distinctly Southern in outlook and habits, except that there were no slaves. Central and northern Kentucky were ostensibly Southern but contained a more diversified economy than the Deep South and more towns—some of which were organized around radical religious sects such as the Shakers at Pleasant Hill. And every region harbored anomalies. Great Lakes Yankees, who could outdo the stodgiest Bostonian in ethnic snobbishness, often found themselves working side by side with German immigrants. And hill-country Appalachians positively hated the slaveholding aristocrats of the flatlands. The West, then, was a mosaic of subcultures—sometimes friendly, often hostile, always unpredictable.

Wherever he went, the settler's life was hard. The very first task for any family was the construction of shelter. Initially, the homesteader might throw up a three-sided hut fashioned from rough logs and intended to last a few weeks or months while the fields were cleared and the first crops planted. All too often, the huts remained for a year or two as settler families worked to clear the tenacious trees that covered their land. Along with the need for shelter was the need for food. Settlers were marksmen by necessity, not choice; the most important single possession of any frontier family was an accurate muzzle-loader and an adequate supply of ammunition. After that came plows, cooking utensils, and—of course—the ever-present draft animal, be it horse, mule, or ox. Slowly, a farm would take shape—often with the aid of others. When the fields were cleared and the crops were in, settlers joined together to raise each other's houses. As soon as money would allow, other accoutrements of civilization trickled in. In the rawest areas, possession of a pane of unbroken glass marked a family as old-timers, founders of the region. After a time came the books, the silverplate, the rugs, and china.

DESPITE the loneliness, the severity, and the capriciousness of frontier life, the settler's most enduring trait was his sense of community. As Tocqueville observed, settlers were not barbarians; they were transplanted republicans. Their persistent, sometimes touching, efforts to preserve the artifacts of civilization on the frontier were testaments to their need for stability in a chaotic world. Yet the fact remained that their world was chaotic. Frontier society was America *in extremis:* fluid, competitive, pluralistic. The two forces—one centripetal, the other centrifugal—existed side by side in an uneasy relationship. Like his Eastern counterparts, then, the settler searched for ways of bringing order into his life.

One offshoot of this drive was the surprising emphasis he placed on religion. Surprising, since Americans were not widely noted for their piety. They drank, fought, and gambled to excess, particularly on the frontier. Yet these excesses were matched by a complementary desire to erect standards of virtue and clean living. The Cane Ridge meeting in Kentucky in 1801 had demonstrated the power religion could exert in even the roughest communities, and for the next half century the revival spirit dominated the West. Revivals introduced the authority of God to areas where other forms of authority often did not exist. They inspired entire communities with a sense of collective purpose, reminding them of their social and ethical obligations to one another regardless of the near-anarchic state of their society. And they served a recreational function by providing a diversion from the lonely rigors of frontier life.

The real impact of the revival began after the camp meetings had broken up. Revivals themselves were transitory and sporadic; their success depended on the charisma of the revivalist and, very often, the weather. Still, they had profound and enduring effects on the frontier. Even though revivals sometimes competed with organized religion, a wave of church building often followed in their wake. These churches served as community centers; sometimes they—and the local saloon —were the only public buildings for miles. Moreover, the revivals enhanced the prestige of the local clergyman. The revivalist—as distinct from the frontier parson—might move on; the parson remained, working long hours in an environment that would have broken the spirit of the most incurable optimist. Revivals gave them a timely boost and reinforced their image as the voice of God. With the aid of the revivals, frontier clergymen commanded respect and deference, becoming, in effect, a kind of elite class that was separate in style and origin from the successful businessman or entrepreneur. The frontier parson, then, personified standards and traditions that were timeless and revered.

Alongside the church came the school. The original plan for distributing federal lands set aside one section—640 acres—in each township to locate and maintain schools, and, while the letter of the law was difficult to follow, settlers adopted its intent eagerly. Larger towns such as Cincinnati very quickly developed an elaborate and well-funded public-school program. Elsewhere, primary instruction was likely to be offered either at home or in Sunday school. Theoretically, this situation should have resulted in an abysmally uneducated citizenry. In fact, literacy was impressively high in even the newest settlements—a testament both to the extent to which Jefferson's dream of an enlightened electorate had taken root and to the settler's own determination to preserve civilization and culture on the frontier.

More astonishing were the number of colleges. Every town had a church, but to have an institution of higher learning suggested that a community had arrived. "Higher learning" in such cases was an elastic term: most frontier colleges were little more than boarding schools run by one or two tutors and funded by local businessmen and a church. They were frankly denominationalist, the offspring of each sect's drive to establish itself and to enhance its prestige. Some enrolled a few students at best; only about one in five lasted more than twenty years. But those that survived—such as Transylvania and Centre in Kentucky or Oberlin in Ohio—were small oases of civilization and learning.

In any community, one of the first tasks was the establishment of some form of law. The need was most obvious in the territories, which were large and only loosely administered by governors appointed in Washington, but it extended to the newer states, where legislatures tended to be weak, poorly financed, and ineffective. In new settlements the preservation of social order was largely an act of faith supported by the combined force of religion and a few courts. Still, the desire to maintain harmony on the frontier resulted in the erection of certain standards and procedures by which justice was defined and administered. The most common problem involved claim jumping or boundary disputes, and the most common remedy was the informal citizen's court. In some territories two-thirds of the claimed land was occupied without benefit of a deed or bill of sale. Settlers stopped where the land looked promising, worked it for a while, and then either saved or borrowed the money to buy it. In the interim they were prey to other settlers with the same idea or to speculators with ready cash. Wherever a dispute arose, the community adopted a priority principle to resolve the contest: those who had arrived first rightfully owned what they had claimed, regardless of the nuances of law. If the case ever actually reached a court, the second-comer, or claim jumper, found his case tried by a judge who was himself a settler and decided by a jury composed of settlers. The verdict was predictable. The same spirit of community, the brotherhood of the frontier, operated whenever civil harmony was threatened.

In time these amorphous communities reached the point where statehood became the logical next step. Given the rapid increase in population, that point was often reached quickly. Five new states— Alabama, Illinois, Indiana, Louisiana, and Mississippi—entered the Union between 1812 and 1819. Maine was admitted in 1820; Missouri, in 1821. From 1821 to 1845 only Arkansas and Michigan achieved statehood; in 1845 the country suddenly pushed west and south again as Texas, Florida, Iowa, Wisconsin, and California were admitted to the Union in the space of five short years. Nothing symbolized the settler's quest for community more than statehood. It filled him with pride to reproduce the republic on the frontier. Inhabitants of a newly admitted state literally fell over themselves in weeks-long celebrations of moonshine whiskey, rococo speeches, and mile-long torchlight parades. Once the celebration had ended, they invested scarce cash in the erection of a statehouse—the monument to their success as a community.

STATEHOOD, however, did not eliminate the hardships of frontier life, nor did it mitigate the problems such headlong expansionism placed before the new nation. The intents and aims of the state government outlined in the carefully worded new constitutions were noble, but the machinery for implementing authority nowhere existed. Given the sheer size of the new states, regional political rivalries and antagonisms among Western subcultures were intense and often violent. Even in Ohio, which was admitted in 1803, the speaker of the state legislature during the 1840s protected his chair with a pair of prize fighting bulldogs. Moreover, most of the land in the new states remained in the hands of the federal government. As each territory was organized into a state, the demand for land shot up. So did the incidence of fraud and corruption. Speculators poured in to acquire land, and wildcat banks appeared with ready, and often worthless, cash for loans. Furthermore, everyone seemed to want a canal or turnpike built to his front door. The West's demand for easy money and faster communications evolved quickly into a nagging dilemma in Washington.

There were other costs to expansionism. Settlers, in their rush to civilize the frontier, brushed aside civilizations that were already there. No Indian tribe, from the Seminoles in Florida to the Shawnees in the Old Northwest, was able to preserve its culture in the face of the advancing tide from the East. Before 1825 the federal government lamely attempted to treat the tribes as protectorates—buying their land where necessary and offering them enclaves secure from white intrusion. State and territorial authorities treated these guarantees with contempt and violence, and in 1825 President Monroe bowed to the inevitable by proposing that all tribes be moved west of the Mississippi River. The removals took twenty years to accomplish; in the process, thousands of Indians died.

And there was environmental damage. The unsettled lands were a vast storehouse of natural resources that fairly begged for exploitation. Americans happily obliged. In an accelerating rush, nineteenth-century pioneers tore, ripped, scarred, and blasted the land, disregarding everything but its material benefits. In the process, much was lost. Indian petroglyphs along the high banks of the Ohio River disappeared at the hands of men who wanted only the stone on which they were inscribed. Rivers were rerouted; forests were leveled piecemeal; miles of prairie grass were burned off, exposing the topsoil to erosion by wind and rain. There is no way to estimate how many acres of prime farmland seeped into the rivers and streams, but by midcentury the Kentucky was a silty mess, and the Mississippi delta was beginning to rise. Nor is there any way of knowing how many species of fish and game vanished without a trace.

The most profound impact of territorial expansion could not be measured. Jeffersonian concepts of republican simplicity and social harmony could not survive such rapid growth intact. No matter how hard the settler tried to reproduce his civilization and his culture on the frontier, the westward explosion—both of territory and of population—was an agent of unsettling change that no part of the new nation escaped. The settler's persistent desire to get there first, to buy low and sell high, fostered competitiveness and mobility. These were not the traits of cooperation and love for the soil that Jefferson had treasured. The settler's need to import durable goods and sell his produce demanded a complex national market economy, one based on fast transportation and easy credit. The ready availability of Western land attracted workers from the East and helped produce a chronic short-

age of labor there. And the pluralistic mix of subcultures, each demanding a political voice, amplified the need for broadly national
institutions of political authority. In short, westward expansion
helped accelerate the new nation's movement from a largely agrarian,
in many respects static, culture to a diversified, complex market economy that stressed innovation and mobility. Nowhere was the impact
of the change more apparent than in the economic transformation of
the new republic.

4

The Contours of
Economic Change

"NO man in America is contented to be poor, or expects to continue so," observed a journalist in 1845. "There are here no established limits within which the hopes of any class of society must be confined, as in other countries. . . . Commerce is to become the universal pursuit of men." During the first half of the nineteenth century, the United States proved to be one of the most enterprising and innovative nations on earth. European visitors universally marveled at how hard Americans worked, how seriously they pursued economic and material gain. It was as if a subtle infection had invaded the entire populace, driving them to rise at dawn, work until dusk, and go home to plot the next day's projects. Even the midday meal, noted one traveler, was given over to business. Americans seemingly did not know how to relax.

The spirit of enterprise fed on many sources. Territorial expansion opened up a continent of almost limitless assets, promising the industrious success and achievement. The egalitarian ideology of the Revolution encouraged mobility and raised expectations. The industrial revolution introduced the tools of technology to economic enterprise. And running through all these forces of change was the American capacity for innovation. It was not innovation in the sense of discovery; very few of the major breakthroughs in technology, for example, originated in the United States. It was innovation in the sense that Americans could adapt their resources to solve problems. Thus, the steam engine was invented in England; the steamboat was invented in the United States.

Innovation was not limited to technology. The most important changes of the era were in the structure and institutions of economic enterprise. In the first half of the nineteenth century the market economy of the new nation reached unprecedented levels of diversification and complexity. The simplicity and self-sufficiency of Jefferson's ideal republic gave way to economic—and, by extension, social—forms that were national rather than local, systematic rather than personal, expansive rather than static. Cities, transportation, and finance assumed strategic importance in stimulating economic growth, as did a correlative need for new methods of production and marketing. These changes were exciting and challenging: they boosted the republic's self-confidence and nationalistic pride; they also placed unexpected burdens on its institutions and its individuals.

LAND and its products remained the basic source of economic expansion. New lands in the South and West, for example, permitted greater regional specialization, which in turn promoted regional interdependence—a critical element in the formation of economic nationalism. As the Appalachian frontier receded, the Ohio Valley emerged as a new source of food and grain. Wheat, corn, and other grains began to move down the Ohio and Mississippi rivers—and, after 1825, along the Erie Canal—in such quantities that the West soon outstripped the Northeast in agricultural production. In an era in which agricultural technology and fertilizers were crude and primitive, it was far easier to expand into new lands than to try to squeeze more productivity from old. The Northeast came to rely on the West for food, and capital in the older regions turned to commerce and industry. This West–Northeast trade was important in forming ties between the states north of the Ohio River and the Mason–Dixon line, since the South grew most of its own foodstuffs.

Yet the South added its own vigor to the expanding economy. With the invention of the cotton gin and the power loom, Southern exports of cotton had soared between 1800 and 1812. The boom continued after the war, as British mills devoured as much of the fiber as Southerners could ship them. Although the price of cotton fluctuated wildly—it was grindingly low throughout the 1820s—the volume of production steadily increased as planters moved west and into the interior. By the 1830s, cotton prices were rising again along with production. Cotton thus gave the United States a solid base in the export trade. Between 1815 and 1845, it accounted for at least one-third—and sometimes more than half—of the entire value of American exports. Southern cotton also helped form the basis of the New England textile development.

THESE changes placed special burdens on trade and transportation. American shipping before the war had been largely confined to the reexport trade, plying the triangle formed by the West Indies, the United States, and Europe. The embargo and the war shut down the trans-Atlantic trade long enough to allow coastal commerce to develop. Once begun, its pace never slackened. Ships churned up and down the Atlantic coast or rounded the Florida Keys and docked at Mobile or New Orleans. Cotton from the South went to factories in New England, and the cloth made there, along with furniture and hardware, was shipped back to the mouth of the Mississippi. Among the Atlantic ports, New York quickly became a giant. It possessed a fine natural harbor; it had a large hinterland—which became even larger after the Erie Canal opened; it was a financial as well as trading center.

New York also led other cities as a commercial innovator. Besides encouraging the building of the Erie Canal and promoting the coastal trade, New York merchants showed their flexibility and inventiveness by establishing in 1817 the first regular packet service between the United States and Europe, the Black Ball Line. Ships left New York and returned on regular schedules, catering to the passenger trade. This made it possible for British and American merchants to deal with each other regularly and easily. The packet ships were so popular that the service moved into the coastal trade within five years. New York also adopted the auction system, whereby buyers of cotton or other products could avoid middlemen and deal directly in raw or finished materials. So could upstate merchants.

But internal, domestic trade was even more important to economic growth. For those who had chosen to move West, trade was impossible without better inland transportation. The small businessman of western Pennsylvania or Ohio could not hope to expand or to fill his orders without a cheap, fast means of getting them to market. Nor could the millions of farmers who raised and sold cash crops. The result was a flurry of turnpike construction during the first decades of the century. The National Road, which joined Washington with the Ohio Valley in 1818, was the grandest attempt to open a highway to the West, but scores of shorter routes also appeared. These early turnpikes connected the backcountry to rivers and ports, giving the small farmer access to markets. Between 1820 and 1840, so many miles of road were built, largely at state and federal expense, that few additional major arteries were cut east of the Mississippi until the twentieth century.

Water travel was more attractive, however. Barges and rafts could carry heavier loads than wagons or carts, and do so smoothly and cheaply. The trouble was that rivers west of the Appalachians ran perversely away from the major markets of the East. A shipment from Cincinnati had to go west to the Mississippi, then down to New Orleans, then up the East Coast in order to reach Baltimore or New York. Or it had to be hauled overland to the Great Lakes, then shipped down the St. Lawrence. Moreover, this commerce was one-way. To ship wheat to New Orleans was one thing; to carry ironware back up to Ohio was quite another. Either traders had to defy the currents or cut new waterways.

They did both. Ever since John Fitch had snorted up the Delaware in 1787 in his crude steamboat, American inventors had been alert to the commercial potential in a ship that could disregard wind and currents. Robert Fulton hit upon the proper combination of power and design in 1807, and soon the rivers were alive with steamboats thrashing about in a gush of red cinders, churning wheels, and burst boilers. Seventeen appeared on Western rivers in 1817; by 1850, that figure had increased to 740. While most used the Mississippi–Ohio route, steam travel was popular on the Hudson and Delaware rivers, the Great Lakes, and the coasts. Steamboats emphasized speed—too often at the cost of their boilers. Captains regularly clamped off safety valves and raced through snags, defying all ordinary laws of physics and navigation. The yearly loss was in wrecked boats and shortened lives, but the yearly increase was in trade and profits.

Although steamboats could navigate against the flow of a river, they could hardly alter its course. Canals offered an alternative. During the 1820s, Americans went very nearly wild over canal building, digging two thousand miles of them between 1820 and 1830 alone. Their model was the Erie in New York. Begun in 1817 and completed in 1825, "Clinton's Big Ditch"—so called after Governor De Witt Clinton—was thirteen times longer than any previously attempted and cost $27,000 per mile, a total of $10,000,000, a staggering sum for the time. The building of the Erie seemed blessed from the start. The terrain between Albany and Buffalo rose and fell only about 650 feet, so the engineering problems of locks and spillways were not acute, even by the standards of the time. Furthermore, the canal could be opened one section at a time, so that profits from a completed stretch could help defray the cost of the unfinished parts. Most important, the Erie connected New York City with the Great Lakes, which in turn served the vast Ohio Valley. Without it, neither that city nor the West could have grown so spectacularly.

The Erie inspired—or perhaps frightened—other states into building their own canals. None was so successful, either because the technological problems were more complex or because the area served was not so rich. An example was the Main Line Canal from Philadelphia to Pittsburgh. Begun in 1826, the Main Line proved a costly and slow enterprise because of the Allegheny Mountains. Rising 2,200 feet to the Erie's 650, it required twice as many locks. Near its highest point, engineers were forced to construct a series of cable cars which inched the barges up the mountains, then down the other side. From an engineering standpoint, the cable cars were a triumph; from a commercial view, they were a time-consuming bottleneck. More successful were the two Ohio canals that connected Lake Erie with the Ohio. But profitable or not, canals sprang up in every section until the mid-1840s, when the railroads began to replace them.

Railroads did not boom until the 1850s, but even by 1840 the potential in rail travel was evident. Railroads were speedy; they could haul enormous loads of all sorts; they could be built almost anywhere. At first, they were designed to carry only passengers. The first line, Baltimore and Ohio, was chartered in 1827 and three years later made its initial run between Baltimore and Ellicott City—about thirteen miles. Other states and cities sponsored similar efforts, and during the 1830s both the extent and the technological sophistication of railroads increased dramatically. By 1840, steam locomotives were capable of a dizzying speed of forty miles per hour, a pace that prompted doctors and scientists to worry gravely if the human body would deteriorate when propelled so fast. Probably more damaging were the smoke and cinders that poured into the open cars, and the occasional wrecks. Even statesmen were not spared the danger; John Quincy Adams helped pull out the dead and dying from a crash on the Boston–Providence line in 1841. Despite the costs and uncertainties, however, railroads were popular. By 1860, over 30,000 miles of track—most of it in short runs of differing gauges—were laid.

But that came later, after 1845. For the 1820s and 1830s, rivers, canals, and roads were the giants of American transportation while railroads were the infants. By linking the states and regions, canals and roads were indispensable to the growth of economic nationalism. They carried goods and opened trade, but equally important, they carried people. Westward migration at best was a tedious, expensive process. With better transportation, the trek to the frontier was made easier. Moreover, as rapid transportation broke down the physical barriers between sections, it erased a fear which had tormented republican thinkers in the eighteenth century—that democracy could not work in a large country. Canals, roads, and railcars carried republican institutions—as well as goods—to the frontier.

As trade grew, so did the cities. Although the United States remained primarily a land of farmers until the end of the century, the growth of cities was enormously significant to the American economy before the Civil War. Their size in the East, their very presence in the South and West, made it possible for capital to flow among the sections, for transportation to establish profitable routes, for farms and industries to find markets. Put simply, cities helped centralize commerce and communications among the diversified elements of a market economy. As surely as the cotton gin helped change the face of Southern agriculture, the city helped change the nature of American commerce.

Along the Eastern seaboard, New York was most important, followed by Philadelphia, Baltimore, Boston, and Charleston. The most dramatic growth, however, occurred in the West. Along the broad river valleys—especially the Mississippi, the Missouri, and the Ohio —new villages sprang up, old villages became towns, and towns grew to the dignity of cities, providing a base of operations for the factors and commission merchants who passed the harvest of farm and plantation along to the ultimate consumer. These urban centers imported or produced manufactured goods and luxuries for the farmer; they spawned the builders, the traders, the speculators, the business venturers of every kind. Pittsburgh and New Orleans were at the two extremes of the long river system that was the major avenue of commerce for the West. In between were Cincinnati, Louisville, and Memphis. St. Louis, still the center of the American fur trade, was the gateway to the lands alluringly described by the Lewis and Clark Expedition. Smaller towns adorned the prairies of Indiana and Illinois and commanded the watercourses of the deeper South.

These were commercial towns, and they depended on trade. Western cities tended to deal in agricultural products; New Orleans was dependent on cotton; New York thrived on the import-export business. Not surprisingly, then, cities located on key trade routes prospered; those that were inaccessible stagnated. Before 1820, for example, Lexington, Louisville, and Cincinnati each competed more or less equally for the business of the Ohio Valley, with Lexington enjoying a slight edge since it was located on the Wilderness Road, which pushed through the Cumberland Gap. The steamboat and the canals, however, made Cincinnati and Louisville more attractive; their populations tripled over the next twenty years. Lexington, however, entered a long period of economic decline.

East, West, or South, most cities were dominated by the merchant. Accordingly, cities were planned and run on business principles, by businessmen. No aspect of urban life escaped their eyes. They built wharves or turnpikes to encourage commerce, but beyond that they meddled openly in the daily life of the marketplace. Through the city governments they fixed prices, supported or opposed monopolies as the situation demanded, and regulated the very scales on which the shopkeeper weighed his produce. Even the price of bread was controlled. Merchants were determined to make their cities commercially successful, so they left little to chance. Each town was the center of a trading area, and very like a city-state. A flourishing, stable market in one town expanded that city's economic domain and attracted new capital and more settlers.

Moreover, orderly growth lent a sense of cultural continuity, especially on the frontier. Having left civilization behind, those who moved west tried desperately to re-create it in their new homes. One offshoot of this attitude was the rage for planned cities. The twisting streets, blind alleys, and cow-paths-turned-thoroughfares that marked old Boston or lower New York were largely absent on the urban frontier. In their place appeared broad boulevards and right angles. The most copied city was Philadelphia, with its classic simplicity and gridiron pattern. Rural life could develop around the haphazard contours of the land; city dwellers preferred regularity. "Curved lines, you know," observed a Cincinnati doctor, "symbolize the country, straight lines the city."

INDUSTRY further spurred economic growth. Before Jefferson's embargo and the ensuing war, the United States had been comfortably content to take its manufacturing goods from mills in Liverpool and Manchester. Jefferson had wanted it that way, of course. Nothing in the arguments of Alexander Hamilton had convinced him that the new republic needed industrial independence. "Let our workshops remain in Europe," he wrote in *Notes on Virginia*. To do otherwise would introduce a class of workers who were separated from the soil and, hence, from the source of true republican values. Thirty years later, however, Jefferson had changed his mind. In a letter to Benjamin Austin in 1816, he admitted that experience had persuaded him that Americans could not be politically independent—and thus could not be free to develop a republican society—so long as they were economically dependent on Europe. The war at sea had triggered his change of attitude, for it had extinguished the myth of freedom of the seas. Piracy and impressment had shown him that "the will of a foreign nation" could reduce Americans "either to dependence on that nation, or to be clothed in skins, and to live like wild beasts in dens and caverns." This he could not accept; hence, "we must now place the manufacturer by the side of the agriculturist."

Jefferson's own embargo had hastened the change, for it had locked up American commercial investment long enough to force New England merchants to channel their money into new enterprises. Stimulated by wartime demands and cut off from the customary sources of supply, American industry reached out into new directions. At Waltham, Massachusetts, Francis Cabot Lowell built the world's first fully integrated cotton mill, where with the aid of improved machinery raw fiber was made into finished cloth under a single roof. William Jarvis, representing the United States in Lisbon, took advantage of Napoleon's sack of Spain to smuggle a stock of fine Merino sheep to his homeland, where they were bred to supply woolen mills in the Eastern states. The years of restriction also enlarged the output of Pennsylvania's iron mills and foundries and turned the skills of artisans and engineers to new projects such as the development of better engines for steamboats.

But the larger, more sophisticated industries demanded power, power that could be had most cheaply along the rivers and waterfalls of the fall line. Thus, the Lowell firm built its textile mills farther inland when the water power at Waltham proved inadequate. In so doing, it founded the first company town—appropriately called Lowell, Massachusetts—and set the stage for an important innovation in the organization and development of American industry.

To make the factory system profitable, entrepreneurs needed to increase its efficiency. Technological innovations such as the power loom were crucial to this process, but so were changes in the organization of labor. Throughout the colonial period, those goods that were not imported were made either in the home or in small artisans' shops for local consumption. For most industries, this pattern persisted with only minor changes until the Civil War. Boots and shoes, for example, were not mass-produced until well into the nineteenth century. The population boom after 1800, however, did modify the ways by which boots were sold. Brokers emerged, who gathered the products of countless shops and resold them in quantity to retailers. Erratic production and uneven quality eventually forced the creation of the central shops, where the leather was cut, then farmed out to craftsmen for sewing, then brought back for fitting to the sole. When even this proved inadequate, the entire process was moved under one roof, where specialists cut, stitched, fitted, and shipped. Similar, if not identical, developments marked the production of clothing. But a modern factory system in both these industries did not emerge until after 1850, when technological innovations in sewing enabled the industry to consolidate.

The textile industry, on the other hand, modernized much more quickly, largely through Lowell's willingness to experiment both with the techniques of production and with the organization of labor. His first move, placing all the machinery for making cotton cloth into one building, created obvious savings in time and transportation costs. Equally important was the way in which he used his labor force. Since making cloth required far fewer skills and less strength than, say, shipbuilding or the fabrication of a steam engine, Lowell and his imitators were able to draw on a much larger pool of labor. For the same reasons, he was less dependent on the men or women he employed, because he could easily replace a worker who quit. Thus, for Lowell the key problem lay not in who worked in his mills but in how the work was organized. In short, he was free to systematize production.

Eli Whitney had already demonstrated the potential of the assembly line in his arms factory in Connecticut, so Lowell quickly adopted the same techniques. Workers labored at specific tasks for a specific number of hours per day, all regulated by the clock rather than by the rising and setting of the sun. By containing all facets of clothmaking in one building, moreover, Lowell was able to keep close watch over both the quality and the quantity of the finished product. His major problem, however, was the chronic shortage of labor which persisted in the United States until well after the Civil War. It was difficult to persuade young men to toil in a factory when opportunities for better jobs were seemingly boundless. The problem persisted after Lowell's death in 1817, and so the Lowell firm turned for its spinners and weavers to the girls of the countryside.

The firm proposed to take unmarried teenagers, pay them a wage, and care for their moral and intellectual growth in the process. At their looms, the girls were taught to work hard, obey their superiors, and be punctual. After hours, they were whisked off to dormitories, given supper, and versed in schemes of self-improvement. In the two hours between supper and bed, the Lowell girls learned basic principles of mathematics and grammar, heavily spiced with moral instructions. In 1840, they brought forth the first issue of the *Lowell Offering*, a journal of poems, essays, and compositions that was published periodically for five years. By the time a Lowell girl left the mill, presumably to marry, she was expected to be a prudent, conscientious woman who would make her family, the commonwealth, and the Lowell factory proud.

Nothing in this regime obscured the fact that the hours were long, the pay low, and the conditions exhausting. From six in the morning until seven at night the girls worked at their looms in stale air and a cacophony of noise. They paid for their bed and board, which left them at week's end with a half dollar or so. The dormitories were crowded and not very sanitary; the food starchy and plain. And if these girls worked hard for meager pay, the plight of laborers in other cities was worse.

By combining the factory and a variation of the finishing school, Lowell attacked one of the major objections to industrialization posed by critics such as Jefferson or John Taylor of Caroline. Jefferson's early fears of cities and factories had centered on their supposedly baneful effects on the virtue and independence of the individual. Since large industries relied on the labor of the poorest elements of society, Jefferson feared the capitalist would keep his workers subservient and discourage the type of independent thought necessary for an enlightened electorate. An inevitable degeneration in the moral fitness of the worker would set in, and the hapless victims of this process would become pawns in a struggle between true republican interests and the schemes of the rich. But Lowell circumvented the issue by using workers who, because of their sex, were not voters and by providing them with the very moral instruction that the factory system was supposed to discourage. Thus, economic independence and moral rectitude were both served.

It is dangerous, however, to make generalizations based on the Lowell experience. Within the textile industry, Lowell was unique both in organization and in scope. Moreover, by 1840 most of the female workers at the factory had been replaced by immigrants, largely Irish, and the moral and educational aspects of the system had been abandoned. And, compared to other industries, textiles were easily the most advanced. The machinery at Lowell was powered by falling water, and the machines themselves were light and relatively inexpensive. Moreover, making cotton cloth is not as technically precise a task as, say, assembling sewing machines or reapers. The production of steel, heavy machinery, or hardware, on the other hand, requires enormous capital, expensive equipment, and massive amounts of power. None of this was common until well after 1850, when the coal furnace and the steam engine had transformed the potential of the factory system. Nor could it develop until the railroads had opened new markets for finished products and new ways of obtaining raw materials. The factory system before 1850 was still in a formative stage.

So were the perceptions of that system. American workers, for example, had not felt the grinding routine of mill life long enough, or in sufficient numbers, to develop a class consciousness. They were not so much alienated from the factory as they were detached from it. An English visitor, J. S. Buckingham, noted in 1842 that the Lowell girls were perfectly willing to endure twelve- and thirteen-hour days, because "none of them consider it as their permanent condition; all look forward to its termination in a few years at the farthest." Men, he observed, tolerated the bad conditions because they fully expected, by working in factories, to "accumulate enough to go off to the West, and buy an estate at 1 1/4 dollar an acre, or set up in some small way of business at home." Worker protest did appear. Trade unions emerged during the 1820s and 1830s, as did workingmen's parties. Yet both were generally led by skilled craftsmen and small businessmen, not factory hands, and were short-lived. They were victims of weak organization, public hostility, and worker apathy.

Primitive as this industrialization was, it had effects far beyond what could be measured in terms of size or wealth. From the 1820s on, industries were the fastest-growing segment of the American economy. They fed on, and in turn helped feed, the spread of urbanization. As economic innovations, their sheer size and the enormous amounts of capital and labor needed to run them helped break the economy free from its small scale, local orientation, and direct it toward large, national enterprise. This resulted—along with the expansion of the West, the growth of a national transportation system, and the rise of the cities—in a critical change in attitudes and outlook among businessmen in all parts of the country.

FOR the real revolution took place in the mind of the American entrepreneur. Praised by mythmakers and damned by romantics, businessmen were slowly but perceptibly demanding changes in the organization of the economy—and, by extension, in the organization of society itself. These demands were voiced not only by Francis Lowell and his peers but by small shopkeepers and merchants up and down the coast and deep in the interior. Practical, hardworking men, they were not ideologues, nor were they, any more than their workers, conscious of belonging to a distinct class—although they did have common interests. Instead, barely aware of the implications of their acts, they groped for a semblance of predictability and rationality in commercial life. If they did not live to see the elevation of system and order to a national faith, as happened near the end of the century, they did set vital precedents.

Their attitudes toward the economic role of government were those of neither Alexander Hamilton nor Adam Smith. Entrepreneurialism was a faith rather than a structured ideology, and laissez-faire or central control of the economy were in a sense denominations within this faith. Each had its apostles. Most American businessmen were remarkably flexible in their approach to the use of governmental authority in promoting economic interests. As men experiencing the bewildering, exciting process of modernization, they were open to change and innovation. Where systemization and public support were desirable, they were quick to call upon government for aid; where individual and private resources were adequate, they desired only to be left alone. For small, local enterprises the latter course was most common, but for larger projects the American entrepreneur used every public agency available.

The federal nature of American government gave entrepreneurs flexibility; they could tap the cities, states, or the national government, or any combination of the three, for aid. Moreover, the division between executive and legislative branches offered other paths of influence. In general, businessmen chose to work through the legislatures, which were more closely attuned to local needs and easier to persuade. Often very little persuasion was necessary, for both investors and officials alike recognized that money was scarce in the early republic. With so little capital in the hands of individuals, it became obvious very early that government would either have to take over the cost of providing vital public services or help businessmen provide them.

Between 1789 and 1830 public aid to the private sector normally took the form of corporate charters granted by the states. In practice, those who were willing to pool their resources in order to furnish some needed service were rewarded with a charter that gave them special privileges, mostly in the form of a monopoly or tax exemption. Insurance and banking—which facilitated trade—and water supply and fire protection were the first to receive such blessings. After 1800, most charters centered on transportation.

Transportation was ripe for the charter system for two reasons: everyone wanted it and it cost dearly. Throughout the great age of turnpikes and canals, state legislatures freely granted charters to almost any group of investors who were willing to take the risks of clearing the forests or moving tons of earth. Often the results were disastrous. Certain canals in Pennsylvania were so remote that they were useless. Turnpikes ended abruptly at a state line. Moreover, the risks involved in such ventures were real. A turnpike or canal, once built, required years to provide a return on the investment. Once profits did trickle in, they were divided among so many investors that only a few became rich. And once the railroads were underway, the savings of a lifetime vanished in the slow currents of obsolete canals.

After 1830, money remained scarce, while expenses climbed. Subsidies and outright grants thus joined the charter as a means of encouraging corporations. The degree of state involvement was directly proportionate to the cost of the project concerned. The Erie Canal was a case in point. The enormous cost of building the Erie was plainly beyond the means of any group of private investors, so the canal became from the start a state project. Other states followed suit, sometimes with disastrous results. When railroads began competing with canals during the 1830s, the response was similar. Either the state would finance a line completely, or, more often, would give land or cash to a corporation. Again, the results were mixed. Some projects were instantly profitable; others pushed out ahead of any real need for them and collapsed.

THE fact remains, however, that states seldom assumed the burden of financing public projects directly. They encouraged private interests to do so, and of course they intervened with regulations whenever necessary and politically popular. But what was notably missing from government's role during the period was any widespread or vigorous use of taxes to pay for public works. The state budget of Massachusetts, for example, remained fixed at $133,000 per year for over three decades before the Civil War—a period of dramatic expansion in one of the nation's most densely populated and industrialized states. Thus, private economic interests very early took over not only large-scale projects such as canals or railroads but also basic public services such as water supply. Corporations were the only business entities large enough to manage such projects.

This situation placed much of the burden for regulating economic growth on the courts. The responsibilities fell not only on the Supreme Court, whose decisions helped define constitutional process, but also on hundreds of lesser federal and state judges who struggled daily with the formidable task of applying the law to an increasingly complex and heterogeneous society. The expanding market economy multiplied the number of cases brought before the courts at a time when law itself was in a highly fluid and malleable state. Courts were thus forced to adapt the law to situations that had no precedent. Any decision that affected economic growth was likely to have far-reaching repercussions on the development of the market economy. The American judiciary accepted this challenge willingly, and in its hands law became an instrument of economic change.

American jurisprudence had inherited many of its basic assumptions from the English common law, which had developed over centuries of tradition and historical precedent. Among the most powerful traditions handed down by the common law were the notions that property existed for the enjoyment of its owner, that the value of goods and services should correspond to their real worth (or "just price"), and that certain inherent standards of morality and fair play lay at the base of all legal relationships. Courts existed to "discover" these standards and apply them to particular legal conflicts. Although the Revolution generated a movement to make all law statutory—the direct written enactments of popular will—the common-law tradition remained strong in the new nation. Common law filled the inevitable gaps in statutory law, which could not possibly cover every type of legal case, and gave judges a guiding philosophy by which they could interpret badly written or inadequate statutes.

The fluid state of American law and the developing market economy, however, produced two notable changes in jurisprudence after the Revolution. Judges began to use their powers of interpretation aggressively to define the law and thus in effect became makers of it. Moreover, the market economy placed stresses on the common law, which was of course rooted in a pre-market, agrarian society. The need to develop property, for example, often conflicted with an owner's right to enjoy it. Under the common law, a landowner could rest secure in the knowledge that the waters on his farm would not be disrupted by the building of a dam upstream. He owned the right to enjoy the stream by title and by the natural configuration of the land. As water-powered mills appeared, however, this tradition came under attack. An 1805 case in New York, *Palmer* v. *Mulligan*, challenged the common-law tradition by pitting the need to develop the river against the landowner's right to enjoy it. The case was decided in favor of development. Thereafter, courts began increasingly to adopt the doctrine that ownership of property implied a correlative responsibility to exploit its economic potential. In this case—and in others that followed it—the courts took a nebulous statute and the assumptions of the common law, interpreted both, and fashioned a new policy.

More instances of like kind followed. Common-law notions of contracts revolved around the concept of the "just price," which assumed that goods or services had a market value based on their inherent worth. Thus, a contract could be abrogated if the court determined that one party had attempted to overcharge the other. The market economy introduced a new and unsettling element into contracts. Goods were often bought or sold before they had actually been produced, or else they might be purchased when the market set their value at one level only to be delivered after the market had changed. The fluctuations of the market made it impossible to determine exactly what a "just price" was, and the rapid spread of corporations and long-distance transactions only complicated the situation. Moreover, if the law had been used to protect antiquated notions of just price, economic growth might have been stifled, for in a market economy goods and services are worth what the buyer will pay—a substitution of supply and demand for inherent value. Faced with these changing circumstances, the courts redefined the bases for contracts. By the 1830s contracts had become limited to the terms of the agreement and no more. If a contracting party fulfilled his part of the bargain, he had satisfied the contract no matter what changes had transpired to change the value of the goods.

These and other redefinitions of the common law were not obvious or startling changes. They earned few headlines. Yet they implied that law was increasingly being used to favor economic growth and the development of the market economy at the expense of traditional, largely agrarian, ideals. The cumulative effect was to relax restraints on development by creating a legal atmosphere in which enterprise could expand and adapt itself to the market without fear of reprisals at the bar.

Soon the Supreme Court endorsed the shift in emphasis. Two decisions were of enduring significance. In 1816 the state of New Hampshire attempted to amend the charter of Dartmouth College in order to bring that institution under state control. The trustees of the college sued, arguing that the original charter, granted in 1769, had created Dartmouth as a private corporation and was protected under the Constitution like any other contract. The case reached the Supreme Court in 1819, where Daniel Webster delivered an emotional and much-quoted plea for the sanctity of his alma mater. The Court, under Marshall, ruled in favor of Dartmouth and the original charter, concluding that charters were contracts and could not be changed arbitrarily by legislative fiat. It was a philosophically curious decision, for charters were of course granted for public purposes, yet the Court was saying that, once granted, they became private contracts, unalterable except by mutual consent of the contracting parties. Philosophy aside, the decision was in keeping with the more general tendency to protect corporations from interference.

Over the next two decades, chartered corporations multiplied at a prodigious rate. Inevitably, they began to encroach on each other's ground. A major conflict arose in the 1830s, when a corporation sought a charter from the Massachusetts legislature to build a free bridge across the Charles River in Boston. Since 1785 the public had been served by a toll bridge owned by the Charles River Bridge Company, and that company naturally sued, maintaining that its charter granted it a monopoly and that another bridge would violate the terms of the contract. The Court—now headed by Roger B. Taney —dismissed the argument. Competing charters, Taney declared, were permissible so long as the public interest was served. This was not a repeal of the Dartmouth decision, for the original terms of the company's charter were not changed. Only its monopoly was lost. The decision removed almost all remaining restraints on the proliferation of corporations and demonstrated the extent to which law had become allied with economic development. Competition and the public interest were assumed to be one, for competition led to enterprise and innovation, and enterprise and innovation created services that benefited the community.

Despite the changed legal environment and the spread of large corporations, there remained areas of economic enterprise that no state or court or private concern could direct. For the larger questions of economic policy—currency and tariffs, for example—the burden fell on the federal government. Here the potential for conflict was far greater than that experienced on the local level. There were more interests, more sectional needs, more people to be served. Additionally, the federal government had to deal with the new and unfamiliar problems wrought by geographical expansion, technological change, and the population explosion. Congressmen and Presidents alike were forced to grope, often blindly, for answers to questions that had no precedent.

JEFFERSON had advocated a policy of federal retrenchment, yet the near-disastrous experience of the War of 1812 produced an urge to give more direction and support to economic development. The shift in emphasis was apparent in the Congress that met in December 1815. Led by Clay, Calhoun, and others, Congress deliberated over policies that, if implemented, would have constituted an "American System" of sectional interdependence and governmental supports. The proponents of this plan based their case on the imperative need for unity, self-sufficiency, and strength if the new nation was to compete in a hostile world. The need for unity outweighed old fears concerning too much concentration of power and left traditional Republicans such as John Randolph vainly arguing that no such power could safely be entrusted to the hands of mortal men. Yet those who favored a more vigorous use of federal power were themselves Republicans, and their dominant voice in Congress suggested that the party of Jefferson was beginning seriously to redefine the ideals of its founder.

The American System was imaginative and many-faceted. To the manufacturers of the New England and the middle states it offered a protective tariff designed to nurture the nascent industries. To Western and Southern farmers and planters it offered a subsidy in the form of improved transportation to facilitate the marketing of their crops. To the nation as a whole it proposed a new national bank to provide a uniform currency necessary to the exchange of goods and indispensable in the regulation of credit. The intent of these proposals was emphatically not to use government as an agency of ownership or total control; rather, they were designed to liberate the individual entrepreneur by creating a stable economic environment and encouraging the fast and profitable development of means of trade.

The second Bank of the United States was frankly patterned on the first: the United States government would put up 20 percent of the Bank's $35,000,000 capital (the old Bank's had been only $10,000,-000), own 20 percent of the stock, appoint five of the twenty-five directors, and be the largest depositor. The Bank was to be centered in Philadelphia, still the financial hub of the country, but the directors might establish branches at will. Only Congress could suspend specie payments—the redemption of the Bank's notes in gold and silver. A few Western Republicans refused to vote for the charter for fear the Bank might curb the easy-money policy that was making their constituents rich, but the losses were made up by Federalist votes from the Eastern commercial centers.

The tariff was especially sensitive to sectional and local interests. Industry could not be established without some form of subsidy to compensate for the lower production costs of better-entrenched and more efficient foreign competitors. The problem of those who framed the tariff of 1816 was to determine, item by item, the extent of the subsidy required, with due allowance for the fact that British manufacturers were already exporting their goods below cost in the hope of destroying American rivals. Three general categories were set up. Articles that could not be produced at home were to be admitted free of duty, and articles that could be produced in quantities sufficient to meet all domestic needs were to be protected by a prohibitively high tax. The third and largest category included all items that could be produced in the United States, but not yet in quantities large enough to meet the entire demand. On these articles the duties were adjusted to encourage the American producer without excluding the foreign. Local self-interest generally governed votes; each congressman sought maximum protection for the products manufactured by his constituents, while he attempted to get goods they consumed onto the free list.

It was agreed by all concerned that three years should be enough to put American industry on a competitive par with that of England, and a provision was therefore included reducing all duties in the year 1819 to a uniform 20 percent by value. As finally established, the average duty under the tariff of 1816 was not much above 25 percent, which proved to be insufficient to enable American industry to compete with Britain. The coarse cotton cloth that made up the bulk of the New England textile output received full protection, however, for Lowell and a handful of others persuaded Congress that the competition of similar fabrics imported from India at five or six cents a yard would be ruinous. Duties of a hundred percent of import value were paid on these textiles.

Another element of the American System was the promotion of internal transportation. Congress proposed to join Eastern bays and estuaries by a series of canals and to create an inland waterway along the Atlantic coast, provide a parallel but more extended coastal highway from Maine to Louisiana, make a water connection between the Hudson and Lake Erie that would bypass Niagara Falls (a plan later realized by the Erie Canal), and link by road or canal the navigable reaches of streams on opposite sides of the Appalachians. The last point was crucial to the success of the system. The West was still closer to Europe by way of the Mississippi than to Washington or New York by existing avenues of commerce. It was hardly realistic to believe the West could be held indefinitely in union with the East unless Western crops could find their way to Eastern markets. Now that British manufactures were to be made more costly or excluded altogether, it had become imperative to make the products of American industry accessible to all America, particularly the West. The National Road was already clogged with traffic, although it still fell short of its Ohio River terminus; its success hinted at rich prospects for the proposed cheaper water routes. The network of roads and canals was to be financed by a bonus to be paid the government by the Bank, and by the dividends from the Bank's stock.

Although the sponsors of the American System conceived of their plan as logical and fair to all citizens of whatever section or political persuasion, each of its elements met resistance. Westerners who favored easy credit were fearful of the regulatory power of the Bank. Southerners who depended on Britain for most of their manufactured goods were hostile to the protective tariff. New Englanders who already possessed a well-developed system of roads and turnpikes were unwilling to help pay the cost of internal improvements in other states. Clay and other proponents of the plan succeeded in passing the measures only by constructing a different coalition of votes for each bill and by relying on votes from Pennsylvania and New Jersey to provide the needed majorities.

They did not, however, expect a Presidential veto. Madison had long since agreed that a national bank was an acceptable risk in a republican society, so he agreed to the bill chartering a second United States Bank. Like his friend Jefferson, he had also concluded that the new nation was not secure from foreign domination without a domestic capacity for producing manufactured goods. He accepted the tariff. But Madison could not reconcile the internal improvement bill with either the commerce clause or the general welfare clause of the Constitution, and his veto, conscientious though it was, delayed for a generation an adequate system of transportation. By the time Congress considered the proposal again, opposition to it had crystallized, and the bill died. Since the American System was intended to be interdependent and self-supporting, the collapse of one of its key elements doomed it to, at best, partial success.

MADISON'S reluctance to endorse all aspects of the American System was only the first suggestion that the road to economic nationalism would be tortuous and slow. Although his successor, James Monroe, tried desperately to preserve the apparent harmony that followed the

War of 1812, the forces of dissent and debate gathered strength. The sudden spurt in the economy, combined with the new and diverse forms of economic enterprise, created both an inevitable tension among conflicting interests and—equally important—entirely new cycles of boom and bust. With an economy that was rapidly becoming far more complex and intertwined than anything experienced before 1815, the United States had entered an era in which fluctuations in one sector had immediate repercussions, for good or ill, in every other. How catastrophic these repercussions could be did not become fully apparent until the Panic of 1837, but the problem was foreshadowed by a sudden dip in economic growth near the end of Monroe's first term.

After the war, the British had begun dumping their manufactured goods on the American market at drastically low prices. Predictably, American buyers took advantage of the situation by buying heavily —largely with borrowed cash. Neither the state banks nor the federal government nor the Bank of the United States did anything to discourage this cycle of spend and borrow; in fact, they were willing accomplices. Exports also increased, but domestic manufacturing, unable to compete with the British, floundered. When, after 1817, the export market began to drop and the price of imports began to climb, the easy access to credit and the free flow of cash dried up. The Panic of 1819 followed

The most obvious sinner, and the one most easily blamed, was the Bank. Managed with incredible laxity and occasional chicanery by its first president, William Jones, the Bank had lent its notes freely and promiscuously to state institutions which were in no way qualified to handle the sudden burst of credit responsibly. State banks, once they had exhausted their own reserve of specie, began to issue notes against the Bank or one of its more solvent Northern branches. Although legally the Bank might have refused to allow this folly, it was impolitic to do so. The results of the Bank's tolerance, however, were costly. Reserves of gold and silver held by the Bank dropped steadily until, by the summer of 1818, they were down to less than half the amount required by law.

Although the Bank began feverishly putting its house in order, it was too late to forestall a congressional investigation. Jones resigned early in 1819, and conservative, widely respected Langdon Cheves of South Carolina took his place. In a matter of weeks, with directors of his own choosing, with specie borrowed from the Barings and other European bankers, and by a sharp contraction of credit, Cheves restored the solvency of the United States Bank. But state banks began to fail as their notes were presented for payment in the specie they no longer had. As they collapsed, they carried with them farmers, traders, and entrepreneurs of all descriptions who were over their heads in debt. A pall of depression, which lasted two years, settled over the land.

The Bank's mismanagement immediately made it the target of renewed political protest. To complicate its problems, Chief Justice John Marshall chose this time to hand down a decision that would simultaneously hurt the reputation of the Bank even more and reaffirm his own doctrine of national power on which the whole American System rested. The Baltimore branch of the Bank had had the misfortune to be staffed by embezzlers and looters, among them its president, James A. Buchanan (not to be confused with James Buchanan of Pennsylvania), and its cashier, James W. McCulloch, who together had robbed the Bank of some $3,000,000 in two years' time. Their corruption, plus the fact that state banks in Maryland chafed under the federal Bank's dominance, prompted the state legislature to levy a tax of $15,000 against the Baltimore branch. McCulloch refused to pay, the state sued, and the case went before Marshall.

Since 1803, when he had first declared that the Supreme Court might overrule an act of Congress, Marshall had refined and enlarged his concept of a strong yet balanced central government, supported by those with an economic stake in the community. He had upheld the inviolability of contracts, had made good the right of the Supreme Court to pass judgment in cases appealed from the state courts, and early in 1819, in the Dartmouth College case, had held that corporate charters such as those under which banks as well as colleges operated were forms of contract. Now in *McCulloch* v. *Maryland* he went further still, explicitly affirming the supremacy of the federal government over the states. Privately, Marshall deplored the thievery that had plagued the Baltimore branch; public interests, however, were his overriding concern. The Court accepted the Bank's argument that the power to tax is the power to destroy, from which it followed that a state could not tax a corporation created by the federal government without placing the government in the unthinkable position of subordination to the state.

Marshall's decision provoked immediate and visceral protest from all sections. The Kentucky and Virginia legislatures replied by reaffirming their resolutions of 1798 and 1799, which were early statements of the states' rights philosophy. Ohio, moreover, endorsed them both and imposed a confiscatory tax of $50,000 on each of the Bank's two branches in that state. As in Maryland, the Bank refused to pay. When the state treasurer seized the money by force, agents of the federal circuit court recovered it by the same means. Once again the power of a state to tax the national government was debated in the Supreme Court, and once again Marshall affirmed his stand.

The tempest stirred by Marshall's opinion was symbolic of the problems that growth and expansion would pose over the next forty years. An incredible diversity of local and sectional interests—multiplied by rapid growth in territory, population, and technological sophistication—placed extraordinary pressures on a political system that was too new, too crude and unformed, to deal with them consistently or effectively. Economic modernization demanded a corollary effort to provide system and predictability to growth, and the American System, Marshall's defense of the supremacy of federal power, and the attempts of capitalists to rationalize their production were all manifestations of this effort. Yet each effort collided with local and particular concerns to produce a tension between national needs and individual desires. Americans had still not developed the attitudes and institutions that would restrain and direct their collective energies while leaving their essential freedoms untouched.

After 1820, the dilemma intensified. The pace of growth and innovation accelerated, and as it did, it exposed profound differences in the way Americans viewed the limits of national authority. The most troubling of these differences was apparent in the growing isolation of the South. It was also evident in the restructuring of American politics during the 1820s and 1830s, in the widespread attempts to "save" Americans through moral reform, and even in the effort to produce a literature that was both natively American and morally instructive.

THE NEW POLITICS

two

5

Political
Realignments

JAMES MONROE'S Presidency brought a deceptive calm to American politics. The old party rivalries between Federalists and Jeffersonians had largely died out after the former's disgrace at Hartford, and the victors were free to pick and choose among Hamilton's policies with little fear that they would be resurrecting his party in the process. Given this apparent unity, there seemed to be little need to maintain party organization. Hostility to the very idea of parties persisted, an extension of the eighteenth-century concept that public servants held office out of devotion to civic virtue—much like Plato's philosopher-kings. Monroe encouraged the idea. He entered the Presidency declaring that the American system of government had approached "perfection" and spent most of his eight years in the office in a cautious attempt to preserve harmony. By the end of his first term, most Americans assumed that an age of cooperation and collective purpose—an "Era of Good Feelings," as one Boston paper rejoiced—had dawned.

The calm did not last. By 1820 the forces of modernization and social change had accelerated, intensifying the strains on American unity. The Panic of 1819 introduced Americans to the cyclical fluctuations of a modernizing economy, and technological and business innovations multiplied the opportunities available to the ambitious. Territorial expansion made harder the task of unifying a diverse republic. Concomitant with territorial growth was the critical problem raised by the expansion of slavery. As both the complexity of the issues and the number of different interests demanding to be served multiplied, new mechanisms of political control were needed.

Slowly the postwar generation turned back to the political party. The parties that emerged during the 1820s and 1830s were new, and they operated in a political climate that had vastly changed since 1800. The electorate, for example, had expanded dramatically. The old freehold restrictions, which dictated that a white male must own a certain minimum amount of taxable property in order to vote, had been steadily disappearing since the middle of the eighteenth century. By the early 1800s, these rules were seldom enforced; by the 1820s, they were gone altogether in most states. In 1824, only six states still chose Presidential electors in the state legislature; eight years later, the only state to do so was South Carolina. Despite the fact that voter turnout was low during the 1820s, the potential number, combined with the startling increase in population, gave the common man power that could not be overlooked.

As voting restrictions relaxed, so did the grip of deferential politics. Well into the 1830s, enough politicians still conceived of parties as groups of constituents clustered around—and obedient to—the "best men" to suggest that the old habits were not dead. But even during Jefferson's two terms there were signs that the Federalists, who personified the deferential system, had recognized that political power was not inherited but had to be won. That meant active campaigning and organization. Young Federalists such as Harrison Gray Otis accepted the need for parties. More particularly, they accepted the fact that they had to join, campaign, and prove themselves worthy of selection, rather than assume that power would flow to them naturally. Federalists were not necessarily less elitist; they had simply begun to realize that their elitism must rest on new foundations.

Deference fell not because the need for leaders had disappeared but because the foundations of leadership had changed. The right to rule no longer rested on birth but on a strict adherence to a constitutional system. To deny that was to deny the Revolutionary attack on privilege and monarchy. Men now exercised power only insofar as they served the people, championed their needs, and reflected their aspirations. The Constitution had indeed produced a second revolution—in the mind.

The extent of this change was aided by the expansion and growing prosperity of the young nation. The move west, the demand for wealth, and the possibility of more movement west and more wealth, all served to emphasize the focus on individual and collective opportunity. The struggles over the American System and the grinding effects of the Panic were proof that this expansiveness would force its way into national politics. A local leader could not hope to have a voice in determining national policy unless he joined with other men. Here he faced a sobering fact: the Founders had done their work well. Without first forming broad coalitions, no one could possibly penetrate the tangle of competing powers within the federal government —and between the federal government and the states.

So new and different parties began to emerge, with new and different functions. These new parties had to be broad and elastic, capable of mediating among countless groups and factions, and they had to be structured so that the common voter was included systematically in the process of decisionmaking. One other factor affected them. Since control of the national government was vital to the life of any party, they must respond to—even create, if necessary—national issues, while at the same time gingerly avoiding ones that would irritate sectional hostilities.

PARTY development began in the states. It could not have been otherwise, for the party leaders were grappling with new organizational forms and new needs, and the sophistication and experience necessary for broad national parties were simply not there. The states, being smaller political entities, were easier to organize and manage. Moreover, most legislation, particularly on economic matters, was decided in the states and not in Washington. And as each state developed economically at a speed different from its neighbors, as each state had different traditions of leadership and participation, so did state parties emerge at different rates.

New York set the pattern. Once finely balanced between Hamilton's Federalists and the Jeffersonian opposition, it had become a Republican stronghold by Madison's first term. Yet, even then, New York politics was a family business. Dutch patroons such as Stephen Van Rensselaer and wealthy landowners such as William Cooper— father of James Fenimore Cooper—were vigorous embodiments of the deferential system. To them, politics was the obligation of gentlemen, who debated policy and made decisions among themselves. Democracy was good in that it gave public favor—and hence legitimacy— to wise decisions and withdrew support from bad ones. By 1815 the living example of this attitude was De Witt Clinton, a born aristocrat with an ego as large as his holdings. Clinton's attitude toward his party was patriarchal. His followers existed to approve his actions, not direct them. To give control of the party to saloonkeepers, he thought, would have been a dangerous step toward mobocracy.

Yet saloonkeepers—or at least their sons—were precisely the ones who wanted control. Martin Van Buren, who began life by sweeping floors and polishing glasses in his father's tavern, was everything that Clinton was not. Short, unpretentious, and initially poor, Van Buren made politics a career, serving in turn as a county judge, state senator, and attorney general. By 1815, he had gathered others of like mind around him, men such as Silas Wright who shared his humble origins and his devotion to Jefferson. These men scorned the paternalism of Clinton. If leadership were to remain the province of the gentry, there was little hope that Van Buren or any of his allies would ever gain high office. They would remain surrogates and errand boys even as their ambitions led them to Albany or Washington. Equally important, Van Buren and his followers had been born after the Revolution. They had no memories or roots in the colonial system; their early political diet consisted of broadsides against John Adams. Partisanship was natural to their concept of democratic politics. Deference had little hold on them.

Clinton's autocratic use of patronage brought about their inevitable battle, from which a new form of party emerged. As governor, Clinton favored friends and associates, even Federalists, when filling key positions within the state government. At first, the Bucktails—as Van Buren's faction was called—did not openly resist. Clinton held his office by the grace of a caucus nomination. Yet the caucus was the very point at which Clinton could be attacked. A caucus nomination presumably reflected the will of the people. Therefore, so long as Clinton won the nomination, his power rested on a popular mandate and was thus worthy of support. But if Clinton lost favor with the majority, he was bound by the party decision to step aside. Swearing allegiance to the Republican Party above all else, the Bucktails slowly and quietly undercut Clinton's power in the caucus until, in 1820, they removed him as the party leader.

Their success was more than simply good strategy, for it implied an entirely new way of approaching politics. The party, not the man, was the agent of the people. It had a life that transcended the talents and ambitions of any individual. Men, personalities, might come and go; parties remained. Since the party was presumably open to all who believed, and since party leadership was presumably open to those who reflected the popular will, to attack the party was to strike directly at democracy. Parties had become not the "baneful influence" Washington feared, but the orderly means by which democratic sentiments found expression.

Unknowingly, the Bucktails were reacting to more than raw greed for office, shrouded in bombastic demagoguery. Their cherished organization was a response to real needs left by the collapse of deferential politics. An expanding population with ready access to the ballot box, money in their pockets, and seemingly limitless opportunities demanded effective leadership. Parties rationalized and made systematic the means of political participation, while providing leadership at the same time. Nothing else could make republicanism workable in a country that was growing so fast.

Parties not only organized the electorate; they articulated ideals. Van Buren, for example, honestly believed that destroying aristocracies was a noble cause as well as an effective means to political power. His disciple William Leggett wrote during the 1830s, at the height of the crisis over the national bank, that plain people had both the right and the duty to organize in order to resist all manifestations of aristocracy. "Have they not the right," he asked, "to act in concert when their opponents act in concert? Nay, is it not their bounden duty to combine" against monopoly and vested interest? Thus were party combinations and the attack on European traditions of aristocracy melded into one, producing political forms and national goals that were uniquely American.

The divisions that appeared during the 1820s and 1830s were less between aristocrats and democrats than between those who saw the future glory of the nation coming from a vigorous use of the government in Washington and those who wanted to see the power of government restrained. Not surprisingly, the tariff, the debate over internal improvements, and the United States Bank became focal points for party appeals. A certain amount of self-interest was always present when one man chose to support or attack these issues, but beyond that there was simply a difference in outlook. Everyone believed in progress and in the sanctity of the democratic experiment. The difference lay in the means by which the former was promoted and the latter enhanced.

Fortunately, the divisions were not strictly sectional, although the South usually favored a reduction in the power of the national government. Van Buren recognized this fact early in the 1820s and attempted to base the new political alignments on grounds similar to those that separated Federalists and Jeffersonians. "We must always have party distinctions," he wrote, "and the old ones are the best. . . . Political combinations between the inhabitants of the different states are unavoidable and the most natural and beneficial to the country is that between the planters of the South and the plain Republicans of the North." Southern proponents of states' rights would thus join hands with ordinary people in the North, who also wanted nothing more than to be left alone. Still, there were enough people in the South who believed that a judicious use of the federal government could promote the interests of all sections to create the probability that an opposition party would develop there. So long as the slavery issue was avoided, a genuinely national two-party system was possible.

IN 1820 Van Buren's party in New York was a prototype, not a norm. Its principles and its form spread slowly, and a national two-party system was not in full operation until 1840. Moreover, the type of leadership that Van Buren provided at the state level was absent in Washington, where the apparent unity among Jeffersonian Republicans was badly decayed. In part, this was due to the weakness of Jefferson's two successors in the White House. Neither Madison nor Monroe possessed the political toughness or the charismatic persuasiveness of Jefferson. Each was by nature cautious when dealing with problems that might encourage conflict or disunity. Monroe was particularly weak. Except for the articulation of the Monroe Doctrine— which was largely Adams's work—Monroe seemed incapable of anticipating and dealing vigorously with knotty issues such as the mismanagement of the United States Bank. His inclination, rather, was to wait, proceed cautiously, and hope that the problems would prove transitory.

Moreover, Madison and Monroe were handicapped in both the means and the extent of influence they could exert on Congress and the nation. While Jefferson used patronage to enforce discipline and loyalty to his programs, Madison and particularly Monroe did not. Monroe lacked Jefferson's immense personal popularity and thus could not appeal directly to the people for support of a controversial policy—as Jefferson had done, for example, in defending the embargo. Had he wanted to go to the people, Monroe still lacked means of mass communication. By contrast, later Presidents, especially Andrew Jackson, could rely on their own prestige and an extensive network of party newspapers and pamphleteers to persuade the public that their actions were proper and just.

Power was fragmented within Washington itself. Monroe often found himself undermined by members of his own Cabinet who used their posts to advance their political careers. It was not uncommon for a Cabinet head to disagree openly with the President's policies if sectional or political interests were at stake. It was assumed, moreover, that the Cabinet was a springboard to the Presidency, as Madison's and then Monroe's success had demonstrated. Departmental heads dealt directly with Congress; each recruited the friendship and loyalty of a clique, which—if large enough—could become instrumental in securing the traditional caucus nomination. These rivalries produced an atmosphere of distrust and intrigue that hampered every effort to develop policies and provide effective leadership.

Even if the executive establishment had been perfectly united, leadership would have remained difficult, because power was so minutely divided on Capitol Hill. Congress during the Jeffersonian era had neither the attitudes nor the institutional arrangements necessary for unified action. Congressmen were zealously defensive of their role as legislators; as the direct representatives of their constituents, they neither wanted nor accepted Presidential direction. To do so, they feared, would create a potential for centralized—and possibly monarchical—power.

This attitude, the natural offspring of ideas formed during the Revolution, was magnified by the nature of the community in which Congress worked. Washington during the Jeffersonian era was a city of transients. Of the senators and representatives who came to the capital at the beginning of any session, little more than half returned two years later. Nor did they spend much time in the city. Except in times of crisis, Congress met only during the winter months; during the rest of the year, Washington was nearly deserted. Moreover, on arrival in the city, a congressman allied himself with one of the several boardinghouses (or "messes") that lined Capitol Hill and served as legislative fraternities. Here members took their meals, slept, played cards, and talked politics. Like any social club, these fraternities were selective and encouraged a certain uniformity among their members. The residents of a mess were almost invariably from the same region; they represented basically the same galaxy of economic, cultural, and sectional interests. In this respect, the sectional character of each mess tended to remain constant from session to session. Once a boarding-house became identified with Southerners, Yankees, or whatever, it stayed that way.

Although the fraternities were superficially models of informality —with congressmen stepping around spittoons in their stocking feet —discipline within each was tight. There was little privacy, for example; even in the larger messes, few had their own rooms. Visitors, therefore, were infrequent and had to be entertained in the common room downstairs. It was impossible for a member of another boarding-house to discuss a delicate political matter in secrecy. This situation continued when congressmen entered the Capitol building, for messmates took desks near one another, within earshot of their colleagues. Not surprisingly, bloc voting was the rule on any issue from the most trivial to the most sensitive. In this greenhouse atmosphere —where ideas and policies took root selectively around the same interests—little else could be expected.

The fragmentation encouraged by the numerous boardinghouses was encouraged by the committee system. Committees were convenient means of handling legislation quickly and thoroughly, and theoretically they gave the leader of the House or the Senate extraordinary power since he determined their membership. But the committee system was in fact one more block to the effective use of power. Speaker Henry Clay, for example, carefully allocated appointments to House committees so that each would contain one or two members of every congressional mess. Chairmanships were similarly divided. While this was a good tactic in Clay's ongoing effort to make himself popular, it produced the same fragmentation and clannishness that characterized the boardinghouses. Committee chairmen fought among each other in an effort to defend their congruent sectional and fraternal interests; similar battles raged within committees. The confusion was made worse by the fact that each committee generally dealt with business that required the attention—at the next higher level— of a member of the Cabinet. This strengthened the political ties between department heads and Congress, but not between departments or with the President. Thus was the legislative process complicated and slow, and thus was the President further restrained from exercising leadership.

FRAGMENTATION among the Republican leadership in Washington and the simultaneous emergence of new political parties in the states meant that the choice of Monroe's successor would not be easy and routine. During his second term, competition for the Presidency was intense. The logical candidate was William Crawford of Georgia, Monroe's Secretary of the Treasury. Crawford had narrowly missed becoming President in 1816, yet he accepted his defeat cheerfully and spent the next eight years in faithful, hard work for both the President and his party. He carefully recruited the support of powerful Republicans in Congress and shrewdly curried the favor of Van Buren—the one man who could bring him support outside his native South. In 1824 the Republican caucus endorsed him overwhelmingly.

It was a pyrrhic victory. Crawford had suffered an untimely stroke in the fall of 1823 which nearly killed him and left him in precarious health. Moreover, Crawford played the game by rules which no longer applied. The caucus had lost its power to dictate candidates. Its actions were not binding even on the senators and representatives who participated in it, and in 1824 barely a third of those eligible were present. With Crawford sick and unable to use his tremendous influence to protect himself, the internecine warfare that raged within Washington erupted into open hostilities.

The chief rivals were John Quincy Adams, Henry Clay, John C. Calhoun, and Andrew Jackson. All except the last represented, not surprisingly, a particular section. After Crawford, the logical choice was Adams. He was a man of remarkable integrity and undeniable intelligence, a latter-day John Winthrop with a Puritan's capacity for exhausting work and selfless dedication. Like Winthrop, however, he was often brittle, detached, and cold. He seemed to defy the world to love him. His diary, scratched out by the light of a solitary candle in the early-morning hours, was a seventy-year record of personal agony. He had few, if any, close friends, but his political assets were formidable: he came from New England, a section that had not been represented in the White House during the long reign of the Virginia dynasty. He was Secretary of State, and had used that post vigorously to advocate American expansionism and hemispheric preeminence. The Monroe Doctrine was largely Adams's creation, and it was a shrewd tactic in his effort to broaden his political base. It weakened charges that he was an Anglophile and demonstrated that he could move beyond his New England heritage to a strong defense of nationalism.

Clay and Calhoun were also nationalists, yet the latter was even more remote, more brittle, and more detached than Adams. Calhoun's support was concentrated almost wholly in his native state of South Carolina, and he was never a serious contender for the Presidency. Clay, on the other hand, enjoyed immense popularity and represented the aspirations of the emerging West. Clay had been born in Virginia and later moved to Lexington, Kentucky, where he built up a profitable law career supported by extensive holdings in real estate. In many ways he personified the new West. Tall and slim, he loved poker, politics, and horse racing, in no particular order. He was also the chief architect of the American System. Clay's keen awareness of the growing isolation of the West made him eager to develop the kind of economic and cultural ties that would bind the region to the rest of the nation. To this end, he was a major contributor to Lexington's status as a center for arts and education—the "Athens of the West"—and a strong proponent of internal improvements and a sound currency. Clay's economic nationalism, moreover, served the same political purpose as Adams's diplomatic nationalism: it helped broaden his appeal beyond the confines of a particular section.

Standing apart, and somehow aloof, from these candidates was Andrew Jackson, a figure so towering that he gave his name to the age. Jackson was at once the most loved and hated man in America. His fame rested entirely on his military exploits, and many saw him as a kind of homegrown Napoleon—imperious, adventuresome, and often cruel. He took orders reluctantly; he spelled badly; he dueled. He called himself a man of the people yet lived in a splendid mansion in Tennessee circled by the cabins of slaves. He gambled. He insisted on wearing his uniform where ordinary clothes would do. Most damaging, his politics were vague. He had spent most of his life either in the saddle or tending his plantation; his political career was spotty and undistinguished.

These peculiarities told only part of the story. Jackson was a complex man who embodied the hopes and fears of a complex nation. Many saw his imperiousness not as arrogance but as the mark of a man chosen by God to fulfill a special destiny. He was an American version of the Byronesque hero: cruder, more impetuous, certainly not a man of letters, but a faithful patriot to the land he served. He belonged to that land in a special way. The fact that he spelled so poorly, while his successes were so great, suggested that his tutor was nature, not books. The connection to nature was vital to his popularity and impact. America existed amid a staggering display of natural resources. To a country schooled in the natural laws extolled by the Enlightenment and fast moving toward the natural mysticism of the Romantics, Jackson seemed more representative of the energetic young republic than did the erudite Adams or the parliamentarian Clay. He was the right man at the right time, the raw material for a monument.

Once the myths are cleared away, Jackson becomes more human. He was not the headstrong tyrant that some believed him to be. He sought advice from his counselors when he was unsure of his course, as he often was. Nor was he the rigid ideologue that his later wars with the Bank of the United States suggested. In the Senate in 1824, for example, he favored both the protective tariff and bills for internal improvements. He had been outspoken enough in his denunciations of banks to endear himself to victims of the depression, yet he was vague enough to avoid alarming investors—to whom he was closely allied. He was against the caucus system, yet his nomination had first been made by a caucus of the Tennessee legislature. Unhampered by political promises, untroubled by consistency, untainted by old partisan associations, Jackson could be and was all things to all people.

These traits served him well in the election of 1824, for when the votes were counted, Jackson's ninety-nine electoral ballots cut sharply across sectional lines. The others were not so lucky. Adams had eighty-four from New York and New England; Clay, thirty-seven from the West; Crawford, forty-one from the Southeast. But Jackson was thirty-two short of the necessary majority. As provided by the Constitution, the three who had polled the highest number of votes were placed before the House of Representatives; each state cast one ballot determined by a majority of the delegation. Clay, out of the running, threw his strength to Adams. The three additional votes needed to give Adams a majority came from Maryland, Louisiana, and Illinois—all states in which Adams had run second to Jackson at the polls. The politicians were still reluctant to accept a popular hero.

Adams's appointment of Clay as Secretary of State gave rise to the charge that the two had made an unseemly deal, although it is difficult to see how Clay could have supported either of the other candidates and still have remained consistent with his own views. Nor is it easy to see where Adams could have found anyone else so well qualified for the State Department. The cry of "corrupt bargain" nonetheless became a rallying point for the opposition and helped prepare the ground for the restoration of the two-party system. Still, the most important aspect of the election was the distribution of the vote. The breadth—as well as the depth—of Jackson's support signaled both his own strength as a candidate and the fact that, thereafter, a successful nominee would have to transcend sectional lines and appeal to all elements of the electorate.

So John Quincy Adams became President, ready to face the four worst years of his life. Adams's Presidency was marked by the best of intentions and the worst of tactics. His first message to Congress in 1825 reflected the pattern. He had prepared the address with more than his usual intense care, for he hoped that it would set the stage for a vigorous and successful Administration. Instead, it doomed him to stalemate.

Adams was a nationalist, and his speech was perhaps the best elaboration of a particular strain of nationalism that was crystallizing during the 1820s. Naturally, he drew heavily on the programs of his father and Alexander Hamilton, stressing the need for tariffs and internal improvements to facilitate commerce and industry. Naturally, he wanted a stable currency and banking system for the same reasons. But Adams went beyond these three traditional points of the American System. They were vital projects, he said, but others were equally important and equally the province of legislation. "Moral, political, intellectual improvement are duties assigned by the Author of our Existence to social no less than to individual man," he stated, calling for endeavors that would uplift the whole society; these efforts, being expensive, would require the aid of government. A national university, coastal and interior surveys, scientific research, and a national observatory—the "light-house of the skies" of which Europe had many and America none—were all projects worthy of national support. "The spirit of improvement is abroad upon the earth," Adams concluded. It was incumbent upon Americans to do their part.

These proposals were not simply the creations of a remote, slightly aristocratic dilettante. They represented, rather, an ambitious sense of nationalism that was shared by a substantial number of Jeffersonians who would later emerge, first as National Republicans, then as Whigs. Adams genuinely believed that the true foundations of national glory lay in the creativity and moral commitment of its citizens. Being a follower of Jefferson, he also believed that all should participate and share in molding and strengthening the culture. To confine the benefits of education and science, as well as commerce and industry, to an elite few would produce nothing. The great mass of people would remain base and depraved; the rest would be incapable of progress. If, on the other hand, everyone prospered and all improved, each individual's happiness would be enhanced.

It was not the ends of Adams's nationalism that troubled his detractors; it was the means. Adams was not at all intimidated or frightened by government. He had been brought up in its highest councils and inner sanctums. He was from Massachusetts, with its Puritan tradition of assigning leaders the responsibility of watching over the moral and economic state of its citizens. He instinctively projected the same function onto the national government. "The great object of the institution of civil government," he preached, "is the improvement of the condition of those who are parties to the social compact . . ." To do so, he continued, "governments are invested with power, and to the attainment of the end—the progressive improvement of the condition of the governed—the exercise of delegated powers is a duty as sacred and indispensable as the usurpation of powers not granted is criminal and odious." He was saying nothing new. The same impulse drove cities to build bridges and states to establish universities. He was simply carrying the role of government to new heights and endowing it with a moral purpose.

What Adams—and his Whig descendants—did not fully realize was the complex tangle of fears that an overzealous or callous use of power could create in the American mind. The nation was new. It hoped for a bright future yet worried that the aristocratic past might return. Not being a party man, Adams failed to comprehend that voters needed at least the appearance of consultation and participation in making decisions. In a disastrous conclusion to his first address, Adams showed his utter ignorance of the currents swirling about him. "While foreign nations . . . are advancing with gigantic strides in the career of public improvement, were we to slumber in indolence or fold up our arms and proclaim to the world that we are palsied by the will of our constituents, would it not be to cast away the bounties of Providence and doom ourselves to perpetual inferiority?" "Palsied by the will of our constituents." The tone was paternalistic and more than a little condescending. It reeked of deference. The irony was that Adams and men like him, who fed on progress and wanted to use institutional machinery to advance it, became outcasts at precisely the time when Martin Van Buren was creating his own institutional machinery for entirely different purposes.

Adams's vision for the new nation remained even as his power dwindled. The outrage and catcalls occasioned by his message to Congress soon found other, more tangible targets. In 1825 he proposed that the United States send emissaries to the Panama Congress, which had been called by Simón Bolívar to discuss hemispheric attitudes toward commerce and Europe. The President's intentions were, as usual, pure, and the meeting would have little binding force. Moreover, the Monroe Doctrine suggested that American policy toward Latin America could be helped by encouraging such conferences. But Adams ignored the probability that some of the delegates from the Caribbean would be blacks. Southern congressmen were alarmed and very nearly killed the mission. Commissioners to attend the Congress were finally chosen and confirmed in March 1826, but not without a disruptive battle in Congress. The Panama Mission was the first and last congressional victory for Adams, and one that gained nothing. One commissioner refused to go during the fever season; the other, less prudent, did go, caught the fever, and died en route.

The off-year elections of 1826 clearly sounded the death knell of Adams's future hopes. The opposition had little trouble in finding issues with which to flail him mercilessly. The Panama Mission crystallized the antagonism to Adams in the South; elsewhere, rivals had only to mock the President's message or, more easily, denounce him as the choice of the politicians and not the people. The real issues dividing the voters, however, were state and local. In Ohio, for example, the aftermath of the depression still weighed heavily in the voters' minds. Those who had been hurt by the closing of the United States Bank branch office in 1820 shied away from Adams and Clay and tended to endorse Jackson's supporters. In Kentucky, a battle over debtor relief raged, with each side perfecting its party machinery. In New York, Pennsylvania, and New England, economic issues were beginning to be matched by the growing hysteria over the alleged subversive power of the Masonic Order. Whatever the local issues, the result of the elections was a stunning defeat for the Administration. The opposition won control of both houses of Congress and of a majority of the state governments.

ADAMS'S troubles signaled the final collapse of the old Jeffersonian coalition. Regardless of the President's personal mistakes—and they were many—the new nation was becoming too large and too diverse to respond well to the informal rules of deferential politics that had served previous generations. An expanding population, territorial growth, and increasing sectional variances all demanded new forms of political machinery. In one respect Adams played a critical role in this realignment: his policies were so far removed from those of Jefferson and his political blunderings so unforgivable that he became a hated symbol against which the opposition could rally. Perceptive observers, especially Van Buren, sensed that the time was right to create a new national party.

What was needed to perfect the coalition was a leader, someone who would be all that Adams was not. Jackson was the man. The elasticity of his political convictions made him acceptable to several factions that otherwise might hate each other. This flexibility was crucial because of the sectional cleavages that plagued every attempt to formulate a unified economic policy. A national bank and federal roads were not pressing problems in New England, which had its own good roads and banks; there the tariff was paramount. Neither tariffs nor banks were indispensable in the West, which needed roads. The South was growing suspicious of any vigorous use of federal power, which could threaten states' rights and possibly slavery. But only by combining these elements into one party could an intersectional alliance be formed.

Because there was so little ideological unity among these disparate elements of the emerging coalition, Jackson served an important symbolic function. His iron will, his patriotism, his identification with the soil and the common man were all transcendent ideals that could be used to inspire devotion to the man and—coincidentally—his party. Van Buren, with his usual perspicacity, saw clearly that modern political parties needed moral symbols, rallying points for the faithful. "I have long been satisfied," he wrote, "that we can only get rid of the present, and restore a better state of things, by combining Genl. Jackson's personal popularity with the portion of old party feeling yet remaining." If that could be done, the new coalition would have not merely Jackson at its head but also the memory of Thomas Jefferson. Thus would two powerful images be fused: Jefferson, the rationalist architect of the Revolution, and Jackson, the energetic, domineering spirit of the expanding republic. Van Buren's intent here was not to deify the man, but to identify him with an organization. The electorate, having voted initially for Jackson, would later vote for the party of Jackson. To encourage loyalty to the organization would "greatly improve the condition of the Republicans of the North and Middle States by substituting *party principle* for *personal preference* as one of the leading points in the contest." The deferential system would be dealt a final, crippling blow.

The first step in implementing this strategy was to make certain that Jackson had a reliable organization. Van Buren easily turned his own political machine in New York to the General's support; other states followed suit. Nationally, the well-oiled Crawford machine became, between 1826 and 1828, the Jackson machine. Its power had declined, of course, but it still provided a useful network of partisans eager for a change of Adminstration. That Crawford's machine had remained in working order was largely Adams's fault, for like Monroe he had failed to see the President's role as party leader. Adams not only refused to remove political opponents from office, he even reappointed most of those who served fixed terms. Yet these same officeholders, most important of whom were the collectors of customs, were Crawford partisans and key figures in state organizations. Their services to Jackson were invaluable.

Recruiting the ordinary voter required more innovative tactics; here newspapers played an essential role. By the 1820s newspapers had proliferated in the United States, providing a cheap, accessible means of mass communications. Most were short-lived and poorly edited, but the best were outlets for literature, politics, factual information, and advertising. As newspapers grew, so did the influence of publishers and editors. Some of the best of these became persuasive spokesmen for the emerging Jacksonian coalition. In the North were Isaac Hill's *New Hampshire Patriot* and Mordecai Noah's New York *Enquirer*, which later merged with James Watson Webb's New York *Courier*. In the West and South, Amos Kendall of Kentucky turned the potent *Argus of Western America* from Clay to Jackson; Thomas Ritchie made the Richmond *Enquirer* into the most influential paper in the South; Duff Green gave up the St. Louis *Enquirer* to edit the new *United States Telegraph* in Washington. The loyalties of these editors reflected the diverse nature of the coalition. In broad terms, Noah and Webb represented the Van Buren wing of the party, Ritchie the Crawford faction, and Green the Calhoun interest. Hill and Kendall gave their undivided allegiance to Jackson.

DESPITE these links, the intersectional nature of the coalition created severe difficulties. The President-makers, especially Van Buren, were determined to center their campaign efforts on the symbolic nationalistic qualities of Jackson's personality, not on real and divisive political issues. Yet issues, particularly the tariff, were unavoidable. Since 1816, when the first protective tariff had been instituted, American manufacturers had regularly pressed for a steady increase, which had reached unprecedented highs in 1824. Still unsatisfied, these interests assembled a convention at Harrisburg, Pennsylvania, in the summer of 1827 to call for even higher duties. At the same time, Southern cotton had fallen to a new low of nine cents a pound—down two-thirds in less than two years. Relentlessly pressured by rising debts and falling income, Southerners viewed protectionism as an open plot by which men of other sections could reduce the South to economic and cultural ruin.

But Jackson needed votes in the North and West as well as in the South. His supporters correctly assumed that Adams would seek a second term and that few Southerners would endorse him, so they concentrated on winning the affections of Northern and Western protectionists. When Congress met in December 1827, Jackson's partisans offered a bill that went so far beyond the proposals of the Harrisburg Convention that New England, too, would likely be hurt by the duties. Tariffs on uncarded wool and other raw materials—on which Northern factories depended—were excessive. Seasoned observers sensed that the bill was a political tactic more than an effort to institute economic policy and focused their attentions on the men behind it. Since the bill was offered by Silas Wright—who would do nothing without first consulting Van Buren—it must have had the latter's approval.

Van Buren's exact intentions remain unclear. Assuming that the South was safe for Jackson and that New England was securely behind Adams, it is possible that the bill was drafted so that it would fail. New England and the South would defeat it, yet Jackson could be put forward as a man of protectionist sympathies. The twisted logic here was that the South, not actually having to endure the torments of the bill, would not be unduly alarmed—particularly since only Jackson's supporters, but not the man himself, put forward the act. It is also possible that Van Buren and his cronies were genuinely behind the bill. It was necessary to win the West and mid-Atlantic states; disaffection in the South would not be enough to overcome that section's distrust of Adams.

Whatever the intent, the tariff did pass the House of Representatives. The West and middle states supported it, as did a crucial portion of New Englanders—who felt that their factories were strong enough to absorb higher costs for raw materials. When the bill reached the more conservative Senate, however, its provisions were reduced, but the level was still substantially higher than existing duties. The reaction in the South was ominous. To Southerners the rates were outrageously high; it was a "Tariff of Abominations." In South Carolina especially, there were those who greeted its passage with demands for forcible resistance, and only the prospect of Jackson's election prevented rebellion.

The convoluted history of this tariff reflected the delicate interplay of political, economic, and sectional forces that were to plague every Administration for the succeeding generation. There was no overriding economic policy in the bill. It was a patchwork assembly of local needs, intense lobbying, and shifting alliances with no internal logic of its own. Certainly Adams would have constructed a more rational, far-seeing law, but Adams was not in control. Nor was anyone else. Presidential power was at its nadir in 1828, political loyalties were shifting and regrouping, and sectional cleavages were becoming daily more apparent. The only fixed goal in anyone's mind was the upcoming Presidential election, and that—more than any economic or social need—provided the focus of organized effort among the lawmakers of the new nation.

THE campaign was one of unparalleled bitterness that left its mark on all concerned. In a contest notable for fraud and dirt, both sides were guilty of misrepresentation, scandalmongering, and outright slander. Friends of Adams dredged up the fact that Jackson and his wife had married before her divorce to her previous husband had become final.

It was an oversight on Jackson's part, but no matter. "Ought a convicted adultress and her paramour husband to be placed in the highest offices of this free and christian land?" asked one pamphlet. Similar trash concerning Jackson's dueling followed. Partisans of Jackson, not to be outdone, portrayed Adams as a snobbish aristocrat who, they incorrectly charged, had fitted the East Room of the White House with a billiard table and an ivory chess set at the public expense. The fact that Adams had paid for these luxuries himself was ignored. More substantive questions were raised concerning the tariff, where Adams was vulnerable and Jackson was vague, but the overall tone of the campaign was strident and intemperate.

Jackson won, though not overwhelmingly. In the electoral college his margin was handsome; Adams carried only New England, New Jersey, and Delaware, and the two split the vote of New York and Maryland. The popular vote was much closer, but still a substantial victory for Jackson. He won about 56 percent of the total. To consider the aggregate vote alone, however, is misleading. The two candidates were approximately equal in only seven states out of twenty-four: New Hampshire, New York, New Jersey, Maryland, Louisiana, Kentucky, and Ohio. But in the rest the vote was lopsided. Moreover, although the total number of votes cast was much greater than in 1824, the percentage of qualified voters participating was generally less than that of the Jefferson era and in many cases less than that cast in state races. The common man, whatever his preferences, remained somewhat indifferent to Presidential elections.

Several conclusions may be drawn from these results. One is that Jackson had not, in 1828, become the demigod of the common man. A healthy support for Adams and the issues he represented remained. But that support was as yet weak and ill organized; a unified opposition to the Jacksonians did not exist. Since the Democrats demolished Adams in nine states, organized opposition to Jackson and the Democrats could hardly be termed national. Hence, the two-party system was not reborn in the campaign of 1828; it awaited later developments in each state.

The campaign did, however, presage many of the characteristics of the emerging two-party system. It must be remembered that Jackson won partly because Adams lost. There is no reliable way of telling how many of the General's votes came from men who were more dissatisfied with Adams than enamored of Jackson, but the latter's ambivalence on the issues, his ability to be all things to all men in heroic form, certainly did not hurt his chances. Sectional preferences also helped. Jackson was from Tennessee, which was far enough West to appeal to Westerners, and far enough South to win votes there. The implications were clear: to be successful, a party must nominate men who were flexible on the issues and attractive to all sections. Finally, they must not, in any way, appear to be aristocrats.

While Adams's party was unorganized and disconnected, the Democrats were only a little less so. Van Buren had been correct; the party needed Jackson's name to get started. But, as Van Buren also knew, Jackson's election would spur the opposition to systematize their efforts, which in turn would help weld the diverse elements of the Democracy together. Nothing was quite so effective in creating tightly knit parties as a close contest and a good brawl.

So the Jacksonians came to power with many tacit promises but no commitments, high hopes but an infant organization. The coalition was, in its first victory, too large to be manageable and its purposes too diverse to be encompassed within a single organization. The South had voted for Jackson in the belief that he would use his influence to reduce the tariff. The middle states had voted for him for the opposite reason. The West expected cheap credit and land reform. The direction the party would take would be determined by Jackson himself. He represented the majority, and he would carry out what he conceived to be its will.

6

The Age of Jackson

NO one who was at Washington at the time of General Jackson's inauguration is likely to forget that period to the day of his death," commented one observer. Thousands crowded into the city to see their hero take the oath and to celebrate the beginning of what they hoped would be a new age for the republic. Their enthusiasm was boundless. The throng cheered Jackson through his speech, then followed him to a reception at the White House, where they horrified dignitaries and servants alike by upsetting punch bowls, snatching away ice cream before it could be properly served, and overturning furniture. Some even stood on damask chairs to catch a glimpse of the new President. "I never saw such a crowd here," sighed Daniel Webster, "and they really seem to think that the country is rescued from some dreadful danger." The almost revivalistic outpouring of enthusiasm puzzled him, for apart from devotion to Jackson—there seemed to be nothing by which this crowd could be distinguished from an ordinary brawl. They "have no common principle," he noted, "—they are held together by no common ties."

Webster's bewilderment was typical. Those who knew Jackson—whether they liked him or not—were certain that he would bring a new style to the White House. They expected him to be a strong President, to reverse the decline in executive leadership that had plagued his three predecessors. But no one really knew what policies Jackson would pursue. His inaugural address was short and dull: he seemed to be on every side of the few issues he raised. This vagueness was a little frightening, for the new President was known to be controversial and unpredictable. But the crowds worshipped him; they treated him as a savior. And that was what puzzled observers the most. The nation was already split into pro- and anti-Jackson camps, yet these divisions appeared to have no basis other than the President himself. If one looked closely at the nature of Jackson's support, only one clear pattern emerged: he ran poorly in New England, where Adams was a favorite son. Beyond that, the nature of his support defied description, particularly if one tried to equate political preferences with the issues. Like the President, Democrats were contradictory and vague when asked to state their positions on internal improvements, the tariff, or the banking system. Yet the enthusiasm that Jackson kindled among his friends and foes was real. It was also robust, quarrelsome, enthusiastic, and fun. Politics had become a national sport, the recreation of the common man.

Jackson's role in changing the style of American politics was important, perhaps crucial, but it can be overstressed. Because Jackson did polarize the electorate, because he did take stands on the major issues facing him, it is tempting to read the history of his Presidency in reverse, to identify his appeal with his actions. Since Jackson's most controversial acts concerned economic policy, it is particularly inviting to link his supporters to certain types of economic or occupational interests. Such an analysis would have been—at least in 1829—premature. Jackson's inauguration was a milestone in political development, certainly, but it was only a milestone in a long and tortuous road toward a new party system.

In 1829 the United States was a mosaic of political subcultures. Within this mosaic were certain patterns. There was a common assumption that ordinary citizens must be given equal access to the structure of power and that talent and work determined who would rise to positions of leadership. In response to this assumption, new organizational forms had appeared and were spreading. The issues that appealed to the electorate were predictably economic. Tariffs, banks, and roads were important to an expanding entrepreneurial society, no matter what position one took on them. These same issues encouraged, although they did not define, sectional animosities, which were daily growing stronger.

But the United States was also maddeningly pluralistic. Sections were subdivided into regions and localities with widely disparate economic pursuits. The needs of a small Virginia farmer, for example, might or might not be congruent with those of a nearby plantation owner, and both differed in outlook from their counterparts to the west and north. Traditions varied. There was a definite hierarchy of social class in parts of New England and the South which was not replicated on the frontier or in the small commercial towns. The bases for such hierarchies were not alike, and their authority was being questioned. Within these sectional subdivisions, moreover, were subcultures based largely on ethnic background or church affiliation. A Congregationalist and a Baptist, even though they might live in the same area and work the same job, viewed the world differently, because each had been brought up to view it differently. Stresses among these subcultures were usually obscured by more pressing, immediate, economic issues, but they contributed much to political antagonisms.

Near the end of the 1820s these antagonisms exploded into open conflict. The near-religious enthusiasm Webster had witnessed at the inauguration was only one manifestation of a crying need to bring order and stability to American life. During the 1830s, Jackson's controversial Presidency would channel much of the anxiety into specific issues, but what was important during the early years was the style in which political topics were debated and expressed. The tone was moralistic and strident. It often conjured up visions of evil conspiracies—no different, really, from the tone of the camp meetings at Cane Ridge in 1801. The structure was systematic, organized, and mechanical—much like the new railroads.

THE clearest example of the new style of politics was the Antimasonic Party. In several ways the Antimasonry was Jacksonian America in microcosm, a colorful blend of hope, fear, openness, and bigotry. In 1827, an obscure New Yorker, William Morgan, threatened to expose the inner secrets of the Order of Freemasons and thus root out what he believed was a conspiratorial threat to American morals and liberty. Almost immediately he disappeared. Morgan's fate remains uncertain, but apparently he was kidnapped by outraged Masons and briefly imprisoned in an abandoned fort near Lake Ontario. When his captors realized that they had committed a felony, they panicked, trussed him in a weighted rope, rowed to the center of the Niagara River, and dumped him overboard. No one ever recovered the body.

When the New York state legislature refused to conduct an official inquiry into Morgan's disappearance, hysteria ensued. Rumors spread that the Freemasons controlled so much of the government that the legislature was nothing more than the political arm of a secret order. The whole affair smelled of a dark conspiracy based, as one writer charged, "on principles dangerous in a free government, subversive of political equality, and hostile to the impartial administration of justice." In the fall elections of 1827, opponents of Masonry elected fifteen men to the legislature by overwhelming majorities. In 1828, they fielded a candidate for governor; by 1830, the fever had spread to most Northern states, especially Pennsylvania, Vermont, and Massachusetts. The Antimasonic Party was born.

Freemasonry was an unlikely cause for such anxieties. A large social fraternity loosely based on Christian principles, it was full of signs, handshakes, and passwords that, taken by themselves, were more seriocomic than threatening. "I always considered the Institution more *ridiculous* than dangerous," one observer sighed. Yet, within the context of Jacksonian nationalism, Masonry was a potential menace. The central issue for Antimasons was power—and its susceptibility to abuse. In that respect, the rhetoric of Antimasonry was typical of Jacksonian America. Independence Day orators spoke grandly and loosely of how the Revolution had broken a conspiratorial threat to American liberties; Jackson worried about the concentrated influence of bankers; Van Buren attacked the power of elites. Similarly, Antimasons convinced themselves that any secret order, no matter how ostensibly benevolent, was "inimical to our EQUALITY, by monopolizing the offices and places of profit and trust, and by contaminating even the *justice* of our country." Masonry, or any other privileged clique, concentrated power beyond its allowable limits and—funneling it through a small group of like-minded men— used it aggressively and undemocratically. As the ultimate absurdity, Antimasons charged that the order was the American agent of a papist conspiracy, when in fact Freemasons were usually anti-Catholic.

This fear of conspiracies was the reverse image of more positive forces in the Antimason's world view. Buried in their naysaying was a strongly nationalistic concept of unity, a unity based on an open, expansive society that protected both its free institutions and its individuals. When Antimasons branded their enemies as aristocrats, they were advocating the rule of law rather than of men. It was to be a law based on moral principles and not on privileges or personalities. "Our call," cried one Antimasonic paper, "is made in behalf of insulted *Law,* and of defiled *religion.*" The attack on Masonry became, then, a concerted effort to rid the United States of any element that upset the natural harmony of a free republic. A democracy worked only when its citizens competed openly and fairly under an absolutely impartial code of law.

This emphasis on law and openness led to the creation of the convention system—the most significant contribution of the Antimasonic Party and one whose impact went far beyond the ideological confines of the movement. Their almost hysterical fear of conspiracies made it imperative that their nominees be selected openly. Conventions were independent of state legislatures, which, as the New York example had shown, were presumably under the control of Freemasons. They were independent of caucuses, which were the secretive domain of professional politicians. Conventions brought the nominating process closer to the ordinary voter, who might even serve as a delegate. And their ritual of deliberation and selection from among a pool of candidates reinforced the Antimasonic appeal for the rule of law, not personalities.

In a broader context, conventions were the logical offspring of the new style of party politics. They married the camp meeting and the machine. Van Buren, for example, welcomed their birth. Since political parties were constructed and organized as machines through which the ordinary voter could participate in making decisions and be rewarded for this service, it was natural that the convention, with its hoopla and its stamp of popular consent, would become a vital link between leaders and led. The convention system did not, of course, eliminate the professional politician. But it did provide a means of harmonizing the interests of the voter with those of the party official. Ideally, any candidate chosen openly by a convention represented the will of the party majority and would champion the interests of all, not just a few. In return, the party itself could coordinate its efforts behind a single man and—since the choice was openly made—demand strict loyalty to him and the institution he represented. Party discipline was thus strengthened and extended. The concept quickly spread to state parties, and by 1840 was the accepted rule in every major political movement.

The Antimasonic movement was short-lived. It was too localized and too narrowly focused to attract a national following. By 1836 it was a political derelict. But its form and structure were typical of the new politics. The movement reflected the anxieties that were erupting among the diverse elements of a pluralistic society. Its aim was to purify the society of unsettling forces; thus, its goals were moralistic and not open to compromise. And it reached out to the voter in an organized, open, and systematic fashion. Other movements, such as the brief Workingmen's parties of Pennsylvania, New York, and Massachusetts, concentrated on different issues, but the style of their response to these issues was much the same.

In time these movements were absorbed into the rivalry between Whigs and Democrats. Because these organizations were broad and national, they were compelled to simplify their appeals while simultaneously extending them. Any issue that fragmented political debate sectionally or that did not transcend the countless subcultures was gingerly avoided. Thus, each party tailored its rhetoric to the common man and his economic aspirations, subjects that engaged every member of the social order. And the rhetoric had a moralistic, urgent tone. Whigs and Democrats portrayed themselves as saviors who possessed eternal truths; each characterized its opposition as unwitting agents of destruction. But though the rhetoric was unambiguous, there was considerable room within each party to accommodate differing interpretations. And each party came to rely on a highly structured bureaucracy to spread its message.

Party lines did not harden until 1840. During the 1830s, the new politics needed controversy in order to define the grounds for political debate, perfect its organizational forms, and polarize the electorate into competing groups. This is precisely what Jackson provided. His election began the process by dividing voters between those who loved him and those who hated him. His aggressive use of Presidential power hardened these divisions and focused attention on the issues. He inspired both friends and foes to create organizations that would continue the debate after his term in office ended, and he did so by attacking his enemies as mortal threats to the progress of the republic. His opponents responded in kind, and politics assumed some of the characteristics of an organized religious crusade. By the time Jackson left the White House, the antagonistic passions he had excited had assumed a life of their own, and loyalty to the party had become largely independent of the issues around which the parties had originally formed.

JACKSON began his term cautiously. The new President was a man of strong convictions and stronger passions, but he was also a seasoned general who insisted on recruiting an able and loyal staff before he launched an attack. His first concern, therefore, was to master the labyrinth of power in Washington and secure control of the executive establishment. The task was far more complicated than anything he had faced in his military career. The election had brought an inchoate mob of partisans to the capital, each determined to capture the President's affections and exploit his prestige. Jackson searched this amorphous mass with a critical eye for men of talent and—above all—loyalty. He could not hope to implement his reforms if his chief aides were not solidly behind him.

The most prominent members of the new Administration were Secretary of State Martin Van Buren and Vice President John C. Calhoun. Each offered formidable assets. Van Buren was a superb organizer and a skilled parliamentarian; Calhoun had been in Washington twenty years, knew the place, and was nationally respected—sometimes feared—for his integrity and ideals. These men represented the extreme poles of the party axis: Van Buren the advocate of majority will; Calhoun the defender of states' rights. Jackson wanted the loyalties of both, for such a combination would have greatly simplified the job of restoring the power of his office. It was not to be.

Van Buren was patient, easygoing, and cooperative; Calhoun was combative, icy, and aloof. Jackson instinctively turned to the former, whose well-known concept of party discipline made him a reliable arm of the President's will. He and Van Buren quickly became close friends, blending their separate personal styles into an executive machine of unprecedented effectiveness. Van Buren's bureaucratic skills extended far beyond the limits of his office; he monitored Congress and the party and performed routine jobs, so that Jackson was free to concentrate on larger issues and problems. Calhoun, on the other hand, was a constant irritant. His ideological rigidity and his personal quest for the White House posed threats to the unity Jackson required, and the President rightly considered him a maverick.

Almost immediately, Jackson's suspicions were confirmed. Early in the term, Calhoun foolishly refused to include Peggy Eaton, the wife of one of the Cabinet members, on his guest lists. Peggy Eaton was lovely, and she had purportedly used her beauty sexually to gain status and favors. Proper Washington—especially Calhoun's wife—accepted the rumors and snubbed her; Jackson rallied to her defense. The President's wife, Rachel, had been similarly libeled during the campaign and had died shortly before Jackson left for Washington.

To a man still in grief, Calhoun's snubs appeared hateful and unchivalrous. The episode would have been minor had not Jackson been so absolute in his demand for loyalty or so passionate in his defense of feminine virtue, but the antagonism it sparked was real. The seed of distrust, once planted, blossomed as Calhoun withdrew deeper into his defense of states' rights—a course that was destined to collide with Jackson's spread-eagle nationalism. By 1831 the two had broken completely.

Similar divisions plagued the Cabinet, which was initially constructed to represent all branches of the party. Jackson waited two years to purge his staff of Calhoun men, but in the meantime he assembled an informal corps of friends and advisers who became known as the "Kitchen Cabinet." This group included former editors Amos Kendall and Isaac Hill, and Major William B. Lewis, an old friend of the President and an architect of his campaign. The Kitchen Cabinet was a brilliant Administrative innovation. Its members served no constituency but the President; it was inconceivable that they would use their post as a stepping-stone to the White House. Their loyalty to the President was unquestioned, and during his tenure in office they provided him the kind of detached, sound advice that enabled him to manipulate Congress and the issues to his benefit.

The issue of loyalty was not simply an extension of Jackson's Presidential ego, nor was it confined to the Cabinet. It was an integral link in the party machinery. Jackson interpreted his election as a mandate to reform a government "corrupted" by its predecessors, so it was necessary and desirable to staff all levels of the government with persons who reflected the popular will. Following a pattern long familiar to local politics, and introduced nationally by Jefferson, the President instituted a process that he called "rotation in office," by which those who were not faithful to the party were replaced by those who were. No man, he reasoned, held office by birthright, and those who remained too long in a position of power might come to regard their posts as private property. This encouraged corruption. "They are apt," he stated, "to acquire a habit of looking with indifference upon the public interests, and of tolerating conduct from which an unpracticed man would revolt." Fresh talent, drawn from those who reflected the majority will, was preferable.

Appointment to office was also a reward for hard work in the service of the party. Van Buren's friend William Marcy justified rotation as the spoils of victory. Van Buren, more pragmatic, saw it slightly differently. A sound political machine owed its success to the support of the people; in return, that machine must be able to pay its debt. Appointments to public offices were tangible incentives to men who had served the party well, more readily identifiable than the slower, indirect rewards of legislation. The payoff also strengthened party discipline. Those who had been honored by the organization would not abandon it lightly. And while Van Buren fully expected to staff the government with Democrats when the party won, he had the common sense to recognize that the opposition would do the same when victory was theirs. Marcy's dictum applied both ways.

Accordingly, Jackson let it be known that he intended to clear the ranks of the unsound, and in no time the capital was overrun by deserving Democrats clamoring for jobs. As the pressure mounted, the President gladly allowed Van Buren to make most appointments. Van Buren filled key positions with men of his own choosing, but he stopped short of a wholesale dismissal in order to avoid replacing old Crawford men, who were generally disposed to favor the President and Van Buren anyway. It was enough to strengthen the party organization and to freeze out the Calhoun faction. Outside the armed forces and the postal service, only about ten percent of the public offices changed hands; they were, however, the positions of power. These officials joined a considerable number of Jackson partisans who owed their original appointments to Crawford and who had survived the Adams regime. By the time Congress met in December 1829, Jackson and Van Buren had developed a formidable Administrative machine.

As Jackson's power grew, he began to confront the issues. Again, he proceeded cautiously. The President was in no hurry to present the nation with controversies until he was certain that he controlled his party. Since the Democracy was a fragile coalition of competing interests, Jackson's use of power during the first three years of his Presidency was largely negative. He declined to make tariff reform an Administrative policy, for example, for that would alienate crucial sections of his support in the North and mid-Atlantic states. He proposed instead that the government use the tariff to pay its expenses and to retire the national debt, then—when the latter task was completed—turn the surplus income over to the states for construction of roads and canals. By offering an alternate source of funds for internal improvements, Jackson freed himself to veto any public-works project that he considered unjustified. This he did in 1830, when he turned down an appropriation that would have built a road from Maysville, Kentucky, to Lexington. Westerners were outraged when he dismissed the proposal as a state, not a national, enterprise, but they were placated when money continued to flow into other projects.

Jackson's personal views on these issues were far stronger than his actions. He did believe as a rule that the tariff should be as low as possible, and he did not believe that the federal government should involve itself in costly public-works projects. But on either issue he was willing to offer compromises whenever possible, in order to keep his party intact. The Maysville veto, then, was a strategic move by which Jackson humiliated his opposition while losing few friends.

The President's use of power was not always so cautious, however. Early in his term he worked hard for a complete removal of the Indian tribes still living east of the Mississippi River. Throughout the 1820s speculators and white settlers had pressed for access to the rich lands occupied by Seminoles, Chickasaws, Cherokees, and other tribes. Jackson backed these efforts in complete political safety; almost no one put tribal claims ahead of American expansionism. In 1830 Jackson persuaded Congress to appropriate funds with which the Indian lands could be bought. Superficially, the President intended to make the removal as legal and as humane as possible. In reality, he was determined to drive the Indians out at any cost. None of the treaties and none of the glowing descriptions of the tribes' promised new homes masked the mismanagement, fraud, and frequent brutality with which the migrations took place. Military force subdued the Sac and Fox Indians in Illinois in 1832; the same power drove the Cherokees west in 1838 and precipitated a long war with the Seminoles in 1835. But every inch of the land thus acquired increased Jackson's popularity and deepened his conviction that he had acted rightly. By 1840 the removals were largely complete, and Jackson looked back on the enterprise with pride. "Rightly considered," he argued, "the policy of the General Government toward the red man is not only liberal, but generous."

All these moves helped Jackson prepare the ground for a dramatic expansion of his role as President. By the end of 1831, he had secured control of the executive establishment and had stripped Calhoun of most of his influence in the Democratic Party. He had made a few thrusts at points where he was assured of victory, and had increased his popularity in the process. With another campaign imminent—a time when most Presidents would have acted discreetly for fear of agitating the electorate—Jackson was ready to confront what he considered to be the two gravest threats to the security of the republic: the growing states' rights movement in the South and the Bank of the United States.

THE nullification crisis will be examined later; although it helped set the stage for the ultimate collapse of the second party system, its direct role in the emergence of that system was limited. But the Bank question was a watershed in the realignment of the 1830s. During the 1820s the Bank had regained much of the prestige it had lost during the Panic of 1819. In part, this recovery was due to its president, Nicholas Biddle. Biddle had been in and out of political life since 1804, when he had served an appointment in the American legation at London. His versatile and retentive mind made him a scholar, lawyer, editor, and politician, and when he took over the Bank in 1823, he extended his talents to finance. Ideologically, Biddle was a Jeffersonian, but he recognized the value of fiscal restraint in an expanding society. The Bank had immense capital reserves founded on the government's deposits; its notes were redeemable in gold or silver; it could expand or contract the circulation of those notes at will. Most importantly, the Bank served as a regulating force over the countless state and local banks across the country. In the absence of a national paper currency, the latter could issue their own notes. There was no guarantee, however, that these could be redeemed for face value. Since the Bank (and its branches) was the one truly national currency exchange, notes from local banks inevitably found their way to it. If Biddle sensed that a local bank was inflating its currency—not backing it with adequate reserves of specie—he could bring that institution quickly into line, even destroy it, by demanding payment in hard cash.

Any institution with such power inescapably made enemies. Despite Biddle's honesty and skill, he could not protect the Bank from criticism by two widely differing groups of opponents. One—which included Jackson himself—advocated a return to "hard money," or the exclusive use of gold and silver coins. Supporters of hard money were a mixed collection of Southerners, Westerners, and Eastern wage earners who clung to the ancient notion that paper money was an artificial creation of speculators and private interests. In their view, the only true currency was that that must be mined from natural resources; anything else contributed to the cycles of boom and bust that—like the Panic of 1819—hurt the common man and left the rich unscathed. On the other extreme was a wholly national and heterogeneous array of speculators and small entrepreneurs who favored "soft money," or an expansion of state bank notes. This group chafed under the Bank's ability to constrict credit. In certain states, such as New York, where a safety fund insured the deposits of local banks and linked them into a single system, such an expansion could be carried out judiciously and safely. In states where there were no controls on banking, the result might well be chaos without the restraining influence of the Bank. The soft-money interests did not see it this way, of course. To them the Bank was a brake on their ambitions.

It is misleading, however, to divide the country neatly into pro-Bank and anti-Bank factions. During the 1820s and early 1830s, most Americans were ambivalent on the issue. Everyone favored economic growth and expansion; no one wanted undue restraints on his liberties. Opinions on the Bank were primarily matters of attitude, and attitudes varied according to one's cultural and regional background. Members of evangelical sects, for example, tended to stress individual thrift and independence; in economic terms, they were the heirs of a strain of republican agrarianism that could be traced directly to John Taylor of Carolina and that resurfaced in the 1820s as the hard-money philosophy. On the other hand, those who had been raised in the more structured, established denominations (e.g., Congregationalist or Episcopalian) saw no conflict between the Bank's attempts to restrain speculation and to regulate currency and the common man's attempts to better himself. Complicating even this dichotomy, at least in the West, were divisions between New England and Southern emigrants to the frontier, each of whom brought with them different attitudes toward the proper limits of federal power. For most of the population, then, the Bank issue was only one of a complex tangle of aspirations and fears.

Jackson made it the primary issue, however. His opposition to the institution could not be ignored, since any major change in the Bank's power was certain to have a profound impact on the economy. In a time of rapid expansion and change, any threat—or promise—of this sort intensified the anxieties simmering within the subcultures of

American society. The Bank problem helped Jackson focus these anxieties on a single issue.

It served the same purpose for his opponents. Initially, Biddle was conciliatory. He moved quickly to change local directors and modify policies in order to placate the President. He was particularly concerned about Jackson's attitude toward a new charter for the Bank, so he sought and received assurances at the Cabinet level that there would be no conflict over that problem if the question were not raised before the election of 1832. Since the original charter would run through 1836, there was no reason for Biddle to provoke a fight. Henry Clay had other ideas. Clay had been nominated for President by the National Republicans in late 1831, and the recharter of the Bank appealed to him as campaign material. There were enough votes in Congress—many of them Democratic—to pass a recharter bill; Jackson could neither sign nor veto, Clay reasoned, without losing a section of his following. The Bank recharter was introduced according to Clay's plan, and passed with Biddle's help early in 1832.

Clay had misread the state of American politics. There were forces working against him that had nothing to do with the Bank. Neither he nor most other National Republicans realized that the new style of Democratic Party politics, with its elaborate system of discipline, its advocacy of party over personalities, and its patronage rewards, was bound to give Jackson a base of support that no opponent could duplicate. Furthermore, Clay had not grasped the significance of the pattern of votes cast either in 1824 or 1828. In both those elections, Jackson had been the only candidate with national appeal. When Clay himself ran against Jackson in 1832, he—a Westerner—lost crucial support in New England, where the sectional origins of a candidate were often decisive. (Martin Van Buren, a Northern man, did much better there in 1836 than Jackson had.) Moreover, William Wirt, the Antimasonic candidate, sapped votes from Clay, leaving the anti-Jackson opposition weak and divided where it might have been organized and strong. In short, Jackson had little to fear from a Bank veto.

AND veto he did. For Jackson, the Bank—and the ideology that supported it—ran counter to the true nature of American values and needs. It was pernicious, he announced in his veto message, to think that society would improve simply by manipulating its institutions. "Equality of talents, of education, or of wealth can not be produced by human institutions," he charged. "In the full enjoyment of the gifts of Heaven and the fruits of superior industry, economy, and virtue, every man is equally entitled to protection by law; but when the laws undertake to add to these natural and just advantages, artificial distinctions, to grant titles, gratuities, and exclusive privileges, to make the rich richer and the potent more powerful, the humble members of society—the farmers, mechanics, and laborers . . . have a right to complain of the injustice of their Government."

This imbalance of power represented by the Bank violated his concept of union. That term meant, in reality, a collective of free individuals and states who shared an absolute equality before the law. Introduce "artificial distinctions," and the Union was perverted, for those distinctions would wield unnatural powers. There was, again, nothing inherently evil about power except its susceptibility to abuse. "There are no necessary evils in government," he stated. "Its evils exist only in its abuses." The net result of creating aristocracies of wealth and privilege was to array "section against section, interest against interest, and man against man, in a fearful commotion which threatens to shake the very foundations of our Union." The Bank, then, was not merely a bad idea; it was a "monster" institution that threatened to corrupt and undermine the natural harmony of a free republic. It had to be stopped, and Jackson counted on the wisdom and moral outrage of ordinary citizens to help him do so. His judgment was sound; he was reelected by a substantial majority.

VICTORY in hand, Jackson turned aggressively against the Bank. He meant to destroy the institution before the opposition could muster its resources for another battle, and the way to do this was to strip the Bank of its capital reserves. In his message of December 1832, Jackson questioned the safety of the public funds deposited in the Bank; the following spring—when congressmen were safely out of Washington—he moved to withdraw federal money from its control. In a bold move that astonished friends and enemies alike, Jackson ordered that no more government monies be deposited in the Bank. The government would continue to pay its debts through the Bank until its deposits there were exhausted; all new revenues were to be placed in seven "pet banks": two in Boston, three in New York, and one each in Philadelphia and Baltimore. The number of these pet banks eventually reached eighty-nine.

Jackson defended his course publicly by portraying the Bank as an unscrupulous power with no interest other than its own preservation. He accused it, in blunt terms, of influence peddling during the election of 1832 by granting loans to congressmen and newspapers. "The bank is thus converted into a vast electioneering engine," Jackson charged, "with means to embroil the country in deadly feuds, and . . . extend its corruption through all the ramifications of society." He branded Biddle as a financial tyrant who granted loans and made policy without consulting his board of directors, and he assured the public that removing the deposits would not lead to a sudden contraction of credit, for the funds from the Bank would immediately flow from the state banks. "What comes in through one bank will go out through others. . . ."

The response among Jackson's opponents was electric. "The Bank veto . . . ," cried a Boston paper, "is the most wholly radical and basely Jesuitical document that ever emanated from any administration, in any country." National Republicans in Congress quickly began to call themselves Whigs, after the eighteenth-century English movement that attempted to limit the power of the king. The name stuck. It was an obvious barb thrown at Jackson's image as the friend of the common man, and it offered a handy label for the rage over his "executive usurpation" of powers. Under the Whig flag a disparate and leaderless coalition found new friends and new life. Nationalists such as Henry Clay joined with states' rights advocates such as Calhoun in an uneasy but vigorous alliance that controlled the Senate in 1834 and would soon spread. The coalition would remake itself over the next six years, but in 1834 it was strong enough to pass a Senate resolution censuring the President for assuming powers "not conferred by the constitution and laws, but in derogation of both."

Biddle, too, was active. It was inevitable, perhaps, that he should seek support from those who were in debt to the Bank, and there were many. Between 1817 and 1828 the Bank averaged about $31,000,000 in loans and discounts per year. For 1829 the figure rose to $39,000,000, reached $44,000,000 for 1831, and leaped to $66,000,000 for 1832—the year in which recharter was vetoed. Many of these loans were "goodwill accommodations" to influential congressmen and editors, but Biddle was also making credit easy for the business community nationwide. He had no doubt that the businessmen, including Jacksonian enterprisers, would repay him by choosing senators and representatives in Congress sympathetic to the Bank. This sudden expansion of credit had a negative value also, for when recharter was vetoed, giving the Bank four years to wind up its affairs, curtailment was necessary. When Jackson removed the government deposits late in 1833, it became imperative.

The removal of the deposits played into Biddle's hand, for it gave him a weapon in his battle with Jackson. Biddle began vigorously calling in loans, thus putting a severe squeeze on the business community. Memorials and petitions were soon pouring in to Congress, recounting business failures and community impoverishment, and praying for restoration of the deposits or a new charter. Even leading Democratic congressmen were staggered by the public reaction, but Jackson himself did not waver. Neither did Senator Thomas Hart Benton, whose Missouri constituents hated the Bank, nor did the New Yorkers who expected their own banks to rise on Biddle's fall. But Jackson was clearly under siege. The tangible and articulate evidence of hard times, more than anything else, made it possible for the Whig coalition to rebuke the Treasury and censure the President for removing the deposits.

The Bank might even have won the fight, had Biddle not overreached himself. In his hostility to Jackson, Biddle carried the contraction to unnecessary extremes. Many of those hurt were Biddle's own sympathizers—Whig merchants and manufacturers who hated Jackson as thoroughly as did Biddle. Shortly after the adjournment of Congress in the summer of 1834, they called a halt, threatening to expose the whole game if Biddle did not relax credit. Under pressure, Biddle blandly announced that the Bank's condition had improved enough to require no further contraction. Business immediately picked up, but many concluded that if the Bank could easily produce prosperity it could also produce hard times. Men otherwise undecided or even friendly toward the institution now agreed that the Bank of the United States had too much power.

THIS political drama obscured certain signs of economic danger. Jackson's understanding of politics was deft, and the destruction of the Bank was to him a great victory. But his understanding of economics was primitive. Since the mid-1820s the United States had prospered; even the price of Southern cotton had begun to rise. Land speculation and demands for new roads and canals increased accordingly. The result was an unprecedented quest for sources of capital that extended beyond the ranks of Eastern investors. Small entrepreneurs of every section—the soft-money advocates—rejoiced in the collapse of the Bank's power. In the absence of a central, restraining authority they anticipated a sudden expansion in the availability of credit.

Their hopes were justified, but the results were unhappy. The pet banks offered no substitute for the ability of the Bank of the United States to regulate currency. On the contrary, the new depositories were prime movers in rushing the country headlong into inflation. The public funds lodged in these banks had naturally swelled their reserves. Since it was understood that the government would not draw on its deposits until it had exhausted its account in the Bank of the United States, the pet banks blithely treated the government deposits as windfall capital. Operations expanded; loans increased; specie reserves declined. Inevitably, however, the federal government used up its deposits in the Bank and turned to the pet banks for cash to pay expenses. Few could honor the drafts without help from the Treasury, and Jackson discovered that in destroying one monster he had created another.

His response only hastened the impending debacle. A hard-money man, he reasoned that the only safeguard against further inflation and wild speculation lay in controlling the pet banks and encouraging the use of specie. In 1836 he persuaded Congress to pass the Deposit Act, which limited government deposits in the pet banks and distributed any surplus revenue to the states. The latter part of the act was necessary because since 1832 the government had been making more money than it spent. Although the distribution was technically a loan, states were free to use the funds for internal improvements. To restrain land speculation, he issued the Specie Circular, which directed that only gold and silver be accepted as payment for public lands.

The effect of these efforts was worse than Biddle's earlier contraction of credit. The Specie Circular actually made the country more dependent on paper currency than on hard cash, because people began to hoard their gold and silver as a hedge against hard times. The fact that the circulation of specie had contracted, however, did nothing to stem the demand for land. Public land sales had quintupled between 1833 and 1836; without specie, however, business at the government land offices dried up. Buyers turned to the speculators who held millions of acres for sale for paper. So the lands were sold, resold, and sold again at ever-inflating prices. The effect of the Deposit Act was equally unhappy, for scores of pet banks held more government funds than the law permitted and were forced to relinquish the excess. This they could do only by calling in their own loans on short notice, putting great pressure on the business community. By the end of 1836 the nation was at economic war with itself. Inflation and speculation burgeoned under an Administration whose policies intended the opposite.

THE election of 1836 was largely a referendum on Jackson and his policies. It also continued the development of a new two-party system. As the campaign drew near, the Whig coalition began the intricate task of organizing and perfecting their party machinery, a duty they had postponed too long. By 1836, anti-Jackson leaders recognized that nothing else would do. In the new style of politics, they could not hope to win elections by depending on local elites to bring out the vote for Whig candidates. Instead, they imitated Democratic tactics, carefully organizing and courting the common man and appealing to his needs by promising economic stability and growth under the American System. The argument was strong and persuasive to a broad spectrum of voters from every section and occupation. Moreover, Whigs wisely stripped their ideals of the lofty rhetoric of Adams's first message and presented them in plain, simple terms the ordinary voter could understand. They were attempting, in short, to show that they and not Jackson were the common man's best friend.

Whigs blundered, however, in their decision to field three candidates. Hoping to split the vote with strong sectional candidates, Whigs ran Daniel Webster for the North, Senator Hugh Lawson White of Tennessee for the South, and General William Henry Harrison for the West. If Van Buren—Jackson's chosen successor—were denied a majority vote, they reasoned, the situation of 1824 would repeat itself and the election would go into the House. Yet Van Buren beat them all. Whigs learned a hard lesson from this: they must nominate one man with appeal in all sections and support him with solid party machinery. Four years later they were to win.

IN the interim, Van Buren was President. His inauguration was a bittersweet affair, for Jackson's lingering presence in the capital overshadowed festivities that should properly have been Van Buren's happiest moment. The same specter haunted his Presidency. Van

Buren was a superb professional politician—a master architect of organization and form. He shared Jackson's ideals and tempered them with his innate good nature and capacity for tolerance. But Van Buren lacked Jackson's flair, and he inherited an economic and political situation that was verging on chaos. Shortly after he settled into the White House, the bubble broke.

Pressure came from an unexpected source. Since 1830 trade with Great Britain had been heavy, but the dollar value of imports from Britain had greatly exceeded that of American exports. This disparity would normally have been equalized by a transfer of specie, but British investors chose instead to absorb the difference by purchasing American securities and cotton. The process amounted to a British loan by which the United States paid for English manufactured goods. It also left the United States vulnerable to fluctuations in the London money market. The arrangement worked only because English financiers were confident that their investments would pay.

The unsettled state of American currency, the collapse of the Bank of the United States, and the Specie Circular shook this confidence. In early 1837 the Bank of England—in a moment of panic—refused to accept the notes of certain British houses with large American investments. A sudden drop in the demand for cotton followed, and prices for that commodity fell sharply. In March the inevitable happened. A New Orleans cotton broker failed, then others, and in chain reaction the panic spread to New York. On May 8 and 9, frightened depositors withdrew a million dollars in gold and silver from New York banks. Not even the strongest could withstand the mounting pressure, and the following day New York banks mutually agreed to suspend specie payments. Banks in other cities quickly followed suit, and the Panic of 1837 had begun.

The depression was intense and long. During 1837 and 1838 real estate prices dropped as much as 90 percent; the price of cotton plunged to half its 1836 level. The market for Western lands was virtually nil, and unemployment in the Eastern cities was staggering. Most damaging, cash was all but unavailable. Those who had specie hoarded it: the rest were left with worthless paper. The Specie Circular contributed to the distress by locking up public funds in custom-houses and land offices, because government deposits in banks were at their legal maximum. As trade and land sales declined, however, the federal surplus disappeared.

Van Buren responded promptly and aggressively. Although his

understanding of economics was little better than Jackson's, he had the good sense to realize that the piecemeal actions of his predecessor were unworkable and ineffective. In a special message to Congress in September, Van Buren blamed the nation's economic distress squarely on the banks, especially the Bank of the United States. But in a startling repudiation of Jackson's alternatives, Van Buren attacked the pet banks. Any system that connected public funds with private institutions encouraged speculation and abuse, he warned, and invited evils "which no precautions can effectually guard." The logical recourse was to deny private banks all access to public money.

Thus the Independent Treasury was conceived. The intent of the system was simple: government funds should be handled only by the government and used only for public purposes. In no way should such funds constitute the working capital of a private institution. The structure of the system was also simple: branches of the Treasury— "subtreasuries"—should be established in key cities to receive and dispense federal income. The Independent Treasury would be a blow to both Whigs and soft-money Democrats. It negated the very concept behind the Bank of the United States and cut the ground from under the pet banks. Conversely, it represented a victory for hard-money Democrats by providing a brake on the influence of the "money power." The former President endorsed the plan eagerly.

But the Independent Treasury plan encountered difficulties from its inception. Opposition to the bill was so intense that not until 1840 was Van Buren able to push it through Congress. That same year the Whigs won the White House, and the act was immediately repealed —only to be passed again five years later. After that, the system existed in one form or another until 1913. Partisan reaction to the measure was mixed and unpredictable. Certain Democrats—especially those who favored a more flexible approach to the currency supply—were so alienated by the dominance of the hard-money faction that they defected to the Whig party. On the other hand, Calhoun and other Southern Whigs saw the plan as evidence of a more general contraction of federal powers and promptly marched back into the Democratic Party. Within these shifting alliances no one was really satisfied—least of all, Van Buren, whose attempts to solve the economic crisis proved inadequate. The Independent Treasury was an ambitious, long-range plan for monetary stability, but it did nothing to cure the nation of its present crisis. After a brief recovery in 1839, the economy sank to new depths, pulled low by the sagging price of cotton. Hard times persisted until the mid-1840s.

In the long run, the economic results of the Panic and the Bank war that preceded it were minimal. The United States expanded so rapidly during the 1830s and 1840s that the harmful effects of the depression were diffused and mitigated. Moreover, it may be argued that the destruction of the Bank actually opened up sources of capital which aided in this expansion. During the 1840s, Whigs and soft-money Democrats often collaborated against the hard-money faction to create systems of "free banks" in the states which released capital from the grip of monopolies and dispersed it to an eager and enterprising population. The price of this expansion was, naturally, a period of instability, but it was an instability that the enormous resources of the new nation and the adaptability of American capitalism easily bore.

But the Panic had a profound effect on party development. The Bank war polarized the electorate into two heterogeneous groups: those who, for whatever reason, approved Jackson's course and those who, for whatever reason, did not. The depression hardened these lines and made possession of the White House the consuming goal of both Whigs and Democrats. Although there was considerable cross-voting between the parties on specific issues, particularly at the state level, the conflicts of the 1830s had engendered attitudes and organizations that were keenly competitive in national elections. Each party worked hard for the loyalty of the common voter, enticing him with visions of a great struggle between absolute good and absolute evil, and recruiting him through minute attention to organizational detail. Once the voter had made his choice, he tended to carry his party label with him until he or the party died.

By 1840, then, two-party conflict was an accepted fact of American political life. In only twenty years the Jeffersonian coalition had fractured, and the simple republican harmony Monroe so desperately wanted had succumbed to the organized warfare of political machines. Politics was no longer a gentleman's game. It had moved through successive stages in which personalities, then issues, and finally organizations captured the loyalties of the electorate and mobilized them into action. In the process, Americans had created perhaps the only really national instruments of authority through which they could channel their energies and still feel that their liberties were protected. "Political parties," a Van Buren Democrat had prophesied in the 1820s, "are inseparable from a free government."

Ironically, the new party system was so delicately balanced, so torn by internal divisions, that its doom was sealed almost before it was born. The antagonistic subcultures that made up the Whig and Democratic parties were incapable of uniting nationally except during Presidential elections. Even then, the success of either party depended on reducing the issues to one or two largely abstract economic problems, and nominating men whose positions on those issues were unknown or obscure. Except for James K. Polk and Zachary Taylor, every successful contender for the White House between 1840 and 1860 was weak and ineffective; even Polk and Taylor were evasive during their campaigns. Tragically for the parties and the nation, the one issue that could not be evaded during the 1840s and 1850s was the one most certain to disrupt the entire system: slavery.

A NATIONAL
CULTURE

three

7

Introspection

T HE Americans appear to me an eminently imaginative people,"
noted a sympathetic Englishwoman, Harriet Martineau, in 1838.
"The unprejudiced traveller can hardly spend a week among them
without being struck by this every day." But Martineau—like other
foreign visitors and a considerable number of Americans—was concerned that the creative energies of the new nation were too focused
on the practical and mundane. Intellectual life in the United States
had a curiously one-dimensional, utilitarian quality. "They do not put
their imaginative power to use in literature and the arts," she complained, finding it "perverse" that they should be "imitative in
fictions" yet "imaginative in their science and philosophy, applying
their sober good sense to details, but being sparing of it in regard to
principles." Charles Dickens reached the same conclusion after a
lengthy visit here. Americans were consumed by materialism and
success; their only recreation seemed to be the reading of newspapers
and political essays. "It would be well . . . ," he wrote, "if they loved
the Real less, and the Ideal somewhat more. It would be well, if there
were greater encouragement to lightness of heart and gaiety, and a
wider cultivation of what is beautiful, without being eminently and
directly useful." Both Dickens and Martineau attributed the intense
practicality of the American mind to the nation's youth, and Dickens
longed for a better day. "I yet hope to hear of there being some other
national amusement in the United States," he sighed, "besides newspaper politics." Other critics were not so generous. "In the four
quarters of the globe," cribbed the *Edinburgh Review* in 1820, "who
reads an American book?"

It was not as bad as all that. The United States did have an intellectual community, a flourishing one, and the life of the mind in the new nation was in good health. But the environment of ideas had definitely changed since the age of Jefferson, Franklin, and Adams. The Founders were collectively one of the most outstanding gatherings of intellectual force anywhere in the world in the latter part of the eighteenth century. Products of a gentry that had both education and the leisure to use it, they defined the problems facing the colonies, constructed an ideological basis for action, and—in drafting the Constitution—applied their training with superb skill. Additionally, they experimented with scientific and natural phenomena, encouraged and sometimes led the efforts of a gifted generation of artists and craftsmen, and left a body of writings that, for lucidity, originality, and variety, has seldom been equaled. In them the role of thinker and doer, of intellectual and politician, was one. They were elites—socially, politically, intellectually. They were also world citizens, participants in an intellectual community that stretched across the Atlantic and across disciplines.

The nineteenth-century intellectual was more isolated and insecure. The rapid expansion of society had created new elites who competed with the thinker or artist for status and prestige. Specialization had set in. The rise of the modern political party, for example, replaced the philosopher-king with the professional tactician. The successful entrepreneur commanded more respect than the educated aristocrat. The engineer began to rival the theologian. In certain respects, this was not so much a social development as an intellectual one. The nineteenth-century intellectual witnessed an incredible burst of information and knowledge that was beyond the means of any one man, or group of men, to assimilate. There was too much to know. And yet the social implications of specialization were the most worrisome. The man of ideas was becoming increasingly isolated from the circles of power.

Most disturbing to many nineteenth-century intellectuals, however, was a change in attitudes. So long as great ideas were the province of great men, there was room for idle reflection and even an occasional foray into the bizarre. An intellectual aristocracy was always present to set standards. But the republican revolution had upset all kinds of aristocracies—including that of the mind—and the standards of the intellectual elite had been replaced by those of public opinion. The beginning of the nineteenth century witnessed a movement to open up culture and learning to everyone, to make ideas as republican as politics. Americans developed a mistrust of the snobbish and refined; they demanded that art and literature and scientific exploration serve some purpose, that it be functional and instructive. Even Benjamin Rush, the premier physician of his age and a veteran of the Revolution, lectured John Adams in 1811 on the uselessness of teaching students to read Latin or Greek. It was better, he argued, to spend time "in communicating the knowledge of *things* instead of the sounds and relations of *words.*" So much for Aristotle. Speculation was fine, added a Yale professor in 1799, so long as it produced workable results on schedule. But there were limits. Too many had wasted their talents on frivolities, like the eccentric in *Gulliver's Travels* who had spent eight years attempting to turn cucumbers into bottled sunshine. "Sunbeams may be extracted from cucumbers," he acknowledged, "but the process is tedious."

Beneath the jeremiads lay a robust and vigorous attempt to come to grips with the changes that were taking place. Nineteenth-century intellectuals sensed that the perfect orderliness of the Enlightenment had been a little unreal and too scientific. A new generation of thinkers and artists looked for other sources of unity and harmony in nature. There had to be a place for the romantic, the passionate, even the supernatural, in the life of the mind. And why should there not also be a place for the ordinary? An age of consolidation and introspection set in, during which the innovations of the eighteenth century were expanded and redefined. In the process, much of the cosmopolitanism of the Enlightenment was lost, but genuinely American forms of artistic and intellectual expression were gained.

ONE of the earliest signs of change was evident in art. Although American painters and sculptors continued the colonial practice of touring England and the Continent to study their craft, the Revolution had brought an urge to develop a more natively American style. As American artists cast about for subjects, they turned to the great men and great events of the Revolution, and the heroic style came into full flower. Painters such as Charles Willson Peale and Gilbert Stuart produced portraits of the Founders (Stuart's likenesses of Washington being the most celebrated), while John Trumbull portrayed battles, heroic deaths, or, in his most famous work, the signing of the Declaration. Although the heroic style was also popular in Europe, its function in the United States was aggressively nationalistic. Paintings of Washington or renditions of great battles were designed to inspire the ordinary citizen with pride in his heritage. Moreover, heroic art was intentionally designed to be accessible to the public. Trumbull's gigantic portrayal of the signing, for example, went on tour before it was installed in the Capitol rotunda. The city of Baltimore commissioned the first monument to Washington—a stone turret rising, appropriately, from Mount Vernon Square—as a towering and easily seen reminder of the nation's glorious past.

And if the public should be able to see the arts, why should it not be able to create them? Charles Willson Peale was convinced that anyone who could hold a brush could, with proper encouragement, paint a masterpiece. To that end he urged each of his seventeen children to try their hand. The most successful—appropriately named Rembrandt, Raphaelle, and Titian—painted portraits, still lifes, and animals and did so well. Others were not so sure that talent was universal. When Samuel F. B. Morse, the painter and inventor, founded the National Academy of the Arts of Design in 1826, it was to cultivate the professional artist and to protest the dominance of a rival organization, led by Trumbull, that catered to the amateur.

Although the heroic style remained strong throughout the century, by 1820 it had been subsumed into a many-faceted and much broader movement—romanticism. Romanticism used a variety of styles and explored a variety of subjects. In landscape art, for example, it spawned the Hudson River School, which included English-born Thomas Cole and Asher Durand. Cole and Durand rejected the formalism and classicism of the past to capture, on canvas, the grandeur and majesty of the American wilderness. Works such as Cole's *In the Catskills* attempted to make the viewer feel the presence of nature through color and line. Paintings by the Hudson River School were not "realistic"; they did not attempt to reproduce the scene in photographic detail. Cole preferred to emphasize color and exaggerate line in order to involve the viewer in the painting. As another artist, Washington Allston, explained, the painting took the eye deeper and deeper into the scene, through "dark draperies of wood and mist," waterfalls, and solitary pines until "the headlong rush of some mighty cataract suddenly thunders upon us." And then the picture released its spell. "In the twinkling of an eye, the outflowing sympathies ebb back upon the heart; the whole mind seems severed from earth, and the awful feeling to suspend the breath." There was a sexual metaphor to this union with Mother Nature that neither Cole nor Allston would have admitted, but it indicated an important break with the cold formalism of more traditional artistic approaches.

All was not beneficence and tranquillity, though. The works of romanticists displayed a preoccupation with death that suggested there were other cosmic forces besides beauty to consider. Adam and Eve, after all, had not remained forever in Paradise, a point Cole illustrated in 1827 in his *Expulsion from the Garden of Eden*. Similarly, civilizations were never permanent. In five sequential canvases entitled *The Course of Empire*, Cole presented the evolution of history, beginning with savagery and running through the pastoral stage, the achievement of civilization and empire, then destruction, and—finally—desolation, in which not a single human remains. The colors were still rich and the lines still exaggerated, but the series exemplified the didactic, morally instructive intent of much of the art of the period. The ruined column that stands at the foreground of *Desolation* is a weed-covered monument to man's insane ability to kill himself. Artists from outside the Hudson River School displayed the same pessimism. Washington Allston's complex and never-completed *Belshazzar's Feast* portrayed civilization in its suicidal debauch. In a more abstract manner, Allston illustrated the fragility of human institutions in a chalk sketch drawn in 1837, *Ship in a Squall*. The chiaroscuro effect of using white, skeletal strokes to outline the ship against the dark and brooding background of the storm was a reminder that nature was more powerful and durable than man, and that nature could be evil.

Between the extremes of the heroic and the romantic were other artists, whose styles and subject matter were probably the most natively American of all. Edward Hicks, for example, was a Pennsylvania Quaker whose talents were entirely self-developed. A carriagemaker by trade, Hicks mourned the divisions that split the Quaker faith of his time and turned to painting to instruct his peers in the joy of harmony and contentment. He painted tranquil Pennsylvania farms and copied a few landscapes from other artists, but his favorite subject was the "peaceable kingdom," taken from a verse in Isaiah, wherein the lion really did lie down with the lamb, while settlers and Indians celebrated an eternal Thanksgiving feast in the background. Hicks never did master technique; proportion and scale were always off in his paintings, which tended to resemble mosaics. He painted only on wood panels, which were likely to warp and split. Yet beneath the untutored crudeness of his style lay originality and conviction. Bears, lions, and wolves symbolized evil, lambs and doves represented good, yet all seemed to coexist in a world that was simultaneously ordinary and divine. The flat, muted colors and the rigid features of the animals—so unlike the lushness and fluid lines of the Hudson River School—were effective testaments to Hicks's belief in an overlying harmony in the universe.

Still other painters concentrated on the prosaic and everyday. The best were William Sidney Mount and George Caleb Bingham, who turned out genre paintings—works that captured a moment or a mood in the life of ordinary people. In *A Barroom Oracle Relates,* Mount made the viewer laugh at the plight of a saloonkeeper patiently listening to a patron's windy views on anything and everything from Jefferson to the price of horses. *Eel Spearing at Setauket* was different: a serene day of crystal clarity and few shadows occupied only by the patient fishermen. Mount delighted in using barns and Negroes in his works. *Music Hath Charm* showed a young black man standing outside a barn door while a fiddler played amid the hay and pitchforks. It was one of Mount's favorite themes. Somehow, despite the crudeness and hard work and isolation of much of American life, civilization kept creeping in. George Caleb Bingham expanded the genre tradition to include politics. *Verdict of the People,* his best-known work, was directly descended from the style of the English engraver William Hogarth, whose prints captured apprentices asleep at their looms and children playing in church. In *Verdict,* Bingham painted the excitement of an election-day rally, complete with orators, workers, blacks, and drunks—none of whom seemed to be listening to the others. Technically, the painting used color and shadow to encourage the eye to roam around, focusing on each figure one at a time and drawing a laugh from each. All this came from a man who was raised in Missouri and had no formal training.

The works of these painters expressed, in different ways, a search for unity and harmony in nature and in society. Peale or Trumbull found it in the heroic examples of the nation's great men. Cole saw it in the omnipresence of nature and the cycles of history. Hicks found harmony in the beneficence of God, while Mount and Bingham saw it in the simplicity of republican life. If there was a central thread knitting these various styles and subjects together, it was their manipulation of the emotions. Each found a way to bypass the head and proceed directly to the heart, where the viewer would be instantly moved to feel inspiration, humor, unease, repose, or any of a hundred other sensations. One did not have to analyze a painting by Cole or Mount; one simply responded to it. Moreover, anyone—from an aristocrat to a chimneysweep—would experience essentially the same thing. Therein lay the achievement. If art must be accessible to everyone, then it must express something everyone could understand. However much critics might complain of the constraints placed on the American artist by public opinion, he had nonetheless devised means of reaching out to his viewers while still maintaining standards of excellence. In the process, he had also broken free of tradition.

THE American writer of the first half of the nineteenth century worked in the same cultural setting as the artist, but under different conditions and often with a different purpose. There were no schools to train writers in their craft, so the novelist or essayist or historian was entirely self-taught. Competition from England and Europe was more intense. A painting by Gainsborough, for example, could not be shipped across the Atlantic and mass-produced for consumption in the United States. A novel could. With no international copyright law in force, it was cheaper and safer for an American publisher to pirate British works than to risk unproved local talent. Sir Walter Scott was easily the most popular novelist; his tales of lords and ladies adorned every bookshelf in the country and fed the American appetite for the heroic. Scores of imitations appeared, none remotely as good. Similarly, the romances of the eighteenth-century English author Samuel Richardson inspired later generations of American writers—a large number of whom were women—to spin tales of unrequited love, illicit sex, duels, suicides, and jealousies—all shrouded in flowery language and redeemed by some obvious moral lesson. Novels such as these could be easily serialized in the newspapers and became early forerunners of the modern soap opera. Americans wept themselves dry as each morning's paper brought a new installment in the life of a doomed lover.

The writer of talent and originality, on the other hand, wept himself dry at the imitative, repetitious, and universally poor quality of such hack work. There was ample material in the New World to develop native themes and styles; why not use it? The frontier and the Indians provided subjects which no European could fathom but which were ripe for exploration in the United States. There was American history, which had its own heroes and villains. And in the most challenging period of social change since the fall of the Roman Empire, there was certainly more to discuss than failed love affairs and lachrymose suicides. Still, the really creative writer worked in the same world as the hacks. He had to make his products interesting and palatable to the common man, for the most exciting and original piece was wasted if it went unpublished. Moreover, he, far more than the hack, had a special responsibility to come to grips with the hopes and fears, the ambiguities and clarities, of the new nation's experiment in democracy. Like the artist or the politician, the American writer was searching for some middle ground between the rigid elitism of the past that set standards only a few could attain and the overeager individualism of the present that seemed to set no standards at all.

History was the most popular and fertile field for the American writer. The enthusiastic reception given Scott's *Ivanhoe* indicated the depth of the American fascination with the past, and the history of the new republic, particularly the Revolution, provided all the raw materials for stories of heroes, tragedies, and moral instruction. Moreover, history could be presented formally or adapted to fiction. It was not expected to be factual and precise but, rather, inspirational and thematic—thus giving free play to the novelist, the pedant, and the social critic. The earliest histories took this latitude to extremes. Mercy Otis Warren's three-volume history of the Revolution, published in 1805, was a sprightly account, but so critical of the Federalists that John Adams considered it vicious. Nonetheless, it was popular. More popular still were the works of Mason Locke Weems, an erstwhile Episcopal minister. Parson Weems tapped a literary gold mine in 1800 with his hastily written *Life and Memorable Actions of George Washington.* The book was so astonishingly well received that Weems expanded it and reintroduced it in 1806 as *The Life of Washington the Great.* Weems had discovered the perfect fusion between the heroic style and the moral lesson, for he made his subject so great, so perfect, as to never lie: Weems invented the tale of Washington, his tiny ax, and the cherry tree.

The heroic appeal of the Founders never faded; as the nation grew in size and complexity, their simple virtues and great achievements became correspondingly more attractive. In 1817 William Wirt published a glowingly flattering biography of Patrick Henry—a great man, perhaps, but also one of the slipperiest and least polished of the Revolutionary heroes. "It is a poor book," commented Jefferson, "written in bad taste, and gives an imperfect idea of Patrick Henry." The book was typical, however, of a genre of works that attempted to prove that a "natural" aristocracy flourished in the new republic. Several authors—a surprising number of them Northern—turned to the image of the Southern cavalier. James Kirke Paulding of New York, for example, abandoned his short stories and witty anecdotes to write in 1835 a two-volume biography of Washington. Washington, as Paulding described him, combined Benjamin Franklin's capacity for hard work and self-control with the ideal Southern qualities of manners and cultivation. In so doing, Paulding married two seemingly contradictory qualities: a forward-looking, common-sense man of industry and a reflective, romantic throwback to a golden age of gentility and taste. Paulding's Washington was a bit too perfect and free of human frailties, but the author's purpose was not to criticize. It was to construct a hero worthy of emulation. Works such as these were not entirely a response to nationalistic pride or the demands of the reading public. They reflected also a profound unease with the increasing materialism and lack of refinement that seemed to plague the new republic.

Other histories and biographies appeared, some of them good, but it was not until 1834 that the United States produced a historian of breadth and skill. In that year George Bancroft, who had studied at Harvard and on the Continent, published the first volume of his *History of the United States from the Discovery of the Continent.* Bancroft's purpose in writing was frankly nationalistic and democratic; he wished to show that the American experience was part of a divine plan by which God was using the New World to establish liberty as the guiding principle of nations. He was also an expansionist and used history to justify every addition to the empire of the new republic. But Bancroft did so with such skill, such thorough research, that he instantly established himself as not only a best seller but a first-rate scholar. Through forty more years of writing and nine more volumes, Bancroft pursued his record of manifest destiny, ending, appropriately, with the signing of the Declaration of Independence.

Along with these achievements, he also served as James K. Polk's Secretary of the Navy and as a minister to England and Germany.

As in art, however, the epic style was balanced by works that reflected on the ordinary and whimsical. Here there was more room to be critical and humorous (no writer would have dared to point out Washington's faults or to crack jokes about his wooden teeth). Washington Irving, for example, used the folklore of his native New York to spin tales of eras gone by and to poke fun at his countrymen. Irving was a literary subversive. He worked puns, satire, and a flair for the absurd into his many stories and fables, with pretense and pomposity his targets. His first book, *Knickerbocker's History of New York*, spoofed the epic style that threatened to make immortals out of so many frail humans. The requisite battle scene, here fought between Dutch and Swedes for possession of some inconsequential piece of the Hudson Valley, is replete with heroes, flashing swords, and, yes, the gods and goddesses of war looking on—just as Providence must have protected Washington when he crossed the Delaware. But chance, not divine intervention, directs the battle. The Swedes discharge a musket volley so fearsome that the Dutch would have been slaughtered "had not the protecting Minerva kindly taken care that the Swedes should, one and all, observe their usual custom of shutting their eyes, and turning away their heads at the moment of discharge." (Later the protecting Minerva forgets about the battle completely when she stops for a pot of beer at a neighboring tavern.) Dutch reserves are late for the battle, having paused to maraud a nearby watermelon patch. In the climactic struggle, the hero—wooden-legged Peter Stuyvesant—is dealt a blow that would have shattered any mere mortal's skull. His, fortunately, is divinely thick. But he is stunned, reels, and:

> at length, missing his footing, by reason of his wooden leg, he came down upon his seat of honor with a crash which shook the surrounding hills, and might have wrecked his frame, had he not been received into a cushion softer than velvet, which Providence, or Minerva, or St. Nicholas, or some kindly cow, had benevolently prepared for his reception.

Stuyvesant finally vanquishes his foe by firing a double dram of Dutch beer at him and sending him into a "death-like torpor." No one, incidentally, is actually killed.

Encouraged by the success of the *History*, Irving developed his craft. The *Salmagundi Papers* was a periodical of burlesque social satire that he edited for a time with his brother and James Kirke Paulding. In 1815 he left the United States for a seventeen-year sojourn in England and the Continent, during which time he published *The Sketch Book* and *Tales of a Traveller,* both collections of his short stories, and other works, including a biography of Christopher Columbus. Throughout, he maintained a delicate balance between sense and nonsense. There was an element of both the social critic and the sentimentalist in Irving. He used satire not only to make his readers laugh but to make them think. In the *History* he attributed the Puritan migration of the 1630s to their propensity for sermonizing and their desire to enjoy, "unmolested, the inestimable right of talking." When Quakers and Anabaptists arrived demanding the same privilege, freedom of speech was quickly transformed into freedom of thought, "provided one thought right." The rapid spread of New England culture he assigned to the Yankee custom of "bundling" and a "certain rambling propensity . . . which continually goads them to shift their residence from place to place, so that a Yankee farmer is in a constant state of migration, *tarrying* occasionally here or there, clearing lands for other people to enjoy, building houses for others to inhabit, and in a manner may be considered the wandering Arab of America." Irving was not far off the mark.

Irving's best-loved stories were whimsical fables that revealed his sentimentality for the past and his unease with the present. Rip Van Winkle goes to sleep in a gentle world where George III is king, illusive Dutch bowlers play ninepins in the clouds, and the only irritation is a shrewish wife. He awakes twenty years later to find the world changed. The shrewish wife is gone, but so is the familiar and the secure. The sleepy hero's first name is an acronym for Rest in Peace: Here lies a bygone era, dead. *The Legend of Sleepy Hollow,* which immortalized headless horsemen, flying pumpkins, and Ichabod Crane, conveyed a similar longing for the simplicity of country life. Crane's mock-heroic contest for a maiden's heart and his midnight encounter with the headless horseman take place in a setting so tranquil, so set in its ways as to be out of place in the busy, changing environment of the nineteenth century. "It is in such little retired Dutch valleys," wrote Irving,

> that population, manners, and customs remained fixed; while the great torrent of migration and improvement, which is making such incessant changes in other parts of this restless country, sweeps by them unob-

served. They are like those little nooks or still water which border a
rapid stream . . .

Irving wrote both pieces in England. Upon his return to the United
States in 1832, his creative talents ebbed, and he turned to writing
histories of the fur trade and descriptions of the frontier.

Irving cloaked his sentimentalism and his social criticism in humor;
James Fenimore Cooper brought the same feelings into the open.
Cooper, more than any other writer who preceded him, used the novel
to probe deeply into the special nature of the American character.
Born to wealthy parents in central New York, he despised at once the
pretensions of aristocracy and the extremes of democracy. True democracy, he wrote in *The American Democrat,* "refuses to lend itself
to unnatural and arbitrary distinctions," but at the same time would
never "level those who have a just claim to be elevated." Like Tocqueville, Cooper recognized the inevitable tension between liberty and
equality inherent in democracy. Like Jefferson, he wanted a republic
that was neither chaotically individualistic nor depressingly standard-
ized. The worst characteristic of democracy was the mediocrity it
engendered; the best defense lay in the possession of land. "As property is the base of all civilization," he argued, "its existence and
security are indispensable to social improvement." Thus, when farmers in upstate New York began to demand possession of the land they
rented in the mid-1830s, Cooper responded by defending the large
landowners. Even though he recognized the poverty and want among
the small farmers, the gentry's right to their land must be protected,
because they alone maintained standards of taste and culture in a
republic.

But standards were apparently in decline in the new nation, victims
of a manic craving for money and cheaply won status. This perversion
of ideals saddened and angered Cooper. Too many of his countrymen
seemed so obsessed with status and the approval of their peers that
they were incapable of individuality. The weakness was best seen
among the ranks of Whig speculators and parvenus. Cooper's description of Steadfast Dodge in *Homeward Bound,* written in 1838 after a
long tour in Europe, was venomous:

> Mr. Dodge came from that part of the country in which men were
> accustomed to eat and drink and sleep, in common; or, in any other

words, from one of those regions in America, in which there was so much community, that few had the moral courage, even when they possessed the knowledge . . . to cause their individuality to be respected.

The trouble with Dodge was that he could not act except through "conventions, sub-conventions, caucuses, and public meetings," or, failing all that, "societies." It is understandable that Cooper failed to realize that such associations were necessary without traditional means of social control. He, after all, was as new to democratic society as anyone else. That he was so vehement against them stemmed from his conviction that democracy was in danger of setting aside excellence in favor of sameness.

Excellence, to Cooper, was a gift of nature, not birth. In place of the status seeker or the snob, Cooper created an alternate ideal—the "natural" man, Natty Bumppo, also known as Leatherstocking or the Deerslayer. In five novels, beginning with *The Pioneers* in 1823 and ending with *The Deerslayer* in 1841, Cooper presented Bumppo as the sturdy backwoodsman who learned from the forest rather than from books, who shunned both barbarity and effeteness. Absolutely selfless, Bumppo willingly risked life and limb in *The Last of the Mohicans* to rescue a British general's daughter from the hands of the Indians. In the process, he proved himself wiser and shrewder than the aristocrats he helped and purer and nobler than the savages he fought. Bumppo, neither primitive nor polished, was an unsullied student of natural moral law.

Cooper was not, however, praising the virtues of crudeness, nor was he deifying the common man, for Bumppo was anything but common. Rather, Cooper was searching for a middle ground between the over-civilization of Europe and the howling wilderness of the American frontier. This was not quite Jeffersonianism, for Jefferson praised the yeoman farmer and not the wandering hunter. Cooper was saying that democracy could free the individual for higher pursuits if only it did not numb him with the comfortable sameness of equality. But even as Cooper held up the ideal, he sensed its failure. The Bumppo novels were a challenge and a lament. If Bumppo was the highest development of mankind, he was also the last of his breed. As civilization moved westward, so did Bumppo, taking his virtues with him. In *The Last of the Mohicans,* both Bumppo and Chingachgook, who embodied the primitive virtues of the noble savage, are like gentle dinosaurs, struggling against a climate hostile to their very existence. In *The Prairie,* in which Bumppo is portrayed as an old man, he finds that he has no place at all, and dies.

This strain of doubt and anxiety came to fruition in the works of Nathaniel Hawthorne. Hawthorne's short stories and novels—brooding, introspective, full of surprise endings and twists of fate—were the products of a man who in his own lifetime could never compete commercially with the "damned bunch of scribbling women" (his words) who poured out forgettable novels at the rate of one or two a year. A Democrat, Hawthorne relied on patronage to support his craft. He wrote *The Scarlet Letter,* for example, while at his post at the Salem customhouse. But in contrast to those (many from his own political party) who preached the innate goodness of the individual and the untarnished blessings of democracy, Hawthorne sensed the persistence of evil. He seemed particularly vexed at the apparent willingness to confuse that which was worthy and enduring with that which was trivial and corruptible. One of his favorite devices was the Faustian legend. In *Ethan Brand* Hawthorne portrayed a man who sold all capacity for love in his quest for knowledge and became "a fiend" when "his moral nature had ceased to keep the pace of improvement with his intellect." In *The Celestial Railroad* Hawthorne wrote a latter-day *Pilgrim's Progress,* describing a society gone wild with gadgets and technology and oblivious to more fundamental achievements of the soul. And in his classic *House of the Seven Gables,* he created, in the figure of Judge Pyncheon, a man so grasping and so tightfisted that his small, hard heart literally burst from its own ambition.

Ambition, of course, could be good. But amid the glitter and euphoria of the expanding republic Hawthorne warned that it could also be, like knowledge, perverted to base and disastrous ends. He was explicit on this point in *The Ambitious Guest,* a sadly overlooked little story which was not great art but which was very good social criticism. Hawthorne presents a contented family living in supreme happiness at the foot of a jagged mountain. Though rocks and landslides might thunder around them, nothing disturbed the tranquillity of the group until a passing stranger stopped for the night. The traveler's conversation was startlingly egocentric. "The secret of the young man's character," Hawthorne explained, "was a high and abstracted ambition . . . Yearning desire had been transformed to hope; and hope, long cherished, had become like certainty that . . . a glory was to beam on all his pathway." As the family listened to their guest's glowing account of his probable destiny, their own ambitions, long forgotten in the comfort of the hearth, awakened. Restlessness and dissatisfaction set in, crowding out all other thoughts, until with a shock they realized that the mountain was crumbling upon them. Fleeing the cottage, they rushed out "right into the pathway of destruction." Ironically, the cottage was untouched. It was a grim and foreboding allegory of a society that, in Hawthorne's eyes, too easily bargained security, harmony, and simplicity for empty dreams of success. Self-made men fashioned only their own destruction.

But Hawthorne was, after all, a Democrat—as was Cooper. Despite his gloomy prediction that the celestial railroad ran only to hell, he saw real progress in the decay of aristocracy and the birth of the democratic man. Alongside the cramped soul of Judge Pyncheon he presented Holgrave, the artist-in-residence of the House of the Seven Gables. The last of a family cheated by past generations of Pyncheons and forgotten by the present one, Holgrave was an independent soul —talented, generous, uncorrupted, and perceptive. He was also a daguerreotypist, an early photographer, who used chemicals and technology to produce a new and very special kind of art. "Altogether, in his culture and want of culture," Hawthorne wrote,

> —in his crude, wild, and misty philosophy, and the practical experience that counteracted some of its tendencies; in his magnanimous zeal for man's welfare, and his recklessness of whatever the ages had established in man's behalf; in his faith, and in his infidelity; in what he had, and in what he lacked,—the artist might fitly enough stand forth as the representative of many compeers in his native land.

Holgrave, in short, was a new man. Perhaps his most endearing trait was his healthy irreverence for the rigidity of the past and his unconcern for the materialism of the present. For Hawthorne, struggling for financial security and obsessed with his Puritan heritage, this was high praise indeed.

Of all critics of democracy in the new republic, none was more pessimistic or more optimistic than Ralph Waldo Emerson. Poet, philosopher, and essayist rather than novelist or storyteller, he surveyed Americans and their institutions with a sharp eye, a gift for the quotable aphorism, and an often devastating honesty for almost five decades after his maiden essay, *Nature,* appeared in 1836. His enemies were, in no particular order, the emotionally stifling atmosphere of overrational religion—what he called the "corpse-cold Unitarianism of Brattle Street and Harvard College"—the equally oppressive materialism and commercialism that turned nature's noblest creatures into clerks and pennypinchers, and the rigidity and artificiality of social institutions that professed to inspire and nurture and ended up stultifying and destroying. He was brought up in Boston, the seat of the emerging industrial revolution and also a major cultural and intellectual center. He found both wanting, because affairs of the purse had so completely, in his view, overwhelmed affairs of the head and heart. "This invasion of Nature by Trade with its Money, its Credit, its Steam, its Railroad," he wrote in 1839, "threatens to upset the balance of man, and establish a new, universal Monarchy more tyrannical than Babylon or Rome." Both major political parties were guilty of promoting this decay. "There is nothing of the true democratic element in what is called Democracy," he concluded; "it must fall, being wholly commercial." The Whigs he dismissed curtly as "the shop-till party."

Yet if Emerson's perception of the society around him was disillusioned and sad, his hope for the future and his belief in the ultimate perfection of man was joyful and, in his own words, "boundless." More than any other writer of his time, Emerson took the promises of dignity and worth held out by the Revolution to the common man and built from them a philosophy that was exuberantly and unabashedly individualistic. Having rejected formal religion, he made his own from shards of Coleridge, Swedenborg, and Oriental mysticism—among others—and called it transcendentalism. Simply because it was a philosophy of individualism, transcendentalism is difficult to define. No two of its followers interpreted it quite the same. As Emerson explained, however, in countless lectures and essays, its basic tenets were a belief in "the new importance given to the single person," and the unity of all in one, through nature, in the Oversoul. The Oversoul was Emerson's concept of a deity—a divine presence that existed in all beings past and present and which gave them meaning and purpose. "We know that all spiritual being is in man," he declared. Locked within each person was an element of the sublime, waiting to be set free if only that person would throw off artificial and meaningless pursuits. A close, emotional tie to nature—sublime, simple, eternal—held the key. To break out of the cramped conventions of materialism and dogma, however, took an act of self-will. "The power which resides in him is new in nature," Emerson wrote of the individual in *Self-Reliance,* "and none but he knows what that is which he can do, nor does he know until he has tried."

Here was a philosophy that closely paralleled the political glorification of the common man. "Democracy, Freedom, has its root in the sacred truth that every man hath in him the divine Reason, or that, though few men since the creation of the world live according to the dictates of Reason, yet all men are created capable of doing so." "The root and seed of democracy is the doctrine, Judge for yourself. Reverence thyself." For Emerson, the effects of this individualistic creed were wholly beneficial, not only in politics but in art and literature. "The same movement which effected the elevation of what was called the lowest class in the state," he wrote, "assumed in literature a very marked and as benign an aspect. Instead of the sublime and beautiful, the near, the low, the common, was explored and poetized . . . It is a great stride. It is a sign . . . of new vigor." Emerson was not calling for mediocrity; quite the opposite. He was convinced that a slavish compulsion to reproduce the institutions and the tastes of other places and other times stunted the potential glory of the individual by separating him from nature and the Oversoul. His was a call for intellectual independence from the Old World and the estates and castes that hemmed in its spirit.

But Emerson remained critical of American society. Like Cooper and Hawthorne, he was mindful—at times agonizingly so—that the celebration of the common man was too often a riotous debauch of the human spirit. Americans, presented with a splendid opportunity to uplift true standards and remake the soul, had succumbed to a materialism so crass and selfish that they very likely would squander their chance. Herein lay the paradox that each writer mourned. All agreed that democracy was the best basis for social and political order, yet it was bringing neither the stability and standards offered by the ruling aristocracy in England nor the true individualism promised by the New World. The United States, it seemed, was a society without a core. There were no canons of good taste, no redeeming goals, no worthwhile institutions, no real individualism.

ONE must read these spiritual self-flagellations with caution and in context. Hawthorne, for example, was a perfect specimen of an aristocrat gone shabby in the cuffs. In the eighteenth century a man of his genius and talent would likely have possessed power and prestige. The democratic revolution had turned the world upside down, however, and now the politician patronized the intellectual—a fact which Hawthorne bitterly resented. Cooper had no such anxieties; his prominence among the landed gentry of upstate New York was secure. But Cooper, too, was aware that an upheaval had taken place in which old and clear standards were being replaced by new and hazy ones. And Emerson delighted in his role as gadfly. If Americans were really as narrow-minded and dull as he sometimes made them out to be, they would not have supported him by paying their hard cash to hear his lectures. If the intellectual elite was in fact separated from the circles of power, it was still an elite that ordinary men respected. Politicians, pundits, shopkeepers, and sages were all searching for some larger meaning, a harmony, to balance the changes that threatened to fragment their lives. They listened to Emerson's lectures on the Oversoul and they read Cooper's glorification of the natural man because they needed standards by which they could measure their lives.

They read, in fact, everything. The plethora of dime novels that saturated the United States was only one response to a restless search for knowledge that gripped the new nation in the age of Jackson. Americans read voraciously, in part because they were a literate people and in part because the invention of the steam press in 1827 made printed material easily available and cheap. Although publishers were slow to take advantage of the steam press because of its initial cost, the 1830s and 1840s witnessed an explosion in every type of literary endeavor. Five major journals, for example, were founded after the War of 1812. The *North American Review* (1815) and its short-lived Charleston counterpart, *The Southern Review* (1828), dealt exclusively with criticism and polemics; so, for the most part, did Irving's *Knickerbocker Magazine* (1833) and the *Southern Literary Messenger* (1834), edited by Poe for three of its first four years. The *Democratic Review,* founded in 1837, offered early stories by Whitman and Hawthorne alongside Jacksonian politics.

More startling was the proliferation of newspapers. Newspapers in the early United States were largely political organs, uncritical in praising their heroes and unsubtle in damning the opposition. Most survived only briefly, existing on the barest margins until an election had passed; some, however, became monuments to the creativity and energy of their publishers. Outstanding were the New York *Evening Post,* edited by William Cullen Bryant after 1829, the New York *Herald* of James Gordon Bennett, founded in 1835, and Horace Greeley's New York *Tribune,* started in 1841. The New York *Sun* became in 1833 the first to sell for a penny. For political controversy none surpassed the Washington *Globe* under Francis Preston Blair, Sr., and the Richmond *Enquirer* of Thomas Ritchie, both organs of the Democrats. These papers and thousands lesser-known served a critical function in the new republic. Where politics and culture were no longer the province of the elite, the newspapers provided a vital link between the ordinary citizen and the society in which he was supposed to have a voice.

This function of integrating the individual and the society led, in time, to the development of newspapers that were less polemical and more concerned with reporting the news—quickly, entertainingly, with fullness and originality. Bennett of the *Herald* was especially eager to separate journalism and partisanship. He was often a sensationalist, and he often stretched the truth. But Bennett initiated many techniques indispensable to the modern newspaper. He was among the first to establish correspondents in Washington, and the first (1838) to employ regular correspondents abroad. He personally persuaded Congress to admit reporters to the House and Senate galleries on a regular basis; he began putting his most startling news, instead of his best-paying ads, on the front page; he first made regular use of the telegraph. Bennett also developed the practice of meeting incoming vessels at sea with small, fast boats in order to get the news quickly.

And each ship, it seemed, brought some new account of America written by a European. Readers devoured the observations of European travelers in the United States, even though the accounts were not always flattering. Europeans watched the American experiment with varying degrees of pleasure and alarm. So did the thousands who, in this country, bought their books. Tocqueville's classic *Democracy in America* sold more volumes in the United States than in England or France, although the author wrote it for European audiences. Whenever a major work appeared, American writers soon followed with a reply. The German-born Jacksonian Francis Grund's *Aristocracy in America* countered Tocqueville's argument that Americans loved equality more than liberty with a wry account of the quest for status in the young republic. A traveler, mentioning his English or French origins, usually met a barrage of boasts that the United States was the best of all possible worlds, then was pestered with a series of questions: What did the foreigner think of the nation and its people? Was American culture as refined as that of Europe? How might the country improve?

THE cultural life of the new nation thus presented stark contrasts. While Americans labored to erect a republic based on the good sense and wisdom of common men, they created heroes who were larger than life. They were fascinated by the beauty and wildness of the land, yet fearful that some of that wildness might extend to their own institutions. They were practical and hardworking, yet they respected the aesthetic. They lived free of traditional restraints, yet they demanded that art and literature instruct them in moral values. These contrasts in the American mind did not reflect conflicting absolutes of right or wrong so much as the predictable confusion of a society in search of its standards. In short, art and literature were subject to the same tension between liberty and authority, between the desire for freedom and the need for restraint, that influenced the development of American political institutions.

8

Toward the Millennium

DURING the first half of the nineteenth century, Americans earned an international reputation for hard work, a boundless desire for self-improvement, and a chronic impatience with the status quo. "An American wants to perform within a year what others do within a much longer period," explained a German immigrant. "Ten years in America are like a century in Spain." No aspect of personal life and no thread in the social fabric escaped this restless search for progress, for Americans really seemed to believe that some cosmic force had blessed them with an unlimited capacity to improve their lot. The result was a persistent tendency to build, tear down, and build again. A Cincinnati newspaper, for example, complained in 1845 that no one seemed content to live or do business in the same building for more than a few years. The streets were always cluttered with stacks of brick and wood for new and bigger edifices, plus heaps of rubble and junk from the remains of old ones. Similarly, Americans attacked and remade the design and structure of their society. They were passionate and incurable reformers, always ready with a new plan for uplifting the individual and society. "We are all a little wild here with numberless projects for social reform," Emerson rejoiced in 1840. "Not a reading man but has a draft of a new community in his waistcoat pocket."

At first glance the American passion for reform might seem out of place. Americans prided themselves on their progress and well-being —the result, they were quick to note, of the most ambitious and successful reform ever attempted, the republican revolution. But in one sense they were victims of their own rhetoric. If, as one Independence Day orator declared, Americans enjoyed "more national happiness and individual prosperity than falls to the lot of any people on the face of the globe," how did they explain the persistence of vice and injustice that afflicted the new nation? If republican self-rule rested on the good judgment of the common man, what accounted for his dogged refusal to stop swearing, stop drinking to excess, stop trying to milk his neighbors of an easy dollar? Nothing was more embarrassing than to find great expectations followed by weak performances. One mission of the reformer, then, was to tinker with society in order to make that last step toward republican perfection.

More worrisome was the fear that the republican revolution would be perverted in its entirety, its grand dreams and visions misused to satisfy the wrong ambitions. Already there were signs that a decay of standards had set in. Materialism and comfort had replaced virtue and self-sacrifice as the guiding ideals of the new republic. And yet financial success had not brought its anticipated gains. Americans seemed to be an insecure, worried lot who were never satisfied. "All strangers who come among us remark the excessive anxiety written in the American countenance," commented one journalist in 1845. Poverty, tyranny, or lack of opportunity could not possibly be the cause in such a prosperous land; rather, a widespread preoccupation with getting more had induced a general sense of frustration. Anxiety had resulted from the "concentration of the faculties upon an object, which in its very nature is unattainable—the perpetual improvement of the outward condition."

In short, the republican revolution had left a vacuum both in attitudes and in institutions that generated intense unease among Americans. The countless schemes for social reform that Emerson remarked were signs of this uncertainty. The reformers seemed to say that man and society could indeed become perfect, but the very need to construct utopias suggested that the society which existed around them was sadly inadequate. Too much individualism—or individualism applied in the wrong manner—could create a society that was rootless and selfish. Institutions that might channel individual effort along creative lines, on the other hand, raised the possibility that new tyrannies, worse than those of Europe, would emerge. The reformer and the ordinary citizen both were searching for a middle ground, some way of uplifting the individual while integrating him with the community.

THE quest was foreshadowed by the great revivals that swept over the nation during the first half of the century. Beginning in Cane

Ridge, Kentucky, in 1801, revivalism spread South and West, then East and North, culminating in the "burned-over district" of western New York during the 1820s. Revivals were not limited to the frontier, although they did have roots in the urge to escape the loneliness and brutality and boredom of frontier life. Certainly they carried an element of the theatrical, with at times thousands of the penitent gathered in clearings, listening to a half-dozen preachers at once in what resembled a political rally more than the worship of God. Simple farmers and sophisticated businessmen might break down, weep, shout, bark, or speak in tongues; the preachers carried on regardless. Hundreds might be saved and, six months or a year later, when the next revival passed through, be saved again. Though the theologians of the East frowned on such raucous enthusiasm, the revivalists knew their audience and redoubled their efforts to save the entire country or, failing that, whole counties and states. "It may be well to state," commented one observer in 1839, ". . . that religious mania is said to be the prevailing form of insanity in the United States."

The revivals were not built on any elaborate theological framework. Indeed, the Second Great Awakening seemed almost hostile to systematic thought or intellectual consistency. Strains of predestination and Calvinism existed side by side with free will and Arminianism. The revival was divinely inspired and directed; the decision to be saved was an act of personal choice. Part of what gave the revivals their intensity and emotional drama was the mechanism of that choice. The revivalists appealed beyond the mind and to the heart. Anyone, whether he or she could read or not, could grasp the message of salvation. The less rationalism, the less logical weighing of alternatives, the less likelihood the individual soul would be led astray to overintellectual theological nitpicking. The need was to act, not to think.

While the Second Great Awakening did not have a Jonathan Edwards, it did have Charles Grandison Finney. Only nine years old at the time of the Cane Ridge meeting, Finney emerged in the 1820s and 1830s as the foremost leader of American revivalism, at once its most compelling spokesman and its most disciplined apologist. Finney, whose influence on the techniques of other reforms was profound, rejected the rigidity and elitism of traditional Calvinism. He agreed that wars, depressions, and revivals could be and were evidence of God's divine plan, but he vigorously denied that man had no free will, that he was a passive reed forever bent to a predestined fate. The individual alone was responsible for his salvation. "Neither God nor any other being can regenerate him if he will not turn," he argued. "If he will not change his choice, it is impossible that it should be changed." Moreover, having chosen regeneration, the sinner had his whole life transformed "from entire sinfulness to entire holiness." In short, if only the person willed it, God could make him perfect.

Free will implied, then, that the individual needed no intermediaries between him and God. Salvation was open to all classes; neither a trained clergy nor a Puritan body of visible saints was necessary to explain and spread the word of God. Finney's contempt for the theologian was complete. While they debated the number of angels who could dance on the head of a pin, whole communities of the lost languished in sin.

To save the individual was to begin the process of redeeming the whole society from chaos and anarchy. To revivalists, the new nation was cursed with a preoccupation with material well-being and greed that threatened to undo the social fabric. Change would come only when each individual recognized his true interests and responsibilities. According to Finney, he who listened to the word of God would be transformed "from a state of entire consecration to self-interest, self-indulgence and self-gratification for its own sake . . . to a state of entire consecration to God and to the interests of his kingdom. . . ." The change in basic attitudes, begun personally, would move outward until no member of society could escape its influence. All would share a unity of purpose that transcended the selfish desires of the individual. Evangelical religion thus provided a common ethos— a religious equivalent of nationalism—that bound the community together literally by an act of faith.

By the 1830s, Finney and those like him who had preached spontaneous regeneration began to turn to the task of institutionalizing their crusade. In providing organized means of spreading the gospel, they were yielding to the certainty that the revivals would ebb, while insuring that the message would persist until the next great wave of enthusiasm. Methodists, for example, began the century with the crying need to form churches. After 1820, their membership extensive, they turned their efforts toward education and voluntary associations of reform. On the frontier, especially, the great wave of revivals was closely followed by the establishment of congregations, which in time themselves produced schools, academies, and colleges. Finney himself joined the faculty of Oberlin College in 1837. A score of denominational colleges were founded in the South alone between 1819—the date of the formation of Centre College in Kentucky by the Presbyterians—and 1850. The purpose of these schools was clear: they protected the revival impulse by giving it continuity and form.

The benevolent society, or Protestant voluntary association, ministered more directly to the people. It had its roots not on the frontier but in the Congregational churches of New England and, beyond that, in the Quaker charitable societies and even the Anglican Society for the Propagation of the Gospel. Benevolent societies reflected the voluntary nature of American Protestantism. By avoiding theological niceties, they opened the way for lay participation. Some were nondenominational. By emphasizing that God's work was nobler and more important than worldly gain, the associations created an alternate ideal: in place of the selfish entrepreneur came the selfless missionary. Individualism was not rejected; it was enhanced with a new purpose.

There was no inherent conflict, then, between personal salvation and the use of organized agencies of reform. The one was an individual, the other a social, expression of Christianity. Here was a close parallel between individual religion and democratic politics. As the political party glorified the common man while organizing him into a collective body, so did the voluntary association. It was a subtle blending of an ideal with the need for giving shape and form to the society whence that ideal sprang.

As the voluntary associations and benevolent societies matured, they, like the political parties, became more professional and more disciplined. In the cities, the local gentry were instrumental before 1830 in starting the associations, but as the decades progressed they withdrew, replaced by a new class of reformers who made benevolence and the work of God their occupation. Increasingly, the informal ideal of an organization staffed by volunteers gave way to one in which the leadership was disciplined, more professional, more committed to fund raising and publicity than to personal acts of sacrifice. By the time of the Civil War, the voluntary associations were led by persons who approached reform as an occupation and a business.

Associations were not confined to evangelical religion; they served an endless variety of purposes, including temperance, abolitionism, and prison and educational reform. Their presence indicated that Americans were deeply concerned about the problem of social order. Without them, action toward common goals was difficult, sometimes impossible. Tocqueville, finding associations everywhere, concluded that they served an essential role in a democracy. "In aristocratic societies," he wrote, "men do not need to combine in order to act, because they are strongly held together. Every wealthy and powerful citizen constitutes the head of a permanent and compulsory association." "Among democratic nations, on the contrary, all the citizens are independent and feeble; they can do hardly anything by themselves." Thus, if "it be proposed to advance some truth, or to foster some feeling by the encouragement of a great example, they form a society. Wherever, at the head of some new undertaking, you see the government in France, or a man of rank in England, in the United States you will be sure to find an association." And so, "the most democratic country on the face of the earth is that in which men have in our time carried to the highest perfection the art of pursuing in common the object of their common desires, and have applied this new science to the greatest number of purposes."

Benevolent associations were especially effective when they merged their efforts with those of state and local governments. An example was the almost total transformation of criminal justice that swept the nation during the 1820s and 1830s. During the colonial era, crime was attributed to the individual's innate depravity, and the usual punishments were exile, humiliation, or death. After the Revolution this attitude gave way to a gentler view that stressed man's inherent goodness. Improper instruction in moral values and a bad environment created the outlaw, and proper instruction and a good environment could reclaim him. To the Boston reformer Samuel Gridley Howe and others like him, a democratic society incurred a solemn responsibility to its outcasts. "When a government seizes upon a person," Howe argued, "especially if he be young, and deprives him of all liberty of action, it assumes at once the offices, and incurs the responsibilities, of a parent and guardian." Good parents simply did not abuse their children with fetters, or dungeons, or scaffolds. They instructed them in wholesome conduct and moral values. The prison, then, was much like a school, "the only school," in fact, ". . . which thousands of its hapless subjects ever enter." "How important, then," concluded Howe, "is the question, whether it is a school of virtue or a school of vice!"

And so new associations for penal reform emerged. In 1825 the Boston Prison Discipline Society organized under the leadership of Louis Dwight, an earnest and rather brittle agent of the American Bible Society. As a youth, Dwight had been headed for a traditional career in the ministry; an accident in a chemistry class injured his lungs and destroyed his plans. For a time he worked as a traveling agent of the American Bible Society—a job that exposed him to the wretched condition of prisons and the miserable lot of convicts. Using the techniques and format of one voluntary association, he began another and became for years the foremost advocate of prison reform in the new nation. Dwight's ideals lost some of their religious content in the transfer, for the Boston society was directed more toward educating the criminal in proper standards of social conduct and moral values than in training him in the tenets of a particular faith. Yet the religious overtones of Dwight's work were unmistakable. It was his intent to remove the prisoner from all evil influences, teach him self-discipline, and prepare him for a wholesome return to freedom.

These ideas and efforts were eagerly seconded by public officials throughout the Northeast. At about the same time Dwight was launching his society in Massachusetts, New York State was busy developing a revolutionary approach to prison discipline. A new facility at Auburn attempted to solve the problem of rehabilitation by a unique combination of military routine, hard work, and total silence. Prisoners awoke at the same hour each morning, spent the day laboring together at collective tasks, and retired for the night in tiny cells three feet wide, seven feet long, and seven feet high. Any communication among prisoners was strictly forbidden. They marched to work in lockstep, ate their meals in rigid silence, and slept alone. Even a glance was outlawed, and violations of the rules were answered with the whip. The only break in this unremitting regime was the occasional visit by some charitable reformer, who provided the inmates with Bibles or simple tracts outlining a moral lesson. The Auburn experiment instantly found advocates—including Dwight—who praised it for the discipline it imposed and the moral instruction it provided. Encouragingly, the Auburn system also returned a profit, and other states eagerly copied it.

Alternate plans appeared, however. Pennsylvania experimented with various formats before settling on a plan of total solitary confinement. Auburn had experienced periods of unrest and one major riot

—the result, explained Pennsylvania officials, of the tiny size of the cells. The obvious solution was to build a larger prison, the Eastern State Penitentiary at Cherry Hill: at the center was an octagonal fortress—very like a medieval castle—from which seven radial arms of cells extended. Each cell was ten by twelve feet and had its own small exercise yard. A turreted wall ringed the entire facility. Solitude was absolute: for the duration of his term a prisoner saw no one (except, again, the occasional missionary), received no letters from home, no news from the outside world, no word from other prisoners. He spent his time, presumably, in quiet meditation on the evil of his ways, read the tracts presented to him, and worked at solitary tasks.

Each system had its advocates who engaged in long, detailed, and often acrimonious debates over which plan worked best. The similarities between the two, however, outweighed the differences. Each was a center for rehabilitation, not penance. Each encouraged discipline, either by a tightly controlled routine or by removing all opportunities for diversion. Each attempted to school the prisoner in moral values. Most of all, each was designed to isolate the criminal from those who would help perpetuate his evil habits. European observers—including Tocqueville and Gustave de Beaumont—who visited them left with praise for their humane and sensible approach to criminal reform. Only later did lockstep, utter silence, and total isolation appear somewhat less than ideal.

What was most notable about these systems was the suddenness with which they appeared and the zealous devotion they inspired. Europeans marveled at the commitment Americans brought to prison reform. The Eastern State Penitentiary, for example, cost Pennsylvania $700,000 and kept a small army of guards and volunteers busy at its maintenance. The success of the Auburn system of congregate labor prompted Connecticut to move its condemned out of the dark squalor of an abandoned copper mine into a modern copy of the New York facility at Wethersfield. New York soon began to differentiate between youthful offenders and hardened criminals, entrusting the former to reform schools financed by private groups.

Behind these efforts were the persistent efforts of the voluntary associations. Dwight almost singlehandedly convinced the Connecticut legislature to build Wethersfield. By 1845 Dorothea Dix had extended the crusade to include separate facilities for the insane. The burden of paying for these changes ultimately fell on the public, but the beginnings were made by men and women who acted, voluntarily, through benevolent societies. However flawed the changes may appear in retrospect, the new prisons were an ambitious and typical testament to the reformer's desire to remake society—and his ability to organize his efforts.

The Jacksonian American, then, was profoundly, and in his own way expertly, concerned with forming institutions. What puzzled so many contemporary observers was the fact that these "institutions" fit no traditional mold. They lacked the elaborate hierarchy of Anglicanism or Catholicism; they carried no inherited legitimacy, as did the English aristocracy. They were, initially, bureaucratically primitive. They were products of a creative tension that existed in the new republic. Combining localism with nationalism, individualism with collectivism, voluntary associations were mechanisms of ordering the community which were open to the participation of all. They fostered their own elites, it is true, but these elites differed fundamentally from those known before. Anyone who gave of his loyalties and his time was eligible. As in the political party, there were rewards, yet to the reformer these were nothing less than the perfection of an entire nation.

THE association provided a means of reforming society without rejecting it. It was inevitable, however, that some would repudiate American society altogether or, more likely, try to remake it by forming alternate examples of social harmony and perfection. They were not unlike the New England Puritans, who, by creating a city on a hill, hoped ultimately to inspire England to mend its ways. Unlike the Puritans, however, these reformers envisioned an earthly utopia based on the innate goodness of mankind. They were, in a variety of ways, perfectionists.

Perfectionists were not so naïve as to think that humanity was without faults. There was far too much evidence to the contrary. Nor did they necessarily believe that all men and women could achieve absolute perfection all the time. They did believe, however, that man's essential nature was good, not depraved; thus, they attacked one of the basic tenets of Calvinism. Their ultimate goal was to construct a society in which neither institutions nor the petty greed of individuals would stifle the better qualities of mankind. Perfectionists, then, attempted to promote harmony, comfort, cooperation, and personal development all at once.

By far the most successful of the perfectionist communities was that started by John Humphrey Noyes. Born in 1811, Noyes possessed both wealth and a religious, inquiring mind. In 1834 he lost his license to preach when, inspired by the revivals, he refused to admit that human nature was basically sinful. From that point the perfectionist spirit grew in his mind, until in 1839 he decided to begin a community that would give shape to his ideas. Originally settling in Putney, Vermont, Noyes and his small band of followers were forced to flee to New York in 1846—primarily because of their unorthodox view of marriage. In 1848 they began anew near the small upstate town of Oneida.

The Oneida community was an experiment in religious communism. All money was held in common; all responsibilities were shared. One labored according to one's talents and endurance, but excessive work and competitiveness were discouraged. The emphasis was on harmony, matched by personal moral development. Women, for example, cooked only once during the day, thus freeing their time for reading and meditation. The food was simple; members of the community ate whenever they wished. At night the community gathered in one of its large rooms for the "criticism," wherein the virtues and faults of a particular member were exposed, discussed, and evaluated. More often than not, a person who thought himself well on the way to perfection emerged from these sessions with a feeling of total failure and self-contempt; no one, certainly, who endured the criticism walked away from it unchanged. It was part of Noyes's emphasis on communal sharing: if the entire group participated in the development of one of its members, the community as a whole improved accordingly.

Noyes's most controversial tenet of collective harmony was his system of "complex" marriage. "Religious love," he wrote, "is very near . . . to sexual love." Thus, if all were united in Christ, all were husband and wife. Noyes avoided the extreme male dominance of Mormon polygamy, while simultaneously rejecting the "feminine" ideal of Shaker celibacy. His goal, again, was to promote harmony and to discourage jealousy and competition. He who could share the marriage bed could share all.

For all its renunciation of competitiveness, the Oneida community proved to be a remarkably successful enterprise in capitalism. Oneida fruits, silks, and silver were praised for their quality and their workmanship. Oneida riding leathers and harnesses were sold as far north as Hudson's Bay. Part of the community's success stemmed from its attitude toward work. Where all labored, but no one met deadlines, there was time for skillful craftsmanship. Part, also, lay in the fact that all profits were poured back into the community, which within a few years possessed a neat, spacious, and valuable physical plant.

In time, neither financial success nor free love could keep the community together. As the first generation died or left, the second failed to develop the intense commitment to religious communism necessary for continuing the experiment. Noyes himself eventually left Oneida in 1877—the same year that his first cousin, Rutherford B. Hayes, became President. For most of its thirty years, however, Oneida had remained the most successful attempt at creating a working utopia in the United States.

Others were not so successful. Experiments in utopianism were usually the products of religious sects such as the Shakers, but in 1824 Robert Owen, the widely known English reformer, introduced the concept of worker communes. Owen had established model villages for the workers at his Lanark, Scotland, textile mills; then he had turned his efforts to the United States. At New Harmony, Indiana, on land he had purchased from disillusioned Shakers, he undertook to rehabilitate 2,400 souls—"the dregs of the dregs of society"—by a work-rest-play-study-meditate regime. When he explained it in Washington to a fascinated audience that included James Monroe and John Quincy Adams, it sounded as if the millennium were at hand; in two years, however, the movement was wrecked by declining funds, personal rivalries, and ordinary laziness. A similar community at Nashoba, Tennessee, at which Frances Wright hoped to colonize slaves who would earn their freedom by their labor, also failed.

The socialist utopian idea reappeared in America in the 1830s and early 1840s, this time inspired by the French socialist François Marie Charles Fourier. Albert Brisbane brought Fourierism to the United States in 1834 and set down its principles in 1840 in *The Social Destiny of Man*. The core of the Fourierist communities was the phalanx, in which labor and capital together built self-sufficient societies based on the sanctity of hard work. As a resident of a phalanx, one labored in the fields or shops, did intellectual or creative work, and meditated. There was no room for the slacker. Fourierism, as Brisbane interpreted it, was a form of industrial perfectionism. Altogether, more than forty such communities were founded; none lasted long. It was a splendid means of reforming oneself, perhaps, and it did have the saving grace of involving communities as well. But the sacrifices were so large and the results so minimal that most simply grew tired and turned elsewhere, concentrating their efforts on particular needs.

WHILE the perfectionist communities always had some ties to the society around them, the Mormon movement attempted to reject American culture altogether. This most complex and ambitious of the several efforts to erect an alternate society began curiously in New York, in the imagination and frustrations of Joseph Smith. Born in Vermont, Smith was descended from a family whose chief distinction seemed to be an utter lack of distinction. Smith's mother, for example, was a naïve, credulous woman who embraced vigorously and randomly any number of the religious enthusiasms of the day and who desperately hoped that one of her sons would grow to prominence as a modern saint. His father drifted through several occupations and several towns (nineteen in one ten-year period) in search of economic success. He was a visionary Yankee, not a shrewd one, and spent much time trooping through the countryside with a divining stick, in search of hidden water. From most reports Joseph Smith was an amiable, gregarious boy with a gift for words, although he was not well-read. He shared his father's instinct for quirky ideas and his mother's passion for the mystical.

In 1816, when Joseph was nine, the family moved to Palmyra, New York. At that time Palmyra was entering a decade of rapid change: a section of the Erie Canal was dug nearby, and the area attracted speculators and families on the move, many of them down-and-out Yankees such as Smith's own. During the 1820s, the village was at the center of the "burned-over district" of religious revivalism and, coincidentally, Antimasonry in upstate New York. In such surroundings Joseph Smith fit well. Like other migrants in the region, he had never known financial security or social status: like others, he found excitement in religious phenomena of all sorts. He cherished a "peek stone" —a small glazed rock—which he was persuaded gave him special powers of vision and which he used to search for buried treasure during his frequent walks in the woods.

On one such walk Smith was seized, as he related it, "by some power which entirely overcame me." Unable to speak, he was surrounded by an intense light from which two figures appeared, God the

Father and Jesus Christ. All religions were a hoax, they informed him; he must renounce them. Smith's mother believed every word of the tale and encouraged her son to seek out the two figures again—a charge that Smith happily accepted. Shortly thereafter he reported finding, with the aid of his peek stone, a set of golden plates on which were inscribed a miraculous story of a lost tribe of Hebrews, the true disciples of Christ, who had wandered into the New World centuries before and whose ragged offspring were the Indians of the American West. The plates also foretold the coming of a new messiah, a Prophet, who would reassemble the lost tribe and establish the kingdom of God on earth. No one else, apparently, ever actually saw these plates. Smith allowed three men to "view" them; one admitted that he had looked through "the eyes of faith . . . though at the time they were covered with cloth." In time angels appeared and bore the mysterious tablets away.

But not before Smith had dictated their contents to a scribe and had them published. *The Book of Mormon* appeared in 1830, and at the same time the Church of Jesus Christ of Latter-Day Saints was born. From its humble and rather bizarre beginnings, the sect made remarkable progress. For fourteen years Smith expanded both his powers and his following in a religious odyssey that took him through three states, several reorganizations, and, finally, to death. In 1833 his small band moved to Kirtland Hills, Ohio—also a center for revivalists and religious eccentrics—and increased their number to several thousand. A second colony was started in Missouri, but both groups were tormented by public hostility—and subverted by Smith's questionable ventures into banking. In 1839 a new town, Nauvoo, in Illinois, was begun, and Mormonism began to prosper.

At Nauvoo, Mormonism began to take form as a hierarchical, authoritarian alternate to the expansive republic from which it originated. Smith's power was such that he could direct his followers to vote as a bloc, and he used that power in the Illinois elections of 1840 to secure a unique charter for the new town. The mayor and aldermen exercised almost unlimited powers; they could pass, amend, or repeal laws at will. The community was strictly governed from the top and was almost entirely self-sufficient, with its own toolworks, factories, and sawmill—even a university. All this was guarded by a town militia of over two thousand troops, of which Smith was the undisputed commander. Within a few years the Mormon hierarchy had produced a city of spacious streets, careful planning, and seductive attractiveness. During the same period Smith's missionaries had reached Europe, and hundreds of immigrants from the factory towns of England were making the long trek to the New World to join their leader.

In 1844 Smith finally overstepped himself. Success bred egotism, and egotism led to the kind of reckless megalomania that could be, and was, fatal. The Prophet outraged the state and a considerable number of his own disciples by his practice of polygamy, which he justified as a logical and divinely ordained extension of the self-sufficient, paternalistic design of the church. The logic escaped many, however, and the movement began to fracture internally. More damaging was his ill-timed candidacy for the Presidency. Smith tried to persuade both political parties, and the federal government, to support his plan for a separate Mormon state. When that failed, he joined the contest directly, on a platform that contemplated, among other things, emancipation for slaves. What little tolerance Smith still enjoyed from Illinois officials disappeared. In June, Smith forcibly exiled the dissidents within his church; they fled to nearby Carthage, and anti-Mormon citizens in the surrounding communities called out their militia. Joseph Smith and his brother were imprisoned in the Carthage jail, promised a fair trial by the governor, and promptly murdered by a mob.

Their leader gone, their membership divided and split, Mormons once again took to the road. One group left for Iowa, another for Wisconsin, and yet a third—under Brigham Young—for the West. In 1847 Young reached the hills surrounding the Great Salt Lake in Utah, surveyed the valley before him, and calmly pronounced: "This is the place." Within a few years the theocratic Mormon government had established a well-run and prosperous colony of several thousand, all living and working outside the laws of any jurisdiction but their own. Young reiterated Smith's approval of polygamy, the faith's most controversial practice. More startling to the discerning observer was the consolidated, hierarchical design of the community. The "State of Deseret" was democratic in name only; each of its citizens was a saint in the Kingdom of God. But work, currency, the law, and families were organized and governed by a paternalistic authority headed, naturally, by Young. The group wanted no part of the government or the society they had left. Their insistent demand for autonomy and their polygamy involved them in a decade of quarrels with Washington, which ruled the Utah Territory after the Mexican War. Only in 1858 was an uneasy compromise reached.

Who would join such a movement? The reasons are as varied and particular as the number of individual Mormons. Some were drawn by the content of the Mormon message, which promised regeneration and a new commitment to Christianity. Some were undoubtedly swayed by the personal magnetism of Joseph Smith, who seemed to grow more confident, more charismatic, as the years went by. But overall, the hierarchical, authoritarian structure of the church and its promise to make saints of ordinary men and women appear to have had their greatest impact on persons whose histories were much like that of their leader. The wandering Yankees, the visionaries, the failed shopkeepers and frustrated artisans who joined Smith had somehow been left behind in the rapid expansion of the new republic. Born into a society that promised them unlimited progress, they had achieved only mediocrity and sour dreams. The English workingmen who responded to the Mormon missionaries had experienced much the same disillusionment in industrial Britain. Mormonism offered them sainthood, an ultimate and eternal realization of their hopes. The hierarchy to which they submitted imparted a sense of order to a changing world. Throughout ran the conviction that the church was a redeemed nation, a state unto itself, chosen by God to preserve morality and obedience to a higher law in a world otherwise corrupted by materialism and vice. Mormons may have rejected American society, then, but in certain ways they owed their very existence to it.

MOST Americans accepted their society, however, and wanted only to improve it. Of the many fields open to reform, education offered both the greatest potential and the most difficult obstacles. Education in the eighteenth century had been regarded primarily as a function of the family, church, private enterprise, philanthropy—by no means ever to be controlled by government at any level. The surprisingly high literacy rate of white Americans in the colonial and Revolutionary periods was the result of home tutoring, a few urban "pay schools," and the apprentice system, which offered in addition to a trade the rudiments of reading and arithmetic. No state had a comprehensive school system before 1815. Ohio and the newer states of the West had grants of public lands, the proceeds from which were to be spent for education, but the money—what little there was—was largely dissipated in sporadic and uneven efforts. In the country districts, the "field school" with its itinerant teacher, the local minister, and the home were the primary educational institutions, and the Bible the main text. Of organized, systematic education, there was very little. Even within higher education, progress was slow. Jefferson's plans for the University of Virginia languished until 1825, the same year that John Quincy Adams's call for a national university fell flat.

After 1825, however, changes began. Education in America, like the nation itself, was at a parting of the ways. One road—the one of few or no schools for the poor, and private schools or tutoring for the rich —led to social stratification, particularism, and provincialism, a reflection of education in colonial society. The other—that of systemization, balance, and public support for every child—led to a modern, nationalistic, and democratic form in which children of all classes were integrated into the educational process. An informed and intelligent people, Jefferson had insisted, could govern themselves; a base and ignorant nation invited despotism. In education, as in government, Americans turned to the democratic ideal and the institutional forms that served it.

There were problems, of course. The extreme shortage of labor in the new nation hampered general education. On the farm, children who labored alongside their parents were isolated from the towns that nurtured schools. In the cities, children often provided a crucial part of the working family's income; parents were naturally reluctant to forego the child's contribution. Beyond that were sharp differences over what constituted an education. Some still advocated a well-rounded introduction to the arts and classics; most preferred instruction in the practical. Even in the Eastern cities there was a feeling that education should be useful—that children should be taught the rudiments of making a living and no more. As late as 1838, many questioned whether the bequest of the English chemist James Smithson to found an institution "for the increase and diffusion of knowledge among men" ought to be accepted. (It was.) A strong strain of anti-intellectualism had grown up in place of the enlightened aristocrat. Education for its own sake, especially with governmental funding, was suspect. As Richard Hofstadter has noted, John Quincy Adams "was the last nineteenth-century occupant of the White House who had a knowledgeable sympathy with the aims and aspirations of science or who believed that fostering the arts might properly be a function of the federal government."

Despite these obstacles, the drive for public education intensified during the 1830s and 1840s. It took nourishment from several ideals. Protestant leaders, for example, saw in the spread of education among all classes one way to maintain religious principles in a country that separated church and state. Universal education, wrote one Western leader, should be taken up "as a great *Christian enterprise.*" Others, mostly the rich, considered education a tool with which the lower classes could be kept under control by being taught to respect the established order. This was a particularly urgent task, since the order was changing constantly. Still others, who had traveled to Germany for their college education, came back full of enthusiasm and a new-found professionalism in their trade. And Jefferson's ideal of an enlightened republic remained a powerful and attractive dream.

These strains of educational thinking were expressed most eloquently by Horace Mann. During the 1840s, Mann worked tirelessly for a complete overhaul of the Massachusetts school system. His ideas spread; they have never become obsolete. Mann welded moral concern, Teutonic thoroughness, a deep dread of social chaos, and a quest for the roots of republican virtue into a program of public instruction that extended to all children. As he explained in 1837, when he became the first secretary of the state Board of Education, universal education was a public duty, not a personal luxury. All persons, rich and poor, contained within them two impulses, good and bad, charitable and selfish, each given by God and each competing for dominance. Childhood, being the most impressionable time of life, was the moment when the "nobler faculties can be elevated into dominion and supremacy over the appetites and passions." Even the most hardened criminal, Mann argued, had experienced an instant when, "ere he plunged into the abyss of infamy and guilt, he might have been recalled, as it were by the waving of the hand." To trust the teaching of moral principles, of discipline and respect, to chance or individual effort was to court failure. "Society is responsible," he charged, "not society considered as an abstraction, but society as it consists of living members. . . ."

The social responsibility for protecting moral virtue was especially critical in a democracy. Monarchies and despotisms might stunt the will to do good, but they at least had the concentrated power to circumscribe evil. In a democracy, the diffusion of power had unleashed the potential of great and widespread improvement, but, since man was also half evil, had also created the possibility of undreamed viciousness. Mann was convinced that the spread of democracy was inevitable. "The oak will as soon go back into the acorn," he stated, "or the bird into its shell, as we return to the monarchical or aristocratic forms of by-gone ages." The need was to channel the energies of a democratic people into wholesome pursuits. "If republican institutions do wake up unexampled energies in the whole mass of a people, and give them implements of unexampled power wherewith to work out their will," Mann declared,

> then these same institutions ought also to confer upon that people unexampled wisdom and rectitude . . . If they quicken the activity and enlarge the sphere of the appetites and passions, they must, at least in an equal ration, establish the authority and extend the jurisdiction of reason and conscience. In a word, we must not add to the impulsive, without also adding to the regulating force.

The "regulating force." Mann had grasped the essential problem that beset the new republic. If democracy was good, it could also be devastatingly evil. If individual fulfillment was desirable, anarchy was possible. Mann had captured two streams of thought in the new nation and combined them into a new ideal. The Founders, fearful of man's innate corruptibility, had constructed checks by which that corruption could be controlled. Romantics, convinced of man's perfectibility, had advocated self-reliance. Mann took them both and, by emphasizing the role of education in shaping the life of the individual and the society, had molded a regulatory institution wherein the two sides—good and bad—of the human personality could be balanced.

Then Mann listed those who were responsible for the moral welfare of the young: clergymen, intellectuals, journalists, legislators—but not the family. His omission indicated a crucial shift from the thinking of the eighteenth century, when it was assumed that virtue—personal and by extension public—was the responsibility of the individual and of his parents and the result of his upbringing. Now the burden lay with society and institutions. External controls, those formed and agreed upon by the general common sense of the community and given structure as institutions, had taken over many of the duties of the conscience. All this from a man who was a contemporary of Emerson, who argued just the opposite.

Mann's reorganization of the public schools reflected his goals. During his tenure at the Board of Education, schools in Massachusetts became structured, highly developed democratic institutions. Pupils were graded according to age and talent; they were taught a standard curriculum; their teachers were trained. Moreover, the concept of a school "system" had arrived, with responsibility for education now a social concern, as he had wanted. It was a strikingly modern institution, and through it any child could receive an education.

Mann's ideas were not adopted everywhere. The very modernity of his program made it innovative; other plans were considered. Typically, these followed the associational pattern set down by the Protestant benevolent societies. The American Sunday School Union, for example, was founded in 1824 as a lay-directed organization to bring books and schools to towns that had none of their own. Its purpose was frankly religious—to preserve sound Protestant values in a changing world. The union was nondenominational and did not survive the sectarian struggles of the 1840s and 1850s, but between its inception and the Civil War it did distribute millions of books and tracts, all at low cost, to persons who would not have had them otherwise. Equally popular was the lyceum. Beginning with local, voluntary organizations in the late 1820s, lyceums spread quickly during the 1830s, forming—as Emerson well knew—one of the major outlets for disseminating knowledge in the young republic. A national group, the American Lyceum Association, was formed in 1831, but the idea worked best in small cities, where it could be tailored to meet community tastes and needs. The aims of the lyceum paralleled many of those of the Sunday schools: moral improvement and patriotic values, as well as scientific and cultural knowledge.

None of these efforts to educate the new nation was entirely successful. Mann's proposals in Massachusetts, for example, were stoutly resisted by a variety of opponents, from church leaders who wanted more emphasis on religious values to schoolteachers who thought Mann's proposals would lead to a breakdown of discipline. (Thirty-one Boston schoolmasters signed a petition to that effect.) The Sunday School Union was more concerned with teaching Protestant values than with spelling; the lyceums were completely voluntary and had no powers of discipline or enforcement. The few attempts to extend state control over colleges and universities met with little success, particularly after Chief Justice Marshall's decision in the Dartmouth

College case in 1819. Thus, higher education remained in the hands of private or, at best, quasi-public, boards of trustees who more often than not kept the institutions either denominational or reserved for the rich.

THE most telling weakness of educational reform, however, was its ultimate failure to reach the poor. However sincerely educators might want to open up the schools to the whole people, their efforts suffered either from misconceptions or poor execution. Two examples are suggestive. In Philadelphia, in 1824, the Franklin Institute for the Promotion of the Mechanic Arts was formed to disseminate both theoretical scientific knowledge and its practical applications. The object was to reach common craftsmen and mechanics and make them both philosophers and artisans—an industrial variety of Jefferson's virtuous agrarian. The institute soon discovered, however, that its audience either cared little for theory or, more likely, was so ignorant of basic scientific principles that the lectures were unintelligible. By 1830, the institute had become almost wholly an organization for professionals, with federal and state funds for such practical endeavors as the study of steam power or the systemization of weights and measures. These were projects that were useful to the expanding nation, but they were carried on largely by the scientific elite in conjunction with government or business. The intelligent artisan had been forgotten.

The development of Harvard presents another story. Primarily a divinity school at the start of the century, Harvard graduated either the sons of established aristocrats or a few deserving, but less wealthy, young men from the countryside. Tuition and costs were fairly low, and the entrance examination was simple. After 1820, members of the rising business elite who made their reputations and their money in the new industries began to look to Harvard as a place where their children might be taught and their own social status confirmed. Costs went up; so did admissions standards. One offshoot of this was the need for wealth and a good preparatory education simply to matriculate. Another was the funding, by the new rich, of buildings, professorships, and specialties. Predictably, the nature of these projects reflected the interests of the donor, such as the Lawrence Scientific School. By 1860, the large majority of Harvard students came from certain families, mostly from Boston, and entered prestigious occupations. While the change insured Harvard adequate funding and community support, it also burdened the school with a reputation for wealthy snobbishness.

Still, beginnings had been made. If Mann's system was unique, it was soon copied. If the lyceums and Sunday schools were informal and only partly successful, they fed the Americans' appetite for more knowledge. If the scientific institutes did not reach the workingman, they did open the way for the proliferation of professional societies later in the century. If colleges were unattainable for most, they were vital for a few. Each in its own way contributed to a new ethos and spirit to extend and organize the spread of knowledge in order to fulfill republican ideals. Both the individual and the community benefited.

REVIVALISM, utopianism, and educational reform were only three of the countless means by which Americans tried to uplift the new nation. For those disgusted with Americans' enormous capacity for cheap whiskey and questionable brandy, temperance societies were formed. Fad diets and water cures were solemnly followed in an effort to purify the soul and the body. Phrenologists turned the search for regeneration inward, exploring bumps on the skull in a perfectly serious attempt to determine the brain's capacity for intelligence and moral judgment. Whatever the cause, there were ample converts. Wherever the converts gathered, a committee would be formed. It was inevitable, then, that the quest for moral purity would turn to the South, and slavery.

EXPANSION AND SECTIONALISM

FOUR

9

The Ambivalent
Society

DURING the first half of the nineteenth century, a romantic legend began to envelop the South. In 1800 the section was one of three loosely defined geographical regions of the United States, no more and no less different in climate, topography, and manners than the others. By 1850 it was the Old South, the solid South, the united South—dominated by slavery and cotton, apparently (although not really) monolithic in its interests, a nation within a nation. The white-columned mansions, the endless rows of cotton dotted with hard-working field slaves, the fierce pride and easy hospitality of the plantation owner had all assumed an almost ethereal, mythical quality. The Old South of legend, wrote Wilbur J. Cash, "was a sort of stage piece out of the eighteenth century, wherein gesturing gentlemen moved soft-spokenly against a background of rose gardens and dueling grounds, through always gallant deeds; and lovely ladies, in farthingales, never for a moment lost that exquisite remoteness which has been the dream of all men and the possession of none." And there were enough examples—tidewater baronies, mostly, built in the eighteenth century—to give the legend force.

The reality was quite different. The South was indeed distinct, as were North and West: the warm, temperate climate—that obvious yet critical element in the development of Southern culture—set the region apart, as did the presence of slavery. But within the South was enough diversity, both of topography and habits and expectations, to render any notion of a monolithic culture almost meaningless. Mountain folk of Tennessee and North Carolina were a breed apart from the cotton planters and tobacco growers of the coastal flatlands, who in turn were different from their counterparts in the Mississippi Valley. Much of the South was starkly primitive, a frontier as little touched as Illinois or the Wisconsin Territory. In these thinly populated areas the mansion and the plantation were absent, as were the cavalier gentlemen and the ladies in crinoline. Elsewhere, in the rough shacks and one-horse farms, the average Southerner cultivated only the soil, not the genteel pursuits of the aristocrat. Most of the South was simply too new for such traditions. Southerners were mobile, brash, perhaps a little crude. What Joseph G. Baldwin, lawyer and storyteller, said of an Alabama friend might be said for all: "Established institutions he looked into as familiarly as a horse's mouth, and with about as much respect for their age."

The long summers and rich soils nourished a society that was every bit as entrepreneurial, as alert to the quick profit and fast sale, as that of the North or West. The Southern economy was exuberantly capitalistic; the Southern farmer, large or small, was a businessman. What he produced, he sold; what he could not (or would not) produce, he bought. Much of this commerce was international. Tobacco, hemp, rice, sugar, and above all cotton were grown in such quantities that they supplied not only domestic needs but a large part of the export trade as well. Cotton alone accounted for about half the value of all American exports from the close of the War of 1812 until the outbreak of the Civil War. The profitability of these crops, in turn, generated a demand for more lands and a restless desire to move. "The new country seemed to be a reservoir," Baldwin wrote of the settlements in the western South, "and every road leading to it a vagrant stream of enterprise and adventure."

But the commercial potential of agriculture so dominated Southern life that other forms of enterprise were neglected. Southern cities, for example, were few and small, and an important element in economic and cultural diversification was thus missing. Most of the major urban centers in the South—such as Charleston or New Orleans—had been founded during the colonial era. They were commercial towns that handled the immense trade in cotton and tobacco, but they contained very little industry—and most of that was of the cottage, or artisan, type. Moreover, Southern cities with few exceptions were located at or near the coast. Away from the seaboard there were no large commercial centers. The boom towns and cities-to-be that dotted the Old Northwest—such as Cincinnati or Detroit—were absent in the South.

In part this resulted from the pattern of Southern transportation. The South was blessed with an ample number of navigable rivers that served the cotton or tobacco trade well enough, but these rivers flowed from the interior to the Gulf or Atlantic coasts. Few connected the region from east to west. The railroads that appeared during the 1840s and 1850s followed the same pattern. Transportation across the region, therefore, was unusually difficult, and the growth of new cities in the interior was slow.

Moreover, the South was overly committed to one crop—cotton. At a time when the North began to industrialize—using, in part, profits from manufacturing Southern cotton—the South remained agricultural. And industry was not the only casualty of this specialization. The transportation network remained poor because the few improvements that were made went primarily to connect plantations to docks and railheads. The dependence on cotton, moreover, made the South nervously sensitive to the fortunes of a single crop. When the market was high and the weather was good, the South flourished. Farmers used the profits to finance more land or more slaves, and the Cotton Kingdom grew. A sudden dip in the world market or a recession at home, however, was instantly calamitous. The Panic of 1819, for example, opened a decade of ruinously low prices during which money became tight and then tighter as planters worked to pay their debts. Often the only recourse was to borrow still more. The few who escaped real hardship were those who grew rice or long-staple cotton (which was of exceptionally high quality and had its own special market), and those who had recently settled new lands where expenses were low and the soil still good. For the rest, hard times closed in.

But every section of the United States experienced cycles of boom and bust; every section was hit hard by the Panic of 1819. What made the South different was the presence of black slavery. At the time of the Panic, slavery in America was two hundred years old, yet its heyday was just beginning. The industrial revolution brought an enormous demand for cotton to supply the textile mills of England and the Northeastern states; as the demand rose, the South's dependency on slavery deepened. Wherever new lands were cleared, slaves and their owners poured in. By 1820 this growth had reached a stage of self-perpetuation. Colonial Southerners had relied heavily on the African slave trade to supply their need for laborers. After the African trade was officially (although not completely) stopped in 1808, planters exploited the natural increase in the black population. Between 1820 and 1860, slaves multiplied at a rate of about 30 percent each decade and produced a cotton crop that doubled every ten years.

Slaves were not uniformly distributed either by ownership or by region. About half of all slaveholders owned four or fewer slaves; three-fourths owned fewer than ten. The really large holdings, however, were concentrated in the hands of a very few: two percent of Southern whites owned half the slaves. There were areas in most Southern states where blacks outnumbered whites two to one; a hundred miles away, still in the same state, nine-tenths of the population or more might be white. And while the number of slaveholders increased with the number of slaves, only a fraction of Southern whites were ever directly connected to the institution. By 1850 slightly under 350,000 persons owned slaves, who totaled ten times that number.

Life for the small slaveholder was hard and far different from that of the large plantation owners. Most were poor. Mark Twain, reminiscing in 1884 about the many "one-horse cotton plantations" in the Mississippi Valley in his childhood, captured their ambience well:

> A rail fence around a two-acre yard; a stile, made out of logs sawed off and up-ended, in steps, like barrels of a different length, to climb over the fence with . . . ; some sickly grass-patches in the big yard, but mostly it was bare and smooth, like an old hat with the nap rubbed off; big double log house for the white folk—hewed logs, with the chinks stopped up with mud or mortar, and these mud-stripes been whitewashed some time or another; round-log kitchen . . . ; log smoke-house back of the kitchen; three little log nigger-cabins in a row t'other side the smoke house; . . . some currant bushes and gooseberry bushes in one place by the fence; outside the fence a garden and a watermelon patch; then the cotton fields begin; and after the fields, the woods.

In such circumstances the farmer, and his wife and children, worked alongside their blacks, suffered from the heat and shivered in the cold. Gentry they were not. If they had time to serve in politics, their offices were likely in the county government. There was simply not enough money and free time to make yearly journeys to Nashville or Montgomery or Washington.

The larger farms and the plantations permitted more leisure, and yet life still remained rough and unrefined. The very wealthiest slaveholders could and often did spend months away from their estates, maintaining town houses in the cities for the fall and spring social seasons and traveling in the North or even Europe for the summer. Most, however, managed their farms personally. They went to town to order supplies, exchange news, and perhaps practice law, but the plantation remained the focus of their lives. Frederick Law Olmsted, who toured the South during the 1850s and reported his observations in the New York *Tribune,* noted a marked difference in the planter's style at home and in town. A Virginia host had purposely remodeled the family home "in the Grecian style" and was "a gentlemen of education," yet his manners on the farm were decidedly informal. "On their plantations," Olmsted wrote, "the Virginia gentlemen seem to drop their full-dress and constrained town habits, and to live a free, rustic, shooting-jacket life." Olmsted was amazed to find that his host had no interest in scientific agriculture and did not care that the endless cycle of growing one crop exhausted the land; he grew only the coarsest grade of tobacco because the finer types required too much attention; he ate starchy, plain food surrounded by four or five foxhounds "grinning or licking their chops" for scraps. All this in a mock-Grecian house. It was on such "estates," however, that slavery reached its peak as an economic system and a form of social organization.

Slavery was profitable. Certainly a worn-out Virginia tobacco plantation was not a thriving concern; the white man who held no slaves or the free black made nothing from the institution; the very lack of economic diversity in the South limited opportunities for everyone. The small slaveholder always hoped for the day when his investment began to pay. More often than not, the very size of that investment plunged him into debt and kept him there. But a planter in new areas could expect a handsome profit. Slavery offered rewards to those able to overcome the initial expense and work the slaves efficiently. That meant hard work for the slaves, of course, but it also required the master to organize his laborers to best advantage.

A large plantation likely employed an overseer, whether the master lived on the estate or not. These overseers might be relatives of the owners, or whites who saw the job either as a career or as a way to earn enough money to start their own plantations. Their treatment of the slaves ranged from decent to abominable. It was the overseer who was most often charged with the task of whipping malcontents and slackers, and the line between ordinary punishment and cruelty was thin. A good overseer respected that line; he recognized that his job was to make the plantation pay, not to beat the slaves into unconsciousness. Not surprisingly, such men were in demand. The rest—and there were all too many—were floaters, moving from one farm to the next, or one state to another, as planters fired them in the wake of slowdowns or outright rebellion.

Beneath the overseer was the black driver. His position on the plantation was at once prestigious and riddled with tension and ambiguity. Drivers were picked for their intelligence and ability to manage their fellow slaves. They were given some rewards not available to the other blacks. Often masters trusted their word more than that of a transient overseer. They were schooled in plantation management. Yet, for all that, they remained slaves. Their duties gave them the complete trust of neither black nor white. An overseer might make the driver punish the hands, and a whip in the hands of a slave was a painful reminder that slavery degraded even the strongest black. Consequently, the driver occupied the most uncomfortable position of all: he was given his job because he was good at it, yet it required him to reinforce the servitude of his own race.

Driver and overseer together were there to see that the crops came in on time. The work was hard. During the long growing season, the hands were in the fields by first light and worked until sundown, with a few minutes off at midday for their meal. At day's end, sacks of cotton had to be weighed, tools put up, and chores done before the slaves could relax for the night. The regimen was especially difficult when the cotton had to be picked. Then schedules were tight; a chance rain might soak the bolls and cost valuable time. If the moon was full and the skies clear, a master might keep his slaves in the fields after dark. Relaxation and sleep were brief.

It must be remembered, however, that the cotton or sugar season did not last the entire year; nor did every slave on the plantation work in the fields. A sane master—and most were that—did not expect children, the elderly or sick, or expectant mothers to plod down the rows of cotton. Moreover, on the large plantations labor was divided and specialized. Older slaves and adolescents would care for the small children; mothers would cook; some males would be carpenters or smiths. During the winter the fields lay fallow, and each slave would work at repairs or at laying up supplies—as corn shucking or hog killing. And there were house servants, whose sole duty was to care for the master and his family.

Slaves demanded and received certain concessions from their masters. When they got them, as they usually did, the plantation ran fairly smoothly. When they did not, work became sloppy and slow; mysterious fires broke out; machinery was broken. A prudent master either gave in or found himself slowly going broke. Most of the slaves' demands were simple and reasonable: to have Sundays free, a holiday and a bonus at Christmas, a garden plot and the right to fish and hunt for meat. Less obvious but equally important was the slave's unspoken insistence that he be adequately fed and clothed, that if he were to be whipped it would not reach the point of extreme cruelty, that his family and his marriage be respected. To make sure that they were being treated fairly, slaves constantly compared the conditions on their own plantation to the descriptions of those on others. As rumors and reports filtered in, a slave could judge whether he had an exceptionally good, merely average, or irresponsibly bad master. In countless subtle ways, he gauged his work accordingly.

American slavery, in short, was not a simple case of domination versus servility. Blacks and whites alike were locked in a system that was a curious blend of entrepreneurialism and paternalism. It could hardly have been otherwise, for the slave was both property and person. As property, he could be sold, exploited, and abused within the limits of the law, as could a horse or mule. As a person, he carried with him human traits, in all their infinite variety. He could be loving or hateful, docile or rebellious, kind or mean. For the master, the task of balancing the two sides of his charge produced a life shot through with ambiguity. One thinks immediately of Jefferson, burdened with the weight of his own words in the Declaration, yet still a slaveholder.

THE Southern slaveholder had always prided himself on his tolerance, even forgiveness, toward his slaves. In the South one seldom heard the word "slave." They were called "hands" or "servants," according to whether they worked outdoors or in the house. The master usually referred to the skilled workers among them by trade, as "my mason," "my blacksmith," "my carpenter," and to the group collectively as "my people" or "the force." These euphemisms masked the essential ambiguity of the master-slave relationship. The slaveholder always emphasized the "my" of slavery; in reality, possession went both ways. The historian U. B. Phillips recognized this in 1918, when he wrote that slaves "were always within the social mind and conscience

of the whites, as the whites in turn were within the mind and conscience of the blacks. . . . This knowledge gave a power all its own.
The general regime was in fact shaped by mutual requirements,
concessions, and understandings, producing reciprocal codes of con-
ventional morality."

To accept this is not to agree with Phillips's further assertion that
slavery was "benevolent in intent and on the whole beneficial in
effect." Undoubtedly a conscientious master genuinely believed that
slavery did the blacks good, as for example the Mississippi planter
who directed his overseer to see that the slaves were "encouraged to
cultivate religious feeling and morality" in order to "elevate" them.
But the same planter also demanded that they be "punished for
. . . profanity, lying, and stealing," and not allowed off the plantation
without a pass. Slaves understood this inherent duality. They responded by forging links among themselves and between themselves
and the whites that bound all in a complex relationship that admitted
no absolutes. Their constant, if subtle, demands, their grief at the
death of a kind master, and their visceral hatred of the whip, their
alternate displays of docility and rebelliousness—all were weapons in
keeping the whites off-balance, in making the responsibility of slaveholding a burden laced with affection, guilt, and fear.

Small wonder, then, that the Southern defense of slavery took many
forms. There was no pat answer to Northern objections or Southern
doubts. To those who charged that slavery was a relic of the barbaric
past, Southerners pointed to the existence of the institution in ancient
Greece and Rome. Classical civilizations had achieved greatness because the slaveholder was free to cultivate the intellect, not spend his
days in worrisome, menial labor. Without slaves, the Parthenon could
not have been built, the pyramids could not have been raised. "We
must recollect," Thomas Roderick Dew proclaimed in 1832, "that the
laws of Lycurgus were promulgated, the sublime eloquence of Demos-
thenes and Cicero was heard, and the glorious achievements of
Epaminondas and Scipio were witnessed, in countries where slavery
existed—without *for one moment* loosening the tie between master
and slave." This idea that slavery encouraged, not retarded, the march
of civilization was given a different basis in 1837 by William Harper
of South Carolina. Slave labor was essential to the production of
cotton, he argued, and "cotton has contributed more than anything
else of later times to the progress of civilization. By enabling the poor

to obtain cheap and becoming clothing, it has inspired a taste for comfort, the first stimulus to civilization."

Other pro-slavery theorists stressed the organic unity of Southern society. Free labor was by nature competitive and insecure. In Britain and France, argued William Gilmore Simms, "millions rise every morning, in doubt where they shall procure the daily bread which shall satisfy the hunger of the next twelve hours." "The free laborer," added Harper, "has few real guarantees from society," and spent a lifetime in miserable alienation. The slave, the planter, the free Southern white, on the other hand, were bound together as a unit. Each played a different role, but each was essential to the organic harmony of the whole. By midcentury George Fitzhugh—a slaveholder of modest means and formidable intellect—expanded the attack on Northern "wage slavery" to a blistering indictment of modern capitalism. Fitzhugh's analysis was socialist, with an odd twist. Capitalism ranged person against person, poor against rich, in a self-defeating system of class warfare. Laborers, he argued, "are at constant war with those above them, asking higher wages but getting lower; ... they are also at war with each other, underbidding to get employment." Slavery solved the problem by uniting the interests of the weak and the rich in a system that used feudal relationships to achieve socialist goals. There was no alienation of labor in the South, no class warfare. "A Southern farm," Fitzhugh concluded, "is the beau ideal of Communism."

The most common defense, however, insisted on the inferiority of the black race. Blacks were assumed to be warm, easygoing, and docile, not calculating, demanding, and aggressive. Set free in white America, they would surely die. Free blacks in the North, exclaimed Dew, "must be considered the most worthless and indolent of the citizens of the United States." This inferiority was not the result of black servitude; it was an inborn trait. Phrenologists—who analyzed a person's qualities by the configuration of bumps on the skull—explained black inferiority as a diminished capacity for thought. Others were more direct. "You can make a nigger work," declared one particularly blunt planter, "but you cannot make him think."

A gentler and more persuasive view combined the organic nature of Southern society with the paternalistic benevolence of the slaveholder. A slave was like a child, human but helpless. He relied on his superiors for protection and for moral guidance. Like all children he needed discipline, which was benevolent even when harsh. He was part of a family that embraced both black and white, and families cared for their own, although their members were not and could not be equal. "Compare his condition with the tenants of the poor houses in the more civilized portions of Europe," John C. Calhoun declared in 1837. "Look at the sick, and the old and infirm slave, on one hand, in the midst of his family and friends, under the kind superintending care of his master and mistress, and compare it with the forlorn and wretched condition of the pauper in the poor house." The implication was clear: slavery was a good, "a positive good." To abolish it was tantamount to destroying the family, with similar results. Chaos, instability, and disorder would follow.

THESE defenses of slavery lacked elaboration and focus before 1820. Circumstances had not yet forced Southerners to turn inward, to contemplate a reasoned justification for the peculiar institution. True, slavery had been challenged in the eighteenth century by a handful of Quaker abolitionists and at the Constitutional Convention of 1787. The Quakers were too few to have much impact, however, and the convention produced compromises that generally favored the South. Before the end of the War of 1812, moreover, the sections were so loosely tied that denunciations of slavery posed no real threat. In fact, Southerners were arguably among the strongest proponents of an integrated, united republic.

In 1819 this attitude began to change quickly. Early that year Congress began debate over a bill that would have admitted Missouri to the Union as a state. All went smoothly and routinely until James Tallmadge, a representative from New York, offered an amendment that would have freed, at age twenty-one, all persons born into slavery in the new state after the date of its admission. The method proposed was essentially the same that had been used to free slaves in the Northern states, where it was commonly assumed that slavery was a dying institution. The amendment was debated briefly and adopted along with the rest of the bill. But in the Senate the slavery restriction was dropped, and the bill died in conference on the final day of the session.

By the time debate resumed, nine months later, both Southerners and Northerners had had time to reflect on the implications of the Tallmadge amendment. The central question was no longer the admission of a state, but the nature of the union among all the states and the place of slavery within that union. The arguments for and against slavery were surprisingly sophisticated and would be repeated for the next four decades. James W. Taylor of New York, for example, delivered an eloquent and passionate synopsis of the antislavery argument: slavery was a burden and a curse; Southerners themselves had often said so. It ran against the principles of democracy and the laws of God. If Congress failed to eliminate slavery in Missouri, Taylor pleaded, "shall we not furnish some apology for doubting our sincerity when we deplore its existence?" Congress had to prohibit the spread of slavery in order to demonstrate its commitment to republican institutions. Moreover, slavery was not even economically desirable; free labor was more productive and deserved encouragement. "If slavery shall be tolerated," Taylor warned, "the country will be settled by rich planters, with their slaves. If it shall be rejected, the emigrants [to the new territories] will consist of the poorer and more laborious classes. If it be true that the prosperity and happiness of a country ought to constitute the grand object of its legislators, I cannot hesitate for a moment which species of population deserves most to be encouraged by the laws we may pass." In one speech Taylor set down the essential elements of the attack on slavery: the moral obligation to purge the country of a great evil; the economic superiority of free labor; the responsibility of a republican government to encourage and facilitate the progress of its independent citizens.

The reply of Charles Pinckney of South Carolina was also eloquent and succinct, appealing to God, economics, and states' rights. Slavery, lines of dominance and servitude, existed by divine decree. To argue that slavery was "against the law of God" controverted the whole of world history back to the time of Abraham (who, Pinckney noted, had owned slaves himself). Furthermore, any attempt to restrict or abolish slavery threatened the economic structure of the South and, ultimately, the entire nation. Southerners would lose not only their capital investment in slaves, Pinckney warned, but also "the value of the lands they cultivate will be diminished in all cases one half, and in many they will become wholly useless." Finally, the Tallmadge amendment struck at the rights of Southerners as defined in the Constitution. Northerners simply did not realize the implications of the bill. "Reposing at a great distance, in safety, in the full enjoyment of all their federal and state rights, unattacked in either, or in the

individual rights," Pinckney warned, "can they, with indifference
. . . risk, in the remotest degree, the consequences which this measure
may produce?" Thus, any attack on slavery, however minor or peripheral, must be resisted to avoid setting a precedent "of the most alarming nature . . . For, should succeeding Congresses continue to push
it, there is no knowing to what length it may be carried." The result
would undoubtedly be civil war.

In the end, both sides agreed to compromise. Missouri was admitted with slavery, while Maine was simultaneously brought into the
Union as a free state. At the same time, slavery was forbidden to enter
all other territory acquired by the Louisiana Purchase lying north of
36° 30" latitude—the line between Missouri and the Arkansas Territory. The two new states were the twenty-third and twenty-fourth,
and their simultaneous admissions maintained the even balance between free states and slave. Thereafter, states were admitted in pairs,
until the annexation of Texas posed the sharp question of extending
slavery into lands not acquired by the Louisiana Purchase. For a time,
the North–South balance was scrupulously maintained.

BUT Southern fears continued to mount. The Missouri controversy
shook the South's faith in the integrity and goodwill of the rest of the
nation; during the 1820s a series of blows—real and imagined—isolated the section even more. In June 1822, an abortive slave rebellion
in Charleston stunned and horrified whites throughout the South.
American slavery had been remarkably free of the insurrections and
revolts that ripped through Brazil and the Caribbean—the most successful and fearsome of which occurred in the French colony of Saint
Domingue in 1791. That had led to the creation of the black republic
of Haiti. The threat of black violence was always present in the
Southern mind, and the news that Denmark Vesey, a free mulatto,
had planned and almost executed an attack on the city of Charleston
was devastating. Vesey had recruited and armed a small group of
slaves, some of them servants in Charleston's finest homes, before
being betrayed by one of his number. Vesey and thirty-five other
blacks were promptly hanged, and evidence was uncovered that he
had read a copy of an antislavery speech delivered in the Senate
during the Missouri debates. If a single speech could incite faithful
house slaves to rebellion, Southerners reasoned, what would happen
if the North made a concerted effort to restrict or even abolish slavery?

Economic worries intensified their concern. At the time of the Missouri controversy, slavery represented a capital investment of $300,000,000. This investment could not be liquidated or transferred to other forms of enterprise, as New England had turned from shipping to manufacturing during the War of 1812. For slavery to pay off, both the price of cotton and the volume of cotton production had to remain high, and that meant expanding the Cotton Kingdom into new lands as soils wore out and profits declined in the older regions. Anything that threatened to upset the productivity of the slaves or limit the availability of lands struck at the very heart of the Southern economy.

The tariff issue only compounded the problem. Before 1819—when prices were high and debts were low—Southerners were eager to have American factories compete on an equal footing with those of Europe: Calhoun especially had supported the tariffs of 1816 and 1818. The Panic, however, obliterated Southern profits and drew a hard line between the self-interest of the South and the needs of the manufacturers. Since the industries that demanded protection were located almost exclusively in the North, Southerners began to view the tariff not as an integral element in the American System but as a malicious device by which one region could grow rich by feeding off another. The South made its money—what little there seemed to be of it—by competing successfully in the export trade. The North, unable to do the same thing, would use the tariff to make the South a captive customer to Northern factories. Thus, an economic question turned into a sectional confrontation. When, in 1824, the North and West demanded higher duties to encourage industrial development, the South resisted fiercely. Tariffs were raised anyway, and so was the level of suspicion and sectional distrust. Worse still was the "Tariff of Abominations," passed in 1828, which imposed even higher duties.

Beyond economics, yet closely entwined with it, was the growing role of the federal government. The admission of Missouri brought into sharp focus a question that would increasingly disturb the Southerners for years to come. The unsettled West was vast, but sure to be populated as time went by. Unlike the states already in the Union, territories were under the absolute control of the national government. There were no state laws to challenge or divide federal rule, no local laws to protect the right to own slaves. Territorial policy was formulated in Washington, where a simple majority in both houses could, with the concurrence of the President, legalize slavery, limit it, or prohibit it. Already the free states commanded a majority in the House and might ultimately do so in the Senate, unless the ratio of free states to slave was carefully balanced. The same arithmetic might produce a Northern President unfriendly to the extension of slavery and forever seal the West to the expansion of Southern institutions. And, again, who could guarantee that the opponents of slavery would be satisfied with a free West? Might they also turn their attack on the South itself?

There were other disturbing signs that the federal government was going too far in assuming control over national affairs. In March 1824, while the tariff bill was still being considered, the Supreme Court greatly extended federal control over interstate trade. For years the heirs of Robert Fulton and Robert Livingston had enjoyed a state-chartered monopoly over steamship navigation on the Hudson, but in *Gibbons* v. *Ogden* the Court, led by Marshall, invalidated the monopoly. The lower reaches of the river, and the bay into which it emptied, were declared interstate waters subject to commercial regulation by the federal government. The ruling limited the power of the states to regulate trade and gave a timely boost to business expansion, particularly since Congress was generally reluctant to intrude its powers into such matters and preferred to let nature, and enterprise, run its course. But the philosophical implications of the decision were disturbing to Southerners. If Washington could interfere in the powers of the states—even if only in theory—it could easily direct its energies to other forms of commerce, including the domestic slave trade.

It was imperative, then, to interpose some kind of protection for the slaveholder against the awesome potential power of the federal government. Here Southerners faced a dilemma. Federal power was based on the exercise of public opinion, the very foundation of republican rule. Every census revealed that the free states were outstripping the slave states in population and, thus, in the number of voters. The arithmetic of demographic growth terrified the South and forced it to reexamine the origins of majority rule. It was the same problem that afflicted every democracy in every age—the inevitable tension between the exercise of personal freedoms and the order imposed by authority—only this time narrowed to a matter of sectional and cultural survival.

10

Half Slave, Half Free

I take it for granted that the present question is a mere preamble," noted John Quincy Adams at the height of the Missouri controversy, "—the title page to a great tragic volume." Between 1828 and 1840 the pages were filled in rapidly. During Andrew Jackson's two terms, the sectional tensions that had lain restless but dormant after the Missouri Compromise erupted into open conflict. It was not a battle with two clearly defined sides, like that of opposing armies in the field. Rather, the sectional struggle was a shifting maze of alliances and counteralliances in which each side was wracked by internal divisions. Moreover, confrontation was often sparked by issues or events that, by themselves, were minor in comparison to the furor they generated. A tariff bill, an isolated act of violence, the appearance of a newspaper—these and other events provoked extreme reactions in every part of the nation. And the entire struggle was waged in the context of an emerging party system that itself depended on sectional harmony for its survival.

There was an eerie quality to sectional strife in the 1830s. American and foreign observers alike were perplexed that a republic which seemed so unified should be torn by sectional problems, particularly those that dealt with black servitude. White Americans cared little for blacks; racism was almost a reflex, an automatic reaction. It was doubly puzzling that the slavery issue should spill over into matters that posed no clear threat to the peculiar institution. "The sectional hatred, if not an abstraction, is founded mainly on abstractions," commented one observer. What was forgotten in this analysis was the highly moralistic tone American nationalism had assumed over the years. Americans were strident in their conviction that the United States represented the best possible form of social order, a model for the entire world. Their achievements in expanding the republic and giving it structure and interconnection were considerable. But as the republic drew closer together through enterprise, transportation, and political machinery, Americans discovered that they still had not reached a consensus over the moral content of their mission. Slavery, being ultimately and irreducibly a moral issue, made the disparities obvious and—in the end—intolerable.

IN 1828, as the controversy over the Tariff of Abominations reached its peak, John C. Calhoun sensed an impending crisis, one that—if not confronted and resolved—would seriously jeopardize the existence of Southern culture in the new nation. Calhoun was deeply concerned over the consequences that the passage of the bill would have on his native section; he was sincerely convinced that the South could not withstand higher prices on manufactured goods. But Calhoun had that rare ability to look beyond immediate issues and search for a wider, and in this case more troubling, context. He was an intense, disciplined thinker, perhaps even a genius, with a mole's capacity for digging under intellectual edifices to discover the nature of their foundations. To him, the central issue in the tariff struggle was not economics or convenience, but power—its origins, its uses, and its limits in a federal republic. The implications of the tariff bill disturbed him and moved him to prepare a defense of Southern rights against the encroachment of majority rule. The result was a pamphlet, published anonymously in 1828, entitled the *South Carolina Exposition and Protest.* In it, and in a public elaboration of it delivered at Fort Hill, South Carolina, in 1831, Calhoun forged the ideological core of Southern sectionalism for decades to come.

The heart of Calhoun's argument was a brilliantly perverse interpretation of the nature of sovereignty in a federal republic. Calhoun was a devoted student of John Locke, the seventeenth-century English philosopher and political theorist who had postulated that all governments were but compacts among sovereigns. As such, Locke had argued, they existed at the pleasure of those sovereigns, who could amend them or even abolish them whenever they became out of touch or repugnant to the contracting parties. Thus far Calhoun agreed, and thus far he was in accord with accepted American political philosophy. But too many Americans, Calhoun claimed, had misread Locke. They equated sovereignty—and thus the formation of the federal government—with the people as a whole. To Calhoun this assumption was a grievous mistake. "The people" lived in states, acted through states, and expressed their will through the medium of states, which functioned as "sovereign and independent communities." In 1787 they had delegated the creation of the federal republic to these states. Thus, the federal government "emanated from the people of the States, forming distinct political communities, and acting in their separate and sovereign capacity, and not from all of the people forming one aggregate political community."

The emphasis was on "distinct." Calhoun realized, even rejoiced, that the South was different from the rest of the nation. He also recognized that its institutions placed it in the minority. If sovereignty rested in the will of the people as a whole—the "aggregate" political community—then the South would be helpless to defend itself from the power of majority rule. If sovereignty was located in the states, however, there would be some interposing authority between Southern culture and the encroachments of federal power. His model here was Georgian England, where authority was mixed and divided among three distinct bodies—monarch, Lords, and Commons. Each was sovereign to itself; each retained its special identity. The English system (which any perceptive observer might have noted was changing rapidly by 1828) gave "each co-estate the right to judge of its powers, with a negative or veto on the acts of the others, in order to protect against encroachments the interests it particularly represents." The same balance existed among the various states of the Union. The authority of these states was absolute; that of the national government—their creation—was limited. If it were otherwise, the "unrestrained will of a majority" of the aggregate could trample on the rights of the minority.

Beneath this tortured prose lay a graceful simplicity and a lethal threat. As the power of public opinion grew—particularly now that Jackson and Van Buren were perfecting means of marshaling it and implementing it—the Southern need to offset the power of the majority increased. Calhoun had devised the ideal solution, states' rights. Sovereigns had rights that no other sovereign could abridge. States were sovereigns; one could not tamper with the rights of another. But this logic, taken to its end, raised an unsettling prospect. A govern-

ment was a compact among sovereigns. If the compact became unworkable, each sovereign—any sovereign—had the right, the duty in
fact, to nullify it and start over.

IN 1828 neither Calhoun nor any other Southerner was prepared to
go that far. There was still hope for a new, lower tariff, and no one
had seriously attacked the institution of slavery. Over the next five
years, however, events pushed the South deeper into fear and farther
down the road to disunion. In 1829 David Walker, a free black living
in Boston but born a slave in North Carolina, published *An Appeal
to the Colored Citizens of the World,* in which he urged slaves to armed
rebellion. "The whites want slaves . . . ," he wrote, "but some of them
will curse the day they ever saw us. . . . They shall have enough of
making slaves of [us], and butchering and murdering us in the manner
which they have." The pamphlet went through three editions before
Walker died, reputedly by violence, in 1830. In January 1831, William
Lloyd Garrison published the first issue of *The Liberator,* a passion-
ately abolitionist newspaper that branded slavery as a moral sin. Eight
months later came the chilling news that sixty blacks—led by an
eloquent and literate slave, Nat Turner—had murdered almost that
many whites in the area surrounding Southampton, Virginia. The
revolt was quickly suppressed and the offending slaves executed, but
the fear remained. Slave codes were tightened, curfews were imposed,
and the state of Georgia, making an unwarranted connection between
the massacre and the appearance of *The Liberator,* offered $5,000 for
Garrison's life.

To make matters worse, it was becoming increasingly apparent that
Calhoun's interpretation of the origin of the Union and the limits of
federal power was not acceptable outside the South. The issue reached
the Senate floor in 1830 when Robert Y. Hayne, also of South Carolina, attempted to use Calhoun's logic to defeat proposed federal
restrictions on the sale of public lands. The question at hand was
entirely unrelated to Southern rights and institutions, except as an
effort, by Hayne, to forge an alliance with congressmen from the
frontier. But Hayne recklessly asserted that the restrictions were part
of a plot by Northern capitalists who wanted to close the West to the
natural migration of laborers and thus, by "adding strength to the
federal government . . . to regulate the whole industry and capital of
the country." He further implied, as Calhoun had done, that the states

might have to use their authority to defeat the conspiracy. This drew a stinging rebuttal from Daniel Webster of Massachusetts. "If the government of the United States be the agent of the State governments, then they may control it . . ." he declared; "if it be the agent of the people, then the people alone can control it, restrain it, modify or reform it." In a concise affirmation of national unity, Webster made his views known. "We are all agents of the same power, the people. The general government and the State governments derive their authority from the same source." And Webster made it clear that he saw no inherent conflict between a strong federal union and individual rights. "Liberty *and* Union," he thundered, "now and forever, one and inseparable."

The Webster–Hayne debate brought Calhoun—and the South— into direct confrontation with Andrew Jackson. Calhoun's authorship of the *Exposition* was an open secret in Washington, and so was the origin of Hayne's remarks. Jackson did not like Calhoun, nor did he subscribe to Calhoun's philosophy. The President was an ardent nationalist who believed, with Webster, that the federal government acted for all the people directly and not through the medium of the states. Certain matters, such as internal improvements, might be served better by using the resources of the states rather than those of the national government, but this did not give the states supremacy over federal policies. To reduce the activities of the federal government was not to reduce its authority, and he, Jackson, was the voice of that authority. At a dinner in April 1830, the President confronted Calhoun publicly and directly. "Our Federal Union," he said in a toast to the memory of Thomas Jefferson, "—it must be preserved."

There was a nightmare quality to the convergence of these events. Walker's *Appeal,* Garrison's *Liberator,* the Nat Turner rebellion, the Webster–Hayne debate, and Jackson's challenge—all suggested that the security of Southern institutions was deteriorating. Southern fears mounted when, in December 1831, the British West Indies were torn by a massive slave rebellion that dwarfed Turner's attempt. For years, the West Indies had been subject to the same kind of pressure from British abolitionists that Garrison represented in the United States. The next month, January 1832, the Virginia House of Burgesses killed a proposal for gradual emancipation by one vote, and later that year Thomas Roderick Dew, professor of political economy at William and Mary, published the first comprehensive defense of slavery as a positive good. It was another point of no return in the slavery controversy.

At that moment the tariff issue flared again. In 1832 a new act was proposed, which did place some additional items on the free list but retained prohibitive duties on essential goods such as wool, iron, and hemp. Southerners were in economic distress. Cotton exported in 1831 had brought an average price of 9.1 cents a pound; the Charleston market had registered an even lower 8.3 cents. The prospect of higher costs for imported goods only added to the burden. While economists of the day—even Southern ones—knew that a lower tariff by itself would not relieve the situation, Southerners reacted with anger and outrage. The tariff had become an emotional issue—the channel through which other frustrations flowed—and was not to be resolved by facts or figures. This opposition notwithstanding, the new tariff was passed by substantial margins in both houses of Congress and was signed into law by Jackson on July 14, 1832. It was not warmly received in the South.

In South Carolina the issue was so critical that it threatened the Union. Several factors contributed to the growing hysteria. One was South Carolina's stubborn adherence to the old political ways. Real political power was exercised by what amounted to a club that largely excluded Charleston merchants and nonslaveholders. This ruling combination of tidewater aristocrats and up-country slaveholders had no intention of submitting its positions of power and influence to an open canvass. Indeed, Presidential electors were still selected by the state legislature until after the Civil War. To tidewater slaveholders, who grew mostly long-staple, high-quality cotton, which had its own market in England and was not severely hurt by the depression of the 1820s, the tariff was not a great economic burden, but it did represent federal interference in their way of life. To up-country slaveholders who grew short-staple cotton, which declined radically in price during the 1820s, the tariff was little better than legalized theft.

The only division of opinion in South Carolina was between those who wanted to nullify the tariff and those who believed that peaceful protest would eventually persuade Congress to compromise. The latter group, called Unionists, was led by Joel Roberts Poinsett. The former was led by Calhoun. Calhoun had taken over direction of the Nullifiers early in 1832, before the tariff bill actually passed, in order to use his prestige (he was still Vice President) to force the Administration to change its tariff policy. When that effort failed, he turned his talents to the fall elections, hoping to prevent Unionists from winning any seats in the state legislature. He was successful. Although the Nullifiers won only a narrow victory in the Charleston city elections, they swept all before them in the state at large. Governor James Hamilton, Jr., himself a Nullifier, immediately called a special session of the legislature, and the newly elected majority authorized the calling of a state convention. After a brief, explosive campaign, delegates were chosen who were overwhelmingly in favor of nullifying the tariff of 1832. The convention met at Columbia on November 19, by which date South Carolinians knew that Andrew Jackson—however much they might detest him—would be President of the United States for another four years.

The Presidential election was overshadowed in South Carolina by the nullification controversy. The state convention, by a vote of almost six to one, declared the tariffs of 1828 and 1832 illegal and forbade anyone in the state to collect any duties under their provisions. The single loophole in this tightly worded decision was the effective date. The Ordinance of Nullification was not to be operative until February 1, 1833 (and was later further postponed), thus giving Congress ample time to act on the objectionable laws. The legislature then chose the tactful and conservative Hayne for governor and elected Calhoun to the seat thus vacated in the Senate. To accept the seat, Calhoun resigned the Vice Presidency of the United States.

Jackson's reaction was typical and sure. On December 10, 1832, he issued a proclamation that was at once a smashing attack on the Nullifiers and a synopsis of his own views of the powers of the Presidency. To the argument that the states could negate federal laws because the Constitution was the creation of the states, he repeated the essence of Webster's reply to Hayne. "The people of the United States formed the Constitution," he declared, not the states. "The terms used in its construction show it to be a Government in which the people of all the States, collectively, are represented." The word that stood out, and the one that separated Jackson's nationalism from Calhoun's, was "collectively." To read the Constitution in any other way would make the federal government a helpless appendage of the states, with no powers of its own. This would lead to chaos. Jackson admitted that the tariff, or any other law, for that matter, might work special hardships on a particular state or section. But redress for unjust laws must be sought through legal means. Otherwise, the Constitution became an "airy bubble that must be blown away by the first breath of disaffection."

It was bad logic, then, to endorse nullification, and treason to proclaim nullification's offspring, secession. Such sentiments struck at the very unity of the federal republic. "To say that any State may at pleasure secede from the Union is to say that the United States are not a nation," Jackson declared flatly. And the President concluded with a warning: if South Carolina persisted in its ill-advised course, it would pay a terrible price. "A compact is an agreement or binding obligation," he warned. Whoever violated its terms invited punishment, and Jackson promised that the punishment would be swift and severe.

Nor did Jackson leave any doubt as to his own course in meeting the crisis. "We are *one people* in the choice of President and Vice-President," he affirmed. But he mentioned no other offices. The President and his second were the only persons chosen by the collective voice of the nation. Neither senators, representatives, nor any other official had such a national base of support. It was Jackson's duty, then, to protect the entire nation from its enemies, and he promised to do so strenuously. "The laws of the United States must be executed," he concluded. "I have no discretionary power on the subject; my duty is emphatically pronounced in the Constitution." The die was cast.

The crisis moved rapidly to a conclusion. Jackson demanded power to force collection of the tariff in South Carolina, by arms if necessary. To some, this reeked of despotism. The governor of Virginia pronounced the President a "tyrant who acknowledges no law but his own will." But whatever their personal opinions of Jackson, all agreed that he was sincere in his threat. Sensing imminent civil war, Congress scurried to fashion a compromise. A new tariff that reduced the duties of 1832 gradually over a ten-year period to a uniform 20 percent was proposed by Clay, accepted by Calhoun, and quickly passed. But a Force Bill was also enacted as a grim reminder that sovereignty lay where the President said it did—with the national government. Jackson signed both bills on March 2, 1833, as his first term of office was coming to its stormy close.

Nullifiers in South Carolina responded lamely but defiantly. They withdrew their ordinance nullifying the tariff, then proceeded to nullify the Force Bill. Jackson, having won, ignored the gesture in silent contempt. More galling to the South Carolinians, however, was the lack of support they received from the rest of the South. Their frenetic pleas to their sister states had met, at best, mixed receptions. No other state possessed the proper blend of elements that produced the special hysteria infecting South Carolina. No other state had such a high concentration of slaves, had been hurt so severely by the depression, or had developed such a close alliance between old and new slaveholders that fostered a unity in fear. South Carolina was, for the time being, unique and alone. For the moment, the great debate between states' rights and majority rule was over.

IN another sense, however, it was just beginning. No one, North or South, seriously believed that the tariff issue was the sole spark to the nullification controversy. Few believed that the weird logic of states' rights was designed simply to resist the growth of federal power. The central issue, as everyone knew, was slavery and the concomitant problem of racial adjustment in a society that generally regarded blacks as inferior. Before 1820 any widespread debate on the subject was infrequent and short-lived. But the Missouri Compromise and the long decade of conflict that followed it unearthed a growing unease in the North over the presence of black servitude in a white democratic republic. The nullification controversy brought the problem into the open.

Northerners were generally hostile to blacks. In several respects their racism was as complete as that of a South Carolina plantation owner. The free Northern black lived a life of poverty and discrimination. He was crowded into slums, given the most menial and worst-paying jobs, and imprisoned for the slightest offense. The very cheapness of his labor provoked hostility from poor whites, who competed with him for the same jobs. In literature and the arts his blackness symbolized savagery and evil. Even his accomplishments went unheralded. Few whites acknowledged the contributions of Benjamin Banneker, the mathematician and astronomer who helped L'Enfant lay out the city of Washington. Nor did they concede the genius of Ira Frederick Aldridge, who had emigrated to England to become one of the greatest Shakespearean actors of the age. Moreover, they were impervious to the artistic expressions of black culture—particularly black music, which by 1830 had already emerged as a complex and subtle blend of African melodies and Protestant lyrics. Racial prejudice was immediately evident in politics: as late as 1850, New York and Ohio still required property bonds from blacks wishing to vote, and courts prohibited them from testifying against whites. Not even Massachusetts had integrated its schools.

Slavery, however, was not a Northern institution, and here the Northern mind made a careful distinction. It was one thing to regard blacks as an inferior race; it was quite another to treat them as property. There was something wrong—and, given the prevailing racism, it was often difficult to say exactly what—in allowing a system of forced human servitude to flourish in a democracy. Northerners were outraged by woodcuts and engravings of the auction block, the lash, the slave mother pleading for her child; these were visual testaments to the institution's potential for cruelty. More immediately, they were vexed by the presence of an actual auction block in Washington, D.C., within sight of the Capitol. Nor did Northerners welcome slave catchers who came to Boston or crossed the Ohio in search of fugitive slaves. The fugitive-slave law of 1793 entitled a master or his agent to capture a runaway—by force if necessary—on no better evidence than the slave owner's oath. Free blacks were often victims of the system, and the North responded with a series of personal liberty laws, beginning with Pennsylvania's in 1825, that complicated the fugitive-slave law and made the master's task more difficult.

More galling was the political influence of the Southern states. Of the first five Presidents, only one—John Adams—had not been from the South (had not, in fact, been from Virginia). Northern states were constantly forced to adjust their needs to the demands of the slaveholding states, especially in the Senate, where Southerners exercised extraordinary influence. Power used in this manner was power abused, and raised once again the specter of conspiracy. The Revolution had been fought to rid the country of the conspiratorial power of George III and his courtiers. Radical Jeffersonians ridiculed Federalists as an elite clan united by wealth and acting in concert. Antimasons saw a conspiracy among Masons, and so on. The South was an easy target for similar fears. Slaveholders, living lives of ease off the forced labor of others, possessed the leisure, the wealth, and the community of interests to force their will on the hardworking republicans of the North and West. The Missouri controversy had demonstrated their power and raised the prospect of an endless struggle between the many and the few.

The unintentioned effect of the Missouri debates was to shift some of this anger away from the political power of the South and concentrate it on slavery. Slavery was the link that united Southerners; slavery was the economic system on which their political influence was based. The more the South became embroiled in political conflict with the rest of the nation, the more Northerners began to question the place of slavery in the republic. By the time of the nullification controversy, a word was beginning to be heard in the North that had rarely been used earlier: abolition.

BEFORE 1820, most plans for ending slavery involved some form of gradual emancipation. Antislavery theorists of the eighteenth and early nineteenth centuries assumed that slavery, being an institution that had developed over countless centuries, could not be obliterated overnight without severe social disruption and possibly chaos. Moreover, it was also assumed that blacks were so racially inferior that they could never compete successfully in a white society; it would be unfair and unchristian simply to turn them loose in an environment for which they were not suited. Thus, the most popular plan for emancipation was colonization, the gradual resettling of blacks either in the Caribbean or in Africa. Prominent Americans, including Jefferson and Henry Clay, subscribed to the idea, which persisted in one form or another until the Civil War. A few attempts were even made—the most successful being the African colony of Liberia. There were two crippling weaknesses to the plan. Slaveholders were reluctant to endorse it and would have demanded compensation anyway—a project that would have cost hundreds of millions of dollars. And the number of available ships to transport blacks could not handle even the yearly increase in the slave population, much less the several million who already labored in servitude.

After 1820 a small and initially unconnected cluster of Americans began to favor a more direct approach. In January 1821, Benjamin Lundy published his first issue of the *Genius of Universal Emancipation.* Lundy was a Quaker reformer who learned to hate slavery while apprenticed to a saddler in Virginia. Passionate, articulate, and erratic, Lundy first published his paper in Ohio, then Tennessee, and finally in Baltimore. He was a gadfly and an irritant, not an original thinker, and for most of its fourteen years the *Genius* searched for places to colonize slaves in Haiti, Texas, and Canada. But Lundy did make one lasting contribution to abolitionism: in 1829 he hired, as associate editor, William Lloyd Garrison.

Thin, owlish, and intense, Garrison brought unflinching dedication and an acerbic, biting style to the antislavery cause. Arrested and imprisoned for libel while working with Lundy in Baltimore, he returned to his native Massachusetts to establish his own newspaper, *The Liberator,* in which he made it clear that gradual emancipation, colonization, or any other scheme to compensate the South for releasing its slaves, was not only inadequate but morally wrong. Abolition —direct and immediate—was Garrison's only goal, and for almost thirty-five years, from 1831 until the passage of the Thirteenth Amendment in 1865, he never moved from his course. "I am in earnest," Garrison wrote in the first issue, "I will not equivocate—I will not excuse—I will not retreat a single inch—and *I will be heard."* He was.

Garrison was the most vocal and controversial spokesman for a group that achieved national prominence with surprising speed during the early 1830s. Apart from Garrison, the dominant figure in the antislavery movement during the early years was Theodore Dwight Weld, who had been converted to revivalistic religion by Charles Grandison Finney. Weld applied techniques of revivalism and moral persuasion to convert Arthur and Lewis Tappan—both wealthy New York merchants who became major financial contributors to the cause. James G. Birney, a former slaveowner, was also one of Weld's protégés; Birney had emancipated his blacks upon being persuaded of the moral sin of slavery. Women participated in the cause. Angelina and Sarah Grimké hated slavery so much that they left their native South Carolina to go on the lecture circuit; Elizabeth Cady Stanton spread the word with her husband, Henry. Diverse, combative, often eloquent, these and others formed the core of a movement that dominated American reform for over a generation.

No single explanation accounts for the sudden emergence of such an articulate and radical group. Many were from New England or that part of the West colonized by New Englanders. In these areas, the old Puritan concept of the visible saints—caretakers of public morality—fused with a more robust and personal strain of individual revivalism to produce a preoccupation with issues of the conscience. Some came from families that had declined in prestige and social influence as the status of parvenus and unprincipled entrepreneurs rose; these needed an outlet, a moral one, to reassert their leadership.

All certainly felt alienated and bewildered by the complex changes occurring in nineteenth-century American culture. Above all, they were men and women who, balancing the twin needs of liberty and authority in a democratic society, concluded that the slave enjoyed too little of the former and submitted to too much of the latter.

Whatever their motives, abolitionists were superb organizers. In 1831 Garrison helped form the Massachusetts Antislavery Society; two years later—along with Weld, Birney, and the Tappans—he founded the American Anti-Slavery Society. A declaration adopted at its first meeting ended with a call to organize, "if possible, in every city, town and village in our land." They determined to "send forth agents," print broadsides and pamphlets, circulate newspapers, and enlist the churches. The techniques were borrowed *in toto* from Finney's revivals and the Protestant benevolent associations, and abolitionists employed them with zeal and inspiration—even occasional eccentricity. One "agent," who decided that the morning service at a New England church was the ideal platform from which to spread his views, found himself unceremoniously picked up and dumped into a nearby stable. He got up, praised the Lord, and kept the coat he was wearing—unwashed, of course—for years as he continued his rounds.

Zealots are predictably combative, and abolitionists were no exception. They quarreled not only with the world around them but with each other, fighting freely and often over such issues as women's rights, pacifism, and tactics. The American Anti-Slavery Society survived intact only six brief years, splitting in 1839 into two wings. One, led by Garrison and keeping the old name, clung tenaciously to the tactics of moral persuasion. The other, led by the Tappans and calling itself the American and Foreign Anti-Slavery Society, was more conservative—particularly on the explosive question of women's rights—and ultimately more congenial to political action. Many of its members joined Birney in forming the Liberty Party in 1840. Those six years of unity, however, witnessed the founding and articulation of an antislavery appeal that forced the question of emancipation before an unwilling country and a horrified South.

AT the core of the abolitionist appeal was a belief in immediate emancipation. Born from revivalistic religion, immediatism explicitly rejected the traditional view that emancipation was best accomplished gradually. The evangelical Protestantism of the early nineteenth century that many abolitionists espoused had replaced the formal, institutional bias of both Calvinism and rationalism with a simple, direct religion of the heart. All men and women were, according to this theology, born into a solemn compact with God, whose salvation they accepted or rejected in a spontaneous, unrehearsed act of conversion. Since each person possessed this moral capacity, neither race nor wealth, birth nor station, prevented anyone from finding redemption. In Weld's terms, every individual was a "free moral agent," capable of determining the fate of his own soul. Abolitionists thus erased the racial barrier that had prevented blacks from entering the ranks of the elect.

Further, anyone who prevented another from fulfilling his compact with God was guilty of sin. The slaveholder, placing his own temporal authority between God and the slave in an "audacious usurpation of the Divine prerogative," obstructed the slave's ability to find salvation. The master was in effect a thief, for he robbed the black of his right to choose between heaven and hell. "He who robs his fellow man of this," Weld charged, "tramples upon right, subverts justice, outrages humanity, unsettles the foundations of human safety, and sacrilegiously assumes the prerogative of God." Moreover, since it was absurd to think that one who stole money or goods should be compensated for giving up his ill-gotten gains, it was ridiculous to pay the slaveholder for returning the souls of his slaves to their rightful owners. Immediate emancipation, then, was "nothing more or less . . . than immediate repentance, applied to this particular sin."

Immediatism also gave the abolitionists a tactical advantage in pressing their case. All previous attempts at abolishing slavery had foundered in the wake of public indifference and Southern hostility. By defining slavery as a sin, however, abolitionists made the peculiar institution a moral—not a political or economic—issue. Economic and political problems were subject to compromise; moral questions were not. Abolitionists were thus able to simplify their appeal and keep it directed at the conscience, not the intellect.

Furthermore, immediatism allowed abolitionists to advance their most controversial tenet: that blacks were created equal with whites. Gradual emancipation tacitly implied that the slave was what the slaveholder said he was, naturally inferior. All forms of gradualism singled out the "most fit," the "best" slaves, and prepared them, one at a time, for eventual emancipation. The rest were presumably not ready to exercise the responsibilities and privileges of freedom. This the immediatists could not accept. To free one soul while leaving the rest to languish in darkness was a crime and an insult against all. It violated the basic premise that all men were created in the image of God. No abolitionist was so naïve as to think that 300,000 Southerners would emancipate their slaves at once. They did realize, however, that those who advocated gradual emancipation assumed the inferiority of persons "having a dark complexion." "Can you change a man's opinions and practice on a subject," asked Amos A. Phelps, "so long as you yield him the main and fundamental principle in debate?"

The religious appeal of the immediatist argument drew strength from the intellectual legacy of the American Revolution. In arguing that blacks were endowed with the same rights to life, liberty, and property as whites, for example, abolitionists had merely carried Jefferson's preface to the Declaration to its logical end. All men meant all men. Similarly, in arguing that God was the ultimate authority over man, they echoed many of the Revolutionary debates over the nature of power, again taking them beyond the confines of political and social institutions and infusing them with a spirit of moral urgency. Repeatedly, they compared their own struggle with that of the Founders, who, they noted, had fought a foreign oppressor with "physical resistance . . . the mortal encounter." Eschewing wars, abolitionists battled a more sinister form of tyranny with love, "the opposition of moral purity to moral corruption."

Abolitionists clung to the Revolutionary concept that power corrupts. Within each person raged a struggle between the intent to use power for good and the tendency to use it for evil. Slavery, being a relationship of "absolute, irresponsible power on one side, and entire subjection on the other," encouraged the slaveholder to give free rein to his basest passions. The abolitionist catalogue of slavery's cruelties —which ranged from rape and brutality to lynching and murder— comprised a morbid list of the excesses to which any person would go when freed from restraint. Moreover, since this power was enjoyed by only a few, abolitionists suspected a malignant Southern conspiracy of slaveholders against the rights of all, North and South, black and white, in a desperate effort to protect and extend the peculiar institution. In words strikingly similar to those directed against George III and his Cabinet, and very like Antimasonic tirades against secret societies, abolitionists described slaveholders as a "privileged aristocracy" that "in all questions touching slavery . . . go together as one man." To rid the nation of the conspiracy was to complete the

Revolution, to finish "an enterprise without which that of our fathers is incomplete."

In each of these arguments, abolitionists welded democratic rights to moral responsibilities. Endowing the black with all the natural rights accorded to whites, they extended the promises of the Revolution to every person. Defining slavery as a sin, and not as a natural estate, they tore down traditions of deference and class and made the improvement of society the direct responsibility of the individuals who constituted it. Fiercely denying pleas for states' rights based on local interests, they envisioned a morally homogeneous society where privileges and duties were not confined by sectional lines. Portraying slaveholders as conspirators, they contended that a democratic republic was workable only when free of artificial distinctions and morally upright.

Yet they mistrusted politics. Politics involved compromise, and compromise was incompatible with the moral absolutes raised by immediatism. One simply could not debate, amend, or attach provisions to repentance. Also, abolitionists had ample evidence that the conspiracy of slaveholders had already eroded the foundations of democratic authority. Living in an era when the political system was passing into the hands of professionals, abolitionists found in neither party a willingness to place moral issues ahead of Southern votes. This suggested that the political system was corrupt and would taint anyone who worked within it. A free, democratic decision concerning the fate of slavery was thus impossible. "FREE," Weld scoffed. "The word and sound are omnipresent masks, and mockers! An impious lie! unless they stand for free *Lynch Law,* and free *murder;* for they *are* free."

This did not mean, however, that abolitionists neglected politics. Quite the reverse. "I have always expected, I still expect, to see abolition at the ballot box," said Garrison in 1839. The abolitionist strategy was to attack the political system obliquely, working through it but not in it. By a skillful use of propaganda, by playing the major parties against one another in competition for antislavery votes, and —most of all—by awakening the consciences of voters so that no party could ignore the surge of abolitionist sentiment, they hoped to convert the parties, much as a revivalist saved his congregation. This emphasis on agitation by moral instruction persisted among abolitionists well into the 1840s and 1850s—long after many had yielded to the inevitable and entered politics through the Liberty Party. The power of the abolitionist, wrote one Liberty Party editor, lay "in the moral influence we exert, and in the moral and reformatory character we give to the enterprize."

To put moral pressure on politics, abolitionists refined the techniques of the benevolent society. An example was the pamphlet campaign. Antislavery societies churned out cheap, readable pamphlets by the hundreds of thousands as part of their educational effort. Usually the pieces had simple texts; often they were illustrated for the benefit of those who could not read. While most of these pamphlets were read by Northerners, a large portion were shipped south to prick the consciences of the slaveowners. Still others were targeted directly to the slave. Abolitionists devised several ways to deliver this literature. It might be consigned to agents who saw personally to its distribution, or it might be slipped in with various manufactured articles delivered to the South. Always it was infuriating and frightening to Southerners, who feared that it might fall into the wrong hands. When a steamboat from New York transported large quantities of such pamphlets to the Charleston post office in July 1835, the Southern reaction was particularly hostile. Some of the literature had been addressed to leading Charleston clergymen and politicians; the rest, in bulk lots, was destined for post offices throughout the state. The Charleston postmaster confiscated it all and wrote hastily to Washington for instructions. Before he could receive a reply, an angry mob crashed his office and burned the material in the street.

The incident immediately became a national political issue. Jackson asked Congress for authority to bar incendiary publications from the mail, but Southerners objected. If a sympathetic Postmaster General had the power to reject abolitionist tracts, an unsympathetic one could also stop delivery of proslavery material. They demanded instead that local offices should decide what literature should or should not be banned. The Southern proposal never became law, but it did become accepted practice. The solution worked well enough to turn abolitionists to other techniques of spreading their appeal.

The most popular was the antislavery petition addressed to Congress. These simple pleas for emancipation were an old tactic, having first appeared in the 1790s. Quakers originated the idea, which was later adopted by abolitionist societies and then taken up by ordinary citizens in almost every congressional district in the free states. During the 1830s, hundreds of thousands of petitions began stacking up (literally in the halls, where congressmen were forced to step around them), creating a time-consuming burden for Congress. Every day some new petition would be presented and referred to an appropriate committee, which invariably refused to take action. By late 1835, Southern congressmen sought some formula to dispose of the requests without consideration—without even acknowledging their existence. The result was the "gag rule," by which any petition dealing with slavery was automatically tabled, never debated, never read. This was too much for ex-President John Quincy Adams, now serving as a representative from his home district in Massachusetts. He had presented an antislavery petition for the first time in 1831, he vigorously denounced the gag rule, and at every opportunity after its passage he denounced it again. Adams kept his hatred of slavery to himself, but his outrage at an act that outlawed debate in a republican society was persuasively open.

Abolitionists took grim and ironic delight at the gag rule. Not only did it demonstrate the innate corruption of the major parties, it mobilized the few outspokenly antislavery congressmen in Washington to action. Joshua Giddings of Ohio was so vigorously antagonistic to Southerners that, in 1842, his colleagues in the House censured him. He resigned his seat, returned home, and was reelected by a landslide. Similarly, Seth Gates of upstate New York and William Slade of Vermont attacked the gag rule not only as cruel usurpation of the right of free speech but as convincing evidence that a conspiracy of slaveholders directed the policies of the national government. What had begun as a peaceful protest on the part of gentle Quakers had turned into a political embarrassment to the South.

Nonetheless, the antislavery crusade recorded few successes during its first years of organized effort. The gag rule was politically explosive —the sort of thing that might help mobilize large segments of public opinion in the North—but it remained in force with the help of Northern congressmen. The pamphlet campaign had made skillful use of modern techniques of propaganda, but it had freed no slaves. The revivalistic appeal of immediate abolitionism had won thousands of converts, but it had not provided the organizational cohesion to keep those converts working in harmony. By 1836 abolitionism was breaking into fragments, each group seeking some better, more effective means of achieving the ultimate goal. What the antislavery crusade needed was some issue that would force all Americans to take action in the great debate over slavery. That issue was Texas.

11

Sectionalism and Democracy

B Y 1840 the American appetite for territorial growth had become insatiable. Since 1800 the expansion of the republic had been so swift, so astounding, that few even remembered the Founders' solemn warning that a democracy might not work when spread over a large territory. Fewer still would have taken the warning seriously. Expansion and progress seemed to go hand in hand, and Americans in every state and section looked greedily outward, beyond the nation's borders. Residents of the North and the Old Northwest regarded Oregon as American property; the presence of British traders there was an irritating—but temporary—obstacle. A few ambitious expansionists were certain that the British would also be driven from Canada, which would naturally join the empire to the south. Southerners, in turn, were impatient to acquire Cuba from Spain—by force if necessary—and spread the Cotton Kingdom into the Caribbean. The problems that such expansion might bring and the resistance it would surely meet were matters to be brushed aside. "We are the nation of human progress," declared a contributor to the *Democratic Review* in 1839, "and who will, what can, set limits to our onward march?"

And yet there were limits. The physical growth of the United States had far outpaced the development of its institutions or the definition of its purpose. "We are a restless people," explained the Unitarian theologian William Ellery Channing, "prone to encroachment, impatient of the ordinary laws of progress, less anxious to consolidate and perfect than to extend our institutions." After fifty years as a constitutional republic, the United States still possessed a central government that was weak and in many respects devoid of power. Most of the nation's business was transacted piecemeal in the states; the few broadly national organizations that could organize the efforts of people in every section were voluntary and generally centered on one issue. The largest organizations, the two political parties, embraced Americans of so many different backgrounds and persuasions that an ideological consensus was impossible to perceive, except in the vaguest terms. And yet ideology played a critical role in American culture. Terms such as democracy, republicanism, and individual rights were heard in every speech, seen in every newspaper. They gave Americans a sense of mission and moral purpose. What they did not give was a definition of that purpose that could be accepted in every section.

Texas illuminated this problem with chilling clarity. The prospect of annexing the Republic of Texas, first officially proposed in 1836, opened years of wrenching and often ugly debate that cast a pall over the spread-eagle optimism of the new nation. Texas appealed to both the grandest hopes and the worst fears of persons in every state and section. Texas was huge; its annexation would be the second largest territorial acquisition the United States had ever negotiated. Texas was the gateway to the great Southwest and, ultimately, to California. Texas was rich and daily growing richer under the efforts of the substantial number of transplanted Americans already there. But Texas was potentially a slave state. It was outside the Louisiana Territory, not subject to the Missouri Compromise line, and large enough to be divided into five states, all with slavery, all with their contingent of senators and representatives in Washington. To the South these promises were bright. To the North and the Old Northwest they raised an unsettling prospect. If Texas were annexed, the spread of American institutions and, by extension, the national purpose, would be tied to the expansion of slavery.

THE desire to annex Texas was old. American explorers had visited the region for decades, and since 1820 American settlers had been moving there in increasing numbers. Led initially by Stephen F. Austin, they quietly submitted to Spanish rule and then—after the revolution of 1824—the authority of various governments in Mexico City. Austin shrewdly advised them not to challenge Mexican authority or involve themselves in politics. "Play the turtle," he directed, "head and feet within your shell." But Texas was vast; the territory at that time extended from the Gulf Coast north to the Red River, then followed the western boundary of the Louisiana Purchase all the way to the northern border of present-day Colorado. The farther one journeyed away from Mexico City, the more remote one was from Mexican rule. Even in central Texas, near San Antonio, the American presence was so great and influential by the early 1830s that the temptation to intrude into politics was irresistible. Americans there objected, first privately and then publicly, to pressures that they adopt the Catholic faith and submit to Mexican customs—and that they have no slaves.

By 1835 these objections had turned to rebellion. The insurgents were led by Sam Houston, a tall, headstrong adventurer who had once been governor of Tennessee and was a protégé of Andrew Jackson. Houston moved to Texas in 1832 and immediately began recruiting and organizing dissidents—mostly men from the South who wanted Texas to be annexed, as a slave state, to the United States. Open fighting began in late 1835 when the insurgents drafted a constitution and selected Houston as general of the Texan army. The Mexican dictator, Antonio López de Santa Anna, had little choice but to crush the rebellion; he quickly moved troops into central Texas. In February 1836, three thousand Mexican regulars, led personally by Santa Anna, surrounded a small garrison of fewer than two hundred Texans at a walled mission, the Alamo, in San Antonio, and for almost two weeks waged a war of attrition and starvation. Finally, the *degüello* (the slaughter) was sounded, and on March 6 the mission was overrun.

Five weeks later, Houston struck back. In mid-April he led eight hundred men in a surprise attack on a Mexican force twice that size at San Jacinto. The Mexican army was utterly routed, and Santa Anna was captured and forced to recognize Texas independence. He did so grudgingly—faced with the obvious fact that, if he did not, he would be executed. Santa Anna was sent home, a new Republic of Texas was created, and the victorious revolutionaries laid claim to all the land north of the Rio Grande. In October, Houston was named the republic's first president, and the Texas congress all but unanimously voted to ask for annexation to the United States.

In Washington, Van Buren received the request as he would a bomb. For several months previous, the petition campaign against slavery had been particularly intense, and most of the documents objected specifically to the proposed annexation of Texas. In the

House, John Quincy Adams had spoken eloquently and at length against annexation only a month after the battle of San Jacinto, while in the Senate, Benjamin Swift of Vermont introduced resolutions from legislators in his home state that protested the admission of Texas or any other slave territory and affirmed the power of Congress to abolish slavery and the slave trade in the District of Columbia. Southern congressmen replied with resolutions of their own, affirming states' rights and denying federal authority the power to intervene in the slavery issue. In this explosive atmosphere, Van Buren rejected the request for annexation without allowing Congress the opportunity to debate it. By October 1838, the Texas legislature had become so disenchanted with the furore that the request was withdrawn.

But the slavery problem refused to disappear. Despite the action of the Texas congress, it was clear that annexation would remain an issue. The political implications were frightening. Van Buren had rejected the initial request partly because he did not want to divert the energies of Congress from the economic crisis and partly because— as a seasoned politician—he realized that the two-party system could not survive a sectional confrontation. He was not alone in these fears. During his term of office, both parties had matured into broad national organizations heavily dependent on discipline and voter loyalty. It was important, indeed necessary, to keep the party foremost in the voter's mind. If a sectional issue took precedence—particularly one that involved a moral problem such as slavery—party discipline would crumble. The Texas question was such an issue, and both parties worked hard to avoid it in the election of 1840. The result was a brassy, showy campaign full of vague rhetoric and meticulous planning in which the most pressing problem confronting the republic was hardly mentioned.

THE campaign began normally enough. Democrats renominated Van Buren, even though many in the country and in the party blamed him for the depression. Whigs sensed victory from the start. They had cut deeply into the Democrats' strength in 1838—even capturing New York—and their state organizations were now better-run and more professional than ever before. As professionals, they were eager to avoid candidates that might generate controversy, so they shelved Clay and Webster in favor of General William Henry Harrison, the hero of Tippecanoe. To give their ticket greater appeal in the South,

Whigs nominated for Vice President John Tyler of Virginia, ex-Jacksonian and a Calhoun nullifier. There was no Whig platform.

There were, however, slogans. A disappointed Clay supporter belittled Harrison with the remark that the nominee was comfortable only in a log cabin with a full barrel of hard cider. Democrats unthinkingly seized the phrase, having misread completely the temper of the times, and Whigs turned what was intended as an insult into a campaign theme. Harrison's very ordinariness was a symbol of the common man, a powerful image by which Whigs could display their devotion to the ideals of democracy. Soon hard cider was everywhere, while miniature replicas of log cabins journeyed by wagon from town to town, to be used as platforms by speakers who addressed thousands. Campaign songs sprang up around the theme that "Tippecanoe and Tyler Too" would beat "little Van, the used-up man." Torchlight parades—some two miles long—rolled papier-mâché balls ten feet in diameter inscribed with party slogans in an untiring and enthusiastic effort to garner votes. "It was a grand national frolic," reminisced one participant.

"No one," wrote the same man, "will now seriously pretend that this was a campaign of ideas, or a struggle for political reform in any sense." He was only partly right. There was certainly more bombast than analysis, more froth than policy. Ideas, however, did not have to be precise to be persuasive. In the log cabin Whigs found a symbol —entirely figurative yet incredibly suggestive—of the republican spirit. The log cabin conjured up the West, the common man, the newness of the nation; it was uniquely American, with no roots in the Old World and no ties to European institutions and customs. So, in a different way, was Harrison. He had been born shortly before the Revolution and had links to the glorious past. He had risen from humble beginnings to national prominence. His victory over Tecumseh was undoubtedly crucial both in opening the West and in winning —as Americans interpreted it—the War of 1812. Van Buren, whose beginnings were also humble and whose successes were if anything harder won, was simply too dull and too much the professional politician. Harrison was idolized precisely because he was common; Van Buren was attacked because he, supposedly, was not.

Harrison also offered a way to avoid the sectional antagonisms that plagued both parties. Being a Westerner, he was not identified clearly with either North or South. A military hero, he was a national figure whose glories belonged to all. Had Clay—a slaveholder—been the Whig nominee in 1840, he would have alienated many in the North. Had Webster been chosen, he would have lost support in the South. The choice of Harrison, then, was a perfect compromise.

Both parties campaigned hard. While Whigs held an obvious advantage going into the campaign, their efforts to organize their voters were intense and thorough. So were those of the Democrats. The slogans, rallies, free food and drink, and the endless gush of campaign literature were all conscious attempts to make the ordinary man part of the political process. Whigs in particular had learned the lessons of democratic party politics well. They did not simply want to win votes; they wanted to create more Whigs, loyal partisans who would stand by the organization in future elections, both state and national. To that end, they were careful to counteract the charge of being aristocrats. They held a convention, nominated a man of the people, and then went directly to those people in a systematic, if often slightly disorderly, fashion. Democrats toiled with equal fervor, but against insuperable odds. The irony was that the very political tools and stratagems Van Buren had perfected in New York two decades earlier were now turned against him.

Neither party was acceptable to abolitionists, and those who had broken from Garrison in 1839 immediately made plans to offer voters yet a third candidate. Slavery, they reasoned, was a political institution as well as a sin and must be attacked by political means. The gag rule, the rifling of the mails, the proposed annexation of Texas, each suggested that the political power of the slaveholders was multiplying, impervious to moral condemnations. They chided Garrison for not facing reality. His "plan of navigating our poor, misguided ship," wrote Elizur Wright, "is to renounce helm, ropes, compass, anchor, all, jump overboard and scream!" The logical recourse was to launch a party that would strike directly at the slave power. Soon the Liberty Party appeared, with Birney its first candidate.

For all their determination, Liberty men were poor politicians. Remarkably effective as volunteers, as petitioners, and as pamphleteers, they lacked political skill and, perhaps more important, eagerness for party politics. Having seen the corruptions that slavery worked on the political process, they were understandably chary about entering the field; a trace of antiparty spirit remained. Birney, moreover, was too reserved and shy to lead an aggressive campaign, even had he possessed the tactical abilities. Though they had denounced Garrison for relying solely on appeals to conscience, Liberty men themselves counted on the moral purity of their ideals to win voters. All but seven thousand of those voters ignored them in the general frenzy for Harrison or Van Buren.

And so the age of the common man reached its showy zenith. Cider disappeared by the barrel, while campaign workers methodically combed polling lists. Webster mourned that he had not had the privilege to be born in a log cabin, while Democrats furiously denied that Van Buren perfumed his sideburns. Issues retreated before symbols, and the voters responded with gratifying zeal. In all, the campaign brought some 2.5 million voters to the polls—more than half again as many as in 1836 and double the total of 1832. On the day after the election, the country awoke—presumably with a grand national hangover—to find that Harrison had been elected. His popular majority was 140,000; his electoral preponderance, almost four to one.

MORE significant than the size of Harrison's victory was the type of party system that emerged from the campaign. The United States now had the most elaborate and most effective framework of party competition it had ever known. It was a system that used personalities but did not depend on them; in that respect the parties differed from Jeffersonian Republicans and Hamiltonian Federalists—and even from Jacksonian Democrats. The key test of a man's political affiliations was not his devotion to a hero but his attachment to a party as it was organized at all levels, local, state, and national. These parties were loosely aligned around issues such as the desirability of a central bank or the tariff, but were flexible enough to allow for some sectional divergence on specifics. Western Democrats, for example, were far more tolerant of national funding for internal improvements than their counterparts in the East, who did not, after all, have to endure such bad roads or generally poor transportation. New England Whigs espoused a high tariff vigorously, but, since they enjoyed a stable banking system of their own, were less eager for a new United States Bank. Most Southerners, both Whig and Democrat, disliked the tariff intensely but were split over the need for a bank or internal improvements.

Both parties were national, and therein lay the immense strength and the fatal weakness of the system. The organizational structures of both parties were similar, although not identical, and extended into every section. Democrats had enjoyed popular support in every section for most of a decade; the election of 1840 brought the system into balance by giving the Whigs a foothold in the South and West which they never fully lost until the party disappeared in the 1850s. Clearly, some states were bastions for one party or the other, but on the whole the electorate was so evenly divided that a different party won the Presidency in each of the four elections from 1840 to 1852.

While neither possessed a completely consistent ideology, each advocated policies designed to liberate the entrepreneurial energies of the new nation. Whigs favored using the power of the federal government to give direction to an expanding economy; Democrats generally preferred to delegate this power to the states or the individual. Both parties, however, championed the common man as the embodiment of the American mission to spread democracy, first to the continent, then to the world. Whigs and Democrats alike were expansionist, optimistic, exuberantly republican. In the midst of political conflict, consensus flourished.

It was a flawed consensus, and the flaw was slavery. All other issues could be compromised or set aside for later resolution. Slavery, however, was a moral question, and nineteenth-century Americans were unwilling to compromise on moral principles. Tacitly recognizing this fact, both parties tried to avoid the question. Neither party was likely to nominate a Presidential candidate who was an abolitionist or who was outspokenly proslavery; it was safer to nominate political nonentities and military heroes. Both major parties quietly agreed that there was no question of introducing slavery into the free states and accepted the fact that there was no likelihood of abolishing it in the South.

The territories were a different matter. They were unsettled lands in which the customs and institutions of neither North nor South had taken root. Moreover, territories—unlike the states—were under the sole direction of Washington. Thus, the campaign for President and control of Congress would have a profound and enduring influence on the type of society, slave or free, the territories would become. It was a question that could not be put off as the clamor to annex Texas grew louder. Despite the Whigs' and Democrats' skillful avoidance of the Texas issue during the campaign of 1840, that election was the last in which they did not have to contend with the sectional crisis.

WHIG unity ended with the counting of the ballots. Like Democrats, Whigs were divided in countless ways over sectional problems and over issues of economic policy. Like Democrats, they were able to work around these divisions, because they shared certain common assumptions concerning the direction economic policy should take. But unlike Democrats, Whigs possessed no tradition of leadership in the White House. Harrison's victory had been the work of propaganda and chance, and even before his inauguration the party had collapsed into bickering and infighting, with Daniel Webster and Henry Clay contending for control of what was, clearly, to be a weak and pliable executive. Worse, no prominent Southern Whig seemed likely to exercise any measurable influence in the new Administration, a situation that caused uneasiness in the South. Webster succeeded in placing himself in the State Department, while Clay controlled most of the other important Cabinet offices and the Congress. When Harrison took office, the party was in a state of uneasy truce.

The peace lasted exactly one month. Harrison was sixty-eight when he took the oath and was unaccustomed to the strenuous schedule he had been forced to keep. While shopping at a public market he caught cold, and the cold, neglected, turned into pneumonia. On April 4, 1841, he died, and John Tyler took command. For a short time it appeared that Tyler would preserve the fragile unity of the Whig coalition. He retained Harrison's Cabinet and seemed receptive to Clay's advice on economic problems. But Tyler was not a Whig. Nor was he a Democrat, for he had renounced his political ties and was not invited to return to the fold. Tyler was, however, a Southerner. Vain, obstinate, and proud, he had entered politics as a Virginia aristocrat determined to protect the rights and institutions of the South. He was ambitious, both for his own political future and for the future of the Cotton Kingdom. Perhaps most of all, Tyler was obsessed with a desire to annex Texas. These traits soon led him into conflict with the party that had elected him and to a much larger confrontation with the North over annexation.

When the members of the new Whig Congress met in May 1841 for a special session, Clay appeared to be in complete control. Harrison had requested the session to deal with the economic crisis, and Tyler reluctantly allowed the order to stand. Clay seized the occasion to introduce a legislative program designed in part to deal with the lingering depression and in part to consolidate the Whig victory. With superb skill he used his legislative talents to drive through, bit by bit, a series of bills that collectively would have dismantled most of the Democratic policies enacted under Jackson and Van Buren. The Independent Treasury, in operation hardly a year, was wiped from the statute books. The tariff, which under the Compromise of 1833 would reach a uniform 20 percent in one year, was modified: the 20 percent ceiling on import duties remained, but articles that had previously been admitted free were given protection—a clear victory for Eastern manufacturing interests. To mollify the West, Clay persuaded Congress to distribute the proceeds from the sale of public lands to the states. Moreover, a preemption policy—giving squatters first option to buy the land they had already settled—was made permanent. Taken together, the bills attempted to give direction and support to economic growth while scrupulously insuring that no sectional or regional interests would be shortchanged.

But the key measure of Clay's ambitious program was the establishment of a new national bank. Called a "Fiscal Bank of the United States" because Tyler had used that curious term, the proposed bank generally followed and improved on the charter of the Second Bank of the United States. In two very critical respects it differed. The Fiscal Bank was to be located in the District of Columbia, where Congress would have undisputed authority over its affairs, and it would have the power to establish branch banks in the several states at will. The proposal was a statesmanlike measure and one that might have served the country well had it been placed in operation, but it was not. Tyler objected to the ease with which branch banks could be added and, after long study and soul-searching, vetoed the bill. He asked Clay to draft a new proposal that would require prior approval from any state in which a branch bank was being contemplated. Clay came back with a modification of the modification: the Fiscal Bank might establish a branch anywhere, but the branch would be dissolved if, within one year, the host state objected. When Tyler received the new bill, he vetoed again, and the measure was lost.

Tyler's objections appear picky and overtechnical; on close inspection they provide a glimpse into the complex workings of a mind that was forced to deal with party politics and sectional loyalties at the same time. Tyler's ambition for a second term had led him to accept much that ran against his Democratic background. He had signed the various measures for a new tariff, land distribution, and preemption, and during his Presidency he approved several internal improvements bills. He would have allowed the bank to begin operation, even though his instincts were completely opposed to a national bank. In short, he wanted to be a good Whig. But Clay's branching plan collided with Tyler's commitment to states' rights. A central bank, located in Washington, was tolerable at best. To give that bank authority to extend its influence into the states without their expressed approval was—to Tyler—a dangerous enlargement of federal power. If Clay had accepted Tyler's changes, the states would have been able to judge what was or was not in their best interests; in effect, they could have nullified a portion of federal authority. To Tyler, Clay's suggestion that the branches be established first, then made subject to state approval, was needlessly complex and not an adequate guarantee of states' rights. Rather than concede a vital principle in order to protect party harmony, Tyler chose to remain loyal to his section. Not surprisingly, he paid a price. The entire Cabinet, with the exception of Daniel Webster, resigned, and the Whig Party renounced its President.

FROM that point on, both Whigs and Democrats treated Tyler's Presidency as an enforced pause, a moratorium between elections. No one, with the exception of a few states' rights Southerners, appeared willing to regard the President as a man of vision and leadership. Webster remained at State only because he was involved in delicate negotiations with Great Britain; the rest of the reconstructed Cabinet was notable for mediocrity. Even after the veto of the second bank bill, Tyler was willing to work with the Whig hierarchy in Congress; their cold rebuffs drove him into isolation and bitterness. As the months wore on, Tyler's only achievement seemed to be his ability to generate hostility. Historians have generally viewed the man in much the same way. Tyler's ill-starred attempts to forge a place of distinction appear selfish and a little sad.

In a larger and somewhat ironic sense, Tyler was one of the most important Presidents of his age. His dogged refusal to compromise on issues of states' rights and his fixation on Texas cost him support in every section and alienated him from the party that elected him. He never stood a realistic chance of being elected in his own right, and his only mechanism of exercising Presidential power appeared to be the veto. But Tyler was a strong-willed man—and he was Chief Executive. The convergence of his personality, his powers, and his goals made him a figure who was easily hated but never ignored, particularly in an age when the Presidency was becoming the focal point of party politics. By being alternately obstinate and aggressive, and by skillfully using the powers that were open to him and him alone as Chief Executive, he set an agenda with which the country had to deal. The significance of his Presidency lay in the types of issues that he chose to pursue. Tyler concentrated his energies on expanding the republic and on extending Southern institutions to the frontier, and he did so vigorously. His four years were notable for the extent to which politics shifted away from problems of economic growth and toward issues of expansionism and sectionalism.

His vetoes, for example, marked the end of any new or imaginative attempts to give direction to economic growth until the Civil War. When Tyler gutted the Whig program by removing its most vital organ, the bank, he delivered a killing setback to Hamiltonian concepts of fiscal stability and regulated change. The more Tyler and the Whig hierarchy fought, the more economic policy lapsed into confusion and drift. The country languished without a clearly defined monetary system until 1846, when Tyler's successor, James K. Polk (a Democrat), resurrected the Independent Treasury. Internal improvements bills were dependent on Tyler's mood—a chancy situation at best. The tariff was increased with Tyler's grudging assent in 1842, then revised down, again under Polk, in 1846. Whigs thus lost their one real chance to implement the American System, for Henry Clay's unsuccessful bid for the Presidency in 1844 forced them back to the strategy of nominating uncommitted and popular national heroes. Even this practice was undermined by bad luck. Zachary Taylor, their only other successful candidate, died in office. In practical terms, this meant that Democrats determined the direction of economic policy, the effect of which was to give very little direction at all.

Economic issues did not disappear from politics, but a subtle shift in responsibility for directing economic growth did take place as the role of state governments became more and more important. During the 1840s and 1850s, several—including New York and Ohio—redrafted their constitutions in response to population increases and economic diversification. States set standards of fiscal policy, regulated the banks, and encouraged investment in transportation. The bewildering disparities in economic development intensified. Private banks in New England, New York, and Louisiana prospered under the stable regulation of state governments; elsewhere, the banking climate was unpredictable and capricious. As the railroads expanded and became national corporations, they were able to manipulate the favors of state legislatures. With no direction or restraint emanating from Washington, this manipulation produced a rail system that by 1860 was disjointed and unevenly distributed. It is doubtful that any President or political party could have effectively reversed such trends, for the problems and demands of an industrializing economy were perplexing to everyone. Tyler's destruction of the Whig program, however, removed an important alternative.

TYLER did not govern by veto alone. As his relations with Congress deteriorated, he shifted his efforts to foreign affairs—the one field in which a President could take decisive action without the need to assemble coalitions in both houses of Congress. Under the Constitution, treaties do, of course, require the advice and consent of the Senate, but the House is not involved. The Senate was where Tyler stood the best chance of finding cooperation, for that was where Southerners exercised considerable influence. This was precisely the kind of situation Tyler could exploit to his own and the South's best interests. The President wanted to protect slavery and to extend it. A skillful manipulation of foreign affairs allowed him to do both.

Protecting slavery through diplomacy initially meant allowing Daniel Webster a free hand at the State Department. This curious situation was not the product of any deliberate design by either Tyler or Webster. The latter was certainly no friend of slavery and was a well-known opponent of sectionalism. The President would have preferred to work through another man. But the crisis in foreign affairs during 1841 and 1842 involved Great Britain, and Webster's advantages in dealing with London were formidable.

For years, relations between the two countries had been deteriorating because of slavery and territorial conflicts. In 1833 Parliament had abolished slavery in the West Indies, and British abolitionists began pressing for emancipation in the United States. Since there was no direct way for the British to involve themselves in American domestic affairs, they worked by cordoning off the slave trade, which still operated between western Africa and South America. Occasionally, American ships transporting slaves along the Atlantic and Gulf coasts ran afoul of the British blockade. One, the *Enterprise,* was storm-driven to Bermuda, where local authorities promptly freed the slaves on board because slavery was illegal on British soil. Another, more delicate case concerned the brig *Creole* in 1841. The *Creole* had been carrying slaves from Virginia to Louisiana when the blacks mutinied, seized the ship, and brought it to the Bahamas. British authorities arrested the ringleaders but allowed the remainder to vanish quietly into freedom. The State Department protested vigorously in each incident, to no avail. Abolitionists, on the other hand, applauded the British actions.

Territorial questions were also volatile. Border disputes were rife in Oregon, where neither British nor Americans were pleased with their joint occupation of the territory. A similar situation existed along the contested boundary between Maine and New Brunswick; tensions there provoked lumberjacks into the armed but bloodless "Aroostook War" of 1839. Complicating everything were unofficial American efforts to aid a brief and unsuccessful rebellion against the Crown in Canada in 1837. During that episode the British had captured and burned an American gunrunner, the *Caroline,* which had been supplying the insurgents from New York. The deed took place in American waters, and an American citizen had been killed. New Yorkers retaliated in 1840 by arresting a Canadian, Alexander McLeod, and indicting him for murder. In time McLeod was acquitted, but not before London had threatened war if he were hanged.

Although few persons on either side of the Atlantic expected these issues to be resolved neatly and quickly, a restoration of good relations was mandatory both for the United States and for John Tyler. The United States was beginning to produce a surplus of grain and foodstuffs that Britain—currently shaken by a series of bad harvests—needed. In return, Americans still relied on English factories for many manufactured goods, and the South urgently needed to protect its market for cotton. Webster recognized this mutual interdependence and worked hard to preserve it. Tyler, meanwhile, was preparing the ground for a possible future confrontation with London over Texas. While British abolitionists kept up their insistence on emancipation in the United States, British diplomats were courting Texas with lower import duties on cotton. If Texas were drawn into economic dependence on England, then the chance of annexing that republic to the United States might well be lost. Worse, the British might use their influence and power to force Texans to emancipate their slaves. Tyler, therefore, needed to relax the tensions with England in order to buy time and turn his attention to annexation.

So Webster did precisely what Tyler wanted him to do. During most of 1841, the Secretary of State made little headway against the rabidly anti-American Foreign Minister, Lord Palmerston, who bluntly asserted his country's right to board and search any American vessel suspected of trafficking in slaves. Palmerston, however, was replaced, and a new Foreign Minister appointed Lord Ashburton to deal with the Americans. Webster and Ashburton liked each other, and by the summer of 1842 the two men had reached an agreement. The Maine boundary was settled; the United States and Canada were guaranteed free navigation of all border waters; each party agreed to police its own ships in an effort to eradicate the slave trade. But all other questions—including Oregon—were shelved for future consideration. Aside from the Maine boundary, nothing much had been won by either side, yet the overall impact of the Webster–Ashburton treaty was to lessen tensions and provide a more favorable diplomatic environment. And Webster, having steered the country out of a potential conflict, finally resigned from the Cabinet in 1843 and joined his fellow Whigs.

WITH Webster gone, Tyler began moving vigorously to acquire Texas. On Calhoun's recommendation he appointed Abel P. Upshur of Virginia as Webster's replacement at State and instructed him to prepare a treaty of annexation—but to do so in secret in order to minimize conflict. Upshur worked fast and hard during the winter of 1843–44 in the midst of an increasingly sensitive situation. Congress was wracked by sectional antagonisms; the British had reaffirmed their campaign to secure emancipation in Texas; a Presidential election was approaching rapidly. Undaunted by these pressures, Upshur drafted a treaty of annexation and persuaded Sam Houston—then serving his second term as President of Texas—that the treaty would be ratified by the necessary two-thirds of the Senate. Both Tyler and Upshur were awaiting the arrival of a Texan envoy with authority to sign the document when tragedy intervened. While inspecting the new steam battleship *Princeton* in late February 1844, Upshur was killed by fragments from an exploding gun. Tyler himself narrowly escaped death.

Upshur's successor was John C. Calhoun, and for slightly less than a year—from April 1844 to March 1845—the United States had a President and a Secretary of State who were both staunch advocates of slavery and states' rights. Calhoun naturally wished to keep the negotiations with Texas private in order to enhance his bargaining position with Congress: a signed document would stand a good chance of speedy passage. To blunt the inevitable outcry from the North, the new Secretary also hoped to reopen the Oregon question as quickly as possible. But secrecy proved impossible. When Texas approved the treaty of annexation on April 12, word of the negotiations leaked to the New York *Herald,* and Calhoun found himself embroiled in yet another bitter sectional conflict.

In such situations Calhoun usually retreated into the iron logic of his own mind. The Texas controversy was no exception. Catching up on his official correspondence, the Secretary found on his desk a letter from Richard Pakenham—the new British ambassador—transmitting assurances that London had no intention of interfering in Texas provided no one else did. The note also reaffirmed Britain's commitment to universal emancipation. Calhoun could have ignored the note; instead, he replied with a detailed defense of slavery. In a carefully worded answer Calhoun chided the British for having already interfered in Texas. He dismissed their interest in emancipation as a foil for their imperialism. Annexation, Calhoun argued, had become a matter of self-defense for the United States against British expansionism. Most important, the Secretary linked annexation with slavery, which he once again defended as a positive good. This last point was an intemperate and blundering move, yet Calhoun seemed unaware of, or oblivious to, its implications. When he posted the letter to Pakenham the press secured a copy, and the President's wish that annexation be handled quickly and quietly died. No prudent senator from a free state could endorse a proposal that was justified, by the Secretary of State, as essential to slavery. The treaty languished in the Senate that term and was not debated again until the following winter.

DURING the interim the Texas issue worked its acid way through the Presidential campaign. On April 21—the same day that Calhoun's letter to Pakenham was made public—Henry Clay and Martin Van Buren released their respective views on annexation. Both statements were long, tortuous, lethally dull attempts to reduce the Texas problem to one simple issue—the probability that annexation would spark a war with Mexico. Mexico had never officially accepted the secession of Texas; even if it had, its boundary with Texas was in dispute. Until the independence of Texas was recognized and the borders firmly drawn, argued both candidates, the United States could not afford to risk annexation. Moreover, since Texas was in the hands of emigrant Americans, the motive behind annexation would surely be suspect in the eyes of the world. "We have a character among the nations of the earth to maintain," Van Buren pleaded; a premature move to acquire Texas would permanently damage American prestige. Both men, however, promised to yield to the will of Congress and the people, even if annexation was the result.

Neither letter was satisfactory. Although Clay secured the Whig nomination with ease, his evasive stand on Texas irritated his supporters in every section. Southern Whigs were vexed that he had not taken a more aggressive view; Northern Whigs were upset that he had not renounced Texas entirely. When Clay steadily modified his letter during the campaign, irritation turned to ridicule. "He is as rotten as a stagnant fish pond, on the subject of Slavery," declared an observer. "Confound him and all his compromises from first to last." Despite these problems, most Whigs accepted Clay's candidacy and set to work to elect him.

The Democratic Party, however, was torn apart. The chief effect of Van Buren's statement was to make him acceptable to almost no one. His opponents in the North were prepared to discard him in favor of Lewis Cass—a Westerner who promised to fight for expansion while leaving the slavery issue to the people in the territories. Southern Democrats wanted Calhoun. In both sections there were men who rejected Van Buren simply because he was identified with the Panic of 1837. When the Democratic convention assembled in Baltimore in May, these factions skillfully pushed through the adoption of a two-thirds rule for nomination. It was a clever mechanism that required the successful nominee to gain what was, in effect, a unanimous vote. Through dozens of roll calls the delegates wearily debated and re-debated the merits of each man; each vote saw Van Buren's support slip. Finally, a series of midnight conferences brought forth a new name: James K. Polk.

Polk was the first "dark horse" candidate in the history of Presidential politics. He had carefully groomed himself for the Vice Presidency, having secured the approval of his fellow Tennessean, Andrew Jackson, in advance. When the convention deadlocked, however, Polk's managers hurriedly raised their sights. Polk was a slaveholder;

he was acceptable to the Calhoun faction. He was Jackson's protégé; therefore, he was popular among Western delegates. He had served faithfully as Speaker of the House during Van Buren's Presidency; the New Yorkers could not in good conscience reject him. When Van Buren's floor manager at last withdrew the former President's name, Polk was nominated unanimously. "Who is James K. Polk?" the Whigs retorted. They would soon find an answer.

The election of 1844 marked a critical shift in American politics. The same organizations that had competed in 1840 were still present, attempting to inspire the same hoopla and near-religious enthusiasm among the voters. But the second American party system was undeniably in trouble, possibly dying. Neither party could avoid the slavery issue. Among Northern Whigs there was ample evidence that Clay's artful dodges and evasions were more confusing than salutary. Northern Whig newspapers spent too much time explaining them. Those who could be persuaded that Southern Whigs did not mean to extend slavery outside Texas demanded that Oregon be admitted simultaneously. A similar rift divided Democrats. And although Van Buren's loyal supporters buried their frustration and worked hard to elect Polk, bitterness and suspicion lingered. "As to Polk and Texas," stormed one, "I consider this nomination brought about by a rascally fraud—one that would disgrace a well-organized den of thieves."

But Polk did hold an edge. Despite the cleavages among Democrats, the party was hungry for office and had not suffered four years of mismanagement under Tyler. Moreover, Polk was a better campaigner. He realized that his slaves and his desire to annex Texas were unpopular among large segments of his party in the North; nothing he said or did could fully overcome their doubts. So Polk left equivocation to Clay. The Democratic platform called for annexing Texas and driving the British from Oregon, and Polk championed both— thus offering rewards to the South and to the North. Against this uncomplicated appeal were Clay's long record of compromise and a deeper, general confusion in the Whig Party.

The confusion was evident in the final returns. The parties were so evenly divided that Polk won only by winning New York, which he carried by a scant 5,000 votes. Some attributed his success there to the 16,000 votes garnered by Birney, once again the Liberty Party candidate. It was easy to conclude that Birney had siphoned off enough disgruntled Whigs to defeat Clay—and elect Polk—in New York. It is more probable, however, that antislavery New York Whigs, thoroughly disgusted with Clay, simply stayed home. However the votes are read, the election in this one state demonstrated an alarming and ultimately fatal trend: once the moral issue of slavery took precedence over party loyalty, the delicate intersectional nature of the second party system was doomed. It was a lesson that Whigs learned well but late. Although they won in 1848, they were unable to survive the dissensions that plagued their party and disappeared after 1852.

As Polk prepared to enter the White House, Tyler tried one last time to acquire Texas. He had worked hard to consummate the deal, and he was not disposed to let the incoming President claim credit for success. Moreover, the British presence in Texas was growing daily more visible, and the Texans themselves showed signs of wavering in their intent to join the United States. When Congress assembled in December 1844, Tyler adopted a new strategy. His efforts to secure annexation by treaty had failed in the Senate, so the President called for a joint resolution by both Houses. The tactic was dubiously constitutional but rewardingly effective, for Tyler had shrewdly ascertained that—with enough pressure at the right points—a majority in both houses could be obtained. It was, and on March 2, 1845—two days before he was to leave the White House—Tyler dispatched the signed resolution to Houston. Four months later came word that the Texans had accepted.

There were optimists in every section who believed that the annexation of Texas resolved—or at least shelved—the slavery controversy. They were wrong. Polk was an expansionist, an aggressive one, who looked beyond Texas to the Mexican territories of New Mexico and California. Early in his term he began looking for means to negotiate a sale with Mexico by which the United States could acquire the Southwestern territories peacefully. He was not, emphatically, eager to reopen the slavery issue; Polk wished simply to buy the land and leave the disposition of slavery to the settlers who would ultimately move there. But unlike Louisiana, California could not be bought, because the Mexicans would not sell. Unlike Missouri, the slavery problem was too obvious and too pressing to be put off or bargained away.

The unintended solution to Polk's quandary was war. When Mexico refused to accept the American definition of the southern boundary of Texas, the President moved troops to the Rio Grande. Border skirmishes followed, and in May 1846 Polk asked Congress for a declaration of war on the grounds that Mexican troops had "shed American blood on American soil." Two years of vicious fighting ensued, during which the United States Army won a series of stunning victories that stretched from Veracruz on the Gulf Coast to Monterey in California. As Mexican resistance crumbled, Polk used the opportunity to negotiate not only a final solution to the boundary dispute but the purchase of New Mexico and California as well. When the war ended in 1848, the continental empire was a reality.

National unity was not. The substantial number of Northern Whigs and Democrats who had protested the annexation of Texas were horrified at the use of violence to defend the acquisition of a slave state. "No moral or political obligation rests upon us," warned Joshua Giddings, to die "dishonorable deaths in defense of Texan slavery." When California was purchased and the South resisted attempts to preclude slavery from being introduced there, the shock was magnified. Even Calhoun was disappointed at the outbreak of hostilities. War, he knew, was the one sure spark that would reopen the slavery controversy, and the South was still in a minority among the American population. This time it would be necessary to assert the rights of the states more forcefully than ever before, and the Union might not survive. In Boston, the aging Josiah Quincy, president of Harvard, foresaw civil war. "Even now I feel the upheaving of the advancing tempest," he mourned. "I see the broken columns of our nation, and . . . the grinding of the massive materials as they dash against each other—*not without blood.*"

Afterword

IN retrospect, the growth of the republic during the first half of the nineteenth century had been no less than breathtaking. In 1800 the United States was a thinly populated, agrarian society huddled against the Atlantic coast. Although a great experiment in republican rule had recently begun, most of the habits, traditions, and assumptions of the new nation were those of the colonial era. Economic pursuits were tied to the soil or the oceans; political power—despite the Revolution—remained in the hands of the "best men." Change, it was assumed, came slowly and by degrees in a continental theater of seemingly limitless proportions, and the presence of that continent was a sobering obstacle to even the most ambitious optimist. "Nature was rather man's master than his servant," wrote Henry Adams, "and the five million Americans struggling with the untamed continent seemed hardly more competent to their task than the beavers and buffaloes."

Fifty years later, all had changed. The twenty million Americans living at midcentury no longer regarded the frontier as untamable but as a vast storehouse of resources waiting to be exploited. Settlers had poured into the West; businessmen had developed new markets and completely new forms of enterprise; political power had shifted from the hands of the gentry to modern, systematic organizations aimed at the common man. The nation had survived a grave threat to its independence between 1812 and 1815, and thirty years later had embarked, successfully, on its first major war of acquisition and expansion. And change, even rapid change, had come to be viewed as a natural and usually beneficent part of life. Nothing seemed entirely

impossible—an assumption uniquely American and doggedly persistent.

And yet the unity they so desperately wanted evaded them.
Throughout the period, Americans struggled to fulfill a promise and
avoid a threat. They wanted to be the strongest, freest nation on earth
—the harbinger of democratic societies to come throughout the
world. They also wanted to escape the anarchy and chaos that deva-
stated a nation when it became too free, too lacking in the means to
restrain itself. By midcentury the incredible flexibility and innovative-
ness of their economic enterprises, the organized and efficient ways by
which they attacked social problems and encouraged reform, and the
systematic means by which political parties gave the common voter
participation in the ruling process—all seemed to suggest that they
had succeeded.

What wrecked the experiment was a failure of purpose, of will.
However effective the new institutions might have been, the expanding republic was so large, so diverse, that its chief source of unity was
an idea. That idea, in all its various and conflicting interpretations,
revolved around the belief that the United States was at the head of
a universal movement by which, in the words of a Kentucky Whig,
"the old, worn-out, effete institutions of Europe," founded on arbitrary power and compulsion, would inevitably be replaced by a new
order based on natural rights and self-rule. During the first half of the
nineteenth century, the idea had assumed a transcendent, moral quality; it was no longer simply a worthwhile objective, but a divinely
appointed duty. The moral imperative to "extend the area of Freedom," in Jackson's terms, became inseparably entwined with the
concept of the Union itself. "Liberty *and* Union," Webster intoned
during his debate with Hayne. And so long as the country remained
loosely connected, all could agree.

But by 1845 both the idea and the institutions had matured to a
point where conflict was inevitable. Americans had persuaded themselves that a consensus had been achieved over the moral goals of their
mission. The persuasion obscured a basic conflict. The traditions of
the deferential society had decayed in the North and West to the point
that any form of obviously arbitrary power was no longer admissible.
Unused to the social stratification and immense concentration of
power that were to accompany the rise of the industrial elite, Northerners defined the idea of the Union as self-rule and limited authority,

a simple but compelling articulation of the Jeffersonian vision. Southerners shared the same vision, but their definition included a defense of slavery and of states' rights. To the Southern mind, anything else opened the way for an unrestrained use of majority rule, a rule that could impose its moral decisions on an unwilling minority.

For, in the end, the sectional problem was a moral one. The United States had drawn for itself a staggering mission—the moral regeneration of the world. It was bitterly disillusioning, then, to discover that Americans could not agree on the terms of this moral mission when applied to their own territories. Each section had been largely content to leave the other and its institutions alone, but each section was determined also to impose its definition of republicanism on the unsettled West. Federal policy in the territories became, then, an expression of national goals, and too late Americans discovered the depth of the divisions that separated them. The struggle for regeneration, for moral purity, turned inward, a point that Lincoln seized with cutting clarity in 1858: "A house divided against itself cannot stand. . . . It will become all one thing or all the other."

Bibliographic Essay

BIBLIOGRAPHIES are by nature selective. What follows is directed primarily to the general reader and not to the professional historian. It includes comprehensive histories and interpretive studies, specialized works on particular topics, and studies that I simply found exciting and worthwhile. There are many more, of course, and for them the revised edition of the *Harvard Guide to American History,* edited by Frank Freidel (1974), is a masterful sourcebook.

GENERAL WORKS: Few historians attempt to write comprehensive works these days. The old masters did, however, and some of their studies are still worthwhile. Among the best are John Bach McMasters, *History of the People of the United States from the Revolution to the Civil War* (8 vols.; 1883–1913), and Edward Channing, *History of the United States* (6 vols.; 1905–25). For graceful style and exhaustive detail, nothing has ever quite matched Henry Adams, *History of the United States during the Administrations of Thomas Jefferson and James Madison* (9 vols.; 1889–91). Adams's first six chapters are classic; they provide a feel for the age that few other writers in any age have approached. There are other, shorter works that are also worthwhile. Raymond H. Robinson, *The Growing of America, 1789–1848* (1973), is quite good despite its short length, and Marcus Cunliffe, *The Nation Takes Shape, 1789–1837* (1959), offers a good overview. See also the general works mentioned in subsequent chapters, below.

General works on broad topics include, for politics, Wilfred E. Binkley, *American Political Parties: Their Natural History* (4th ed.; 1963), and Arthur M. Schlesinger, Jr., ed., *History of United States Political Parties, Volume I: 1789–1860: From Factions to Parties* (4 vols.; 1973). For an overview of Presidential elections, see Arthur M. Schlesinger, Jr., and Fred L. Israel, eds., *History of American Presidential Elections* (4 vols.; 1971). Diplomatic history is covered by William Goetzmann, *When the Eagle Screamed: The Romantic Horizon in American Diplomacy, 1800–1860* (1966), and Thomas A. Bailey, *A Diplomatic History of the American People* (8th ed.; 1969). Intellectual history is admirably covered in Vernon L. Parrington, *Main Currents in American Thought* (3 vols.; 1927–30), and Merle Curti, *The Growth of American Thought* (3rd ed.; 1964). See chapter 4 for economic histories.

The interpretive study, if it is good, provides a context for understanding and raises questions that inspire additional study. The best are David Potter, *People of Plenty: Economic Abundance and the American Character* (1954); Robert H. Wiebe, *The Segmented Society: An Introduction to the Meaning of America* (1975); Rowland Berthoff, *An Unsettled People: Social Order and Disorder in American History* (1971); and Richard D. Brown, *Modernization: The Transformation of American Life, 1600–1865* (1976). Although mostly limited to the period before 1800, Michael Kammen's *People of Paradox: An Inquiry Concerning the Origins of American Civilization* (1972) is instructive reading for those interested in the first half of the nineteenth century. Frederick Jackson Turner's "frontier thesis" has inspired scores of elaborations and critiques. The original is contained in a collection of Turner's essays, *The Frontier in American History* (1930). Both Louis Hartz, *The Liberal Tradition in America* (1955), and Richard Hofstadter, *The American Political Tradition and the Men Who Made It* (1948), attempted to find an underlying consensus in American political thought. For all the evidence to the contrary, these works still endure.

The unique quality of American nationalism is explored further in Hans Kohn, *American Nationalism: An Interpretative Essay* (1957), which should be read in conjunction with his *The Idea of Nationalism: A Study in Its Origins and Background* (1944). Yehoshua Arieli, *Individualism and Nationalism in American Ideology* (1964), includes a section on the utopian strain in American thought. Paul C. Nagel, *One Nation Indivisible: The Union in American Thought, 1776–1861* (1964), is an exemplary piece of intellectual history, as are Fred Somkin, *Unquiet Eagle: Memory and Desire in the Idea of American Freedom* (1967), and Major L. Wilson, *Space, Time, and Freedom: The Quest for Nationality and the Irrepressible Conflict, 1815–1861* (1964). A short essay by David Potter, "The Historian's Use of Nationalism and Vice Versa," *American Historical Review*, 67 (1962): 924–50, offers perceptive cautions to those interested in the subject, and Seymour Martin Lipset's *The First New Nation: The United States in Historical and Comparative Perspective* (1963) is an innovative effort to consider the American experience in the context of developing nations.

Four works that go well beyond their particular subjects are A. K. Weinberg, *Manifest Destiny: A Study of Nationalist Expansionism in American History* (1935); Arthur A. Ekirch, *The Idea of Progress in America, 1815–1860*

(1944); Irvin G. Wyllie, *The Self-Made Man in America* (1954); and John G. Cawelti, *Apostles of the Self-Made Man* (1965). All are first-rate.

CHAPTER 1. The fullest account of the United States during Jefferson's Presidency remains Henry Adams's study, cited above, which is fortunately available in abridged versions. Marshall Smelser, *The Democratic Republic, 1801–1815* (1968), is a witty and useful survey, and Thomas P. Abernethy, *The South in the New Nation, 1789–1819* (1961), adds important perspectives on the role of the South. These largely political studies are well complemented by Russel B. Nye, *The Cultural Life of the New Nation, 1776–1830* (1960), and Ralph Brown, *Historical Geography of the United States* (1948).

On the growth of moral reform and revivalism, see the works cited in chapter 8, below. On Jefferson and Jeffersonianism, the best place to begin is Dumas Malone's multivolumed biography—especially volume 4—*Jefferson the President: First Term, 1801–1805* (1970). Jeffersonian politics is examined in William N. Chambers, *Political Parties in a New Nation, 1776–1809* (1967), and Noble Cunningham, Jr., *The Jeffersonian Republicans in Power: Party Operations, 1801–1809* (1963). A broad and useful description of political relationships within the capital is James Sterling Young, *The Washington Community, 1800–1828* (1966). Administrative history is thoroughly examined in Leonard D. White, *The Jeffersonians: Administrative History, 1801–1829* (1951). Paul Goodman, *The Democratic-Republicans of Massachusetts: Politics in a Young Republic* (1964), is an excellent state study with implications for the national scene. David Hackett Fischer, *The Revolution of American Conservatism* (1965), is the best study of the Federalist response to Jefferson and to the changing nature of party politics. Fischer's work should be accompanied by Linda Kerber, *Federalists in Dissent: Imagery and Ideology in Jeffersonian America* (1970). Richard Hofstadter, *The Idea of a Party System: The Rise of Legitimate Opposition in the United States, 1740–1840* (1969), is one of the last works by a master of synthesis and context.

There are several good works on the growth of Jeffersonianism as an ideology. The best are Lance Banning, *The Jeffersonian Persuasion: Evolution of a Party Ideology* (1978), and Richard Buel, Jr., *Securing the Revolution: Ideology in American Politics, 1789–1815* (1972). Charles M. Wiltse, *The Jeffersonian Tradition in American Democracy* (1935; 1960), and Merrill Peterson, *The Jefferson Image in the American Mind* (1960), are wonderfully ambitious and comprehensive treatments of an enduring subject. The chapter on Jefferson in Robert Kelley, *The Transatlantic Persuasion: The Liberal Democratic Mind in the Age of Gladstone* (1969), is a superb comparative study of Jeffersonian and British liberal thought.

The judiciary has received extensive treatment. The starting point is Albert J. Beveridge, *The Life of John Marshall* (4 vols.; 1919), which is still the standard work. R. Kent Newmyer, *The Supreme Court under Marshall and Taney* (1969), is a more recent survey. Edward S. Corwin, *The "Higher Law" Background of American Constitutional Law* (1955), explores the origins of judicial review, as does Charles G. Haines, *The American Doctrine of Judicial Supremacy* (1932). Jefferson's struggles with Marshall are ably covered in Beveridge's biography and in Richard E. Ellis, *The Jeffersonian Crisis: Courts and Politics in the Young Republic* (1971).

The Louisiana Purchase is examined in E. Wilson Lyon, *Louisiana in French Diplomacy, 1759–1804* (1934), and in Thomas J. Farnham, "Federal– State Issue and the Louisiana Purchase," *Louisiana History,* 6 (1965): 5–28. See also George Dangerfield, *Chancellor Robert R. Livingston of New York, 1746–1803* (1960).

CHAPTER 2.   Three works by Bradford Perkins, *First Rapprochement: England and the United States, 1795–1805* (1955), *Prologue to War: England and the United States, 1805–1812* (1960), and *Castlereagh and Adams: England and the United States, 1812–1836* (1964), provide an exhaustive and well-argued survey of relations between the two countries before, during, and after the War of 1812. Dumas Malone, *Jefferson the President: Second Term, 1805–1809* (1974), traces the attempt to remain neutral. Louis M. Sears, *Jefferson and the Embargo* (1967), is the best treatment of that disastrous experiment.

The issues and controversies that led to war have received extensive treatment. A. L. Burt, *The United States, Great Britain, and British North America* (1940), stresses the issue of impressment. Julius W. Pratt, *Expansionists of 1812* (1949), overstresses the role of the War Hawks, who are put in better perspective by Norman K. Risjord, "1812: Conservatives, War Hawks, and the Nation's Honor," *William and Mary Quarterly,* 18 (1961): 196–210. The American preoccupation with honor and the sanctity of republican institutions is ably treated in Roger H. Brown, *The Republic in Peril: 1812* (1964).

Harry Lewis Coles, *The War of 1812* (1965); Reginald Horsman, *The War of 1812* (1969); and Patrick C. T. White, *The Nation on Trial: America and the War of 1812* (1965), are the best histories of the conflict. Irving Brant, *James Madison: The Commander in Chief, 1812–1836* (1961), is generally sympathetic to Madison's executive abilities, but Ralph Ketcham, *James Madison* (1971), and the relevant parts of Perkins's *Prologue to War* are better balanced. Of the various accounts of battles and campaigns, Alfred Thayer Mahan, *Sea Power in the War of 1812* (2 vols.; 1905), remains the best.

Peace negotiations and the Treaty of Ghent are examined in the works by Perkins and Burt, above, and in F. L. Engelman, *The Peace of Christmas Eve* (1962), and Samuel Flagg Bemis, *John Quincy Adams and the Foundations of American Foreign Policy* (1949). The social and cultural forces that led to the

Hartford Convention are imaginatively treated in James M. Banner, Jr., *To the Hartford Convention: The Federalists and the Origins of Party Politics in Massachusetts, 1789–1815* (1970).

CHAPTER 3. The best introduction to the opening of the West and American expansionism is Ray A. Billington, *Westward Expansion: A History of the American Frontier* (3rd ed.; 1974). Frederick Jackson Turner, *The Frontier in American History* (1930) and *The Rise of the New West, 1819–1829* (1906), offer what is probably the most challenging and enduring interpretation of the effect of the frontier on American institutions and politics that has yet been written. Turner's works, for all their originality, were somewhat dry reading. Daniel J. Boorstin, *The Americans: The National Experience* (1965), is lively and absorbing and offers its own special perspective on the influence of the frontier. A. K. Weinberg's *Manifest Destiny,* previously cited, is a sensitive and often ironic study of the expansionist drive, and Henry Nash Smith, *Virgin Land: The American West as Symbol and Myth* (1950; 1970), is a remarkable piece, drawn primarily from literary sources, that examines the magnetic appeal of the frontier. Leo Marx, *The Machine in the Garden: Technology and the Pastoral Ideal in America* (1964)—also a literary study—does not deal with the West directly, but its treatment of the American concept of the "garden" is simply excellent.

The diplomatic history of expansionism has been explored by several good works. The acquisition of Florida is traced by Philip C. Brooks, *Diplomacy and the Borderlands: The Adams–Onís Treaty* of 1819 (1939). United States relations with Latin America are covered by Arthur P. Whitaker, *The United States and the Independence of Latin America* (1941). Dexter Perkins, *The Monroe Doctrine* (3 vols.; 1927–37), is the standard work on that subject, and George Dangerfield provides an excellent survey in *The Era of Good Feelings* (1963). In *The Making of the Monroe Doctrine* (1975), Ernest R. May stressed the importance of the approaching Presidential election in the decision to issue a unilateral statement.

The study of the settlement of the West can begin with a history of two of its earliest explorers: Paul R. Cutright, *Lewis and Clark: Pioneering Naturalists* (1969). Boorstin's excellent chapters on settlement patterns are complemented by more specialized works, including Richard C. Wade, *The Urban Frontier: Pioneer Life in Early Pittsburgh, Cincinnati, Lexington, Louisville, and St. Louis* (1959), and Harry W. Scheiber, *The Old Northwest: Studies in Regional History, 1787–1910* (1969). Harlan Hatcher, *The Western Reserve: The Story of New Connecticut in Ohio* (1966), and Lois K. Mathews, *The Expansion of New England: The Spread of New England Settlements and Institutions to the Mississippi River* (1909), are two very good books that show the transplantation of traditions from East to West. John B. Boles, *The Great*

Revival: The Origins of the Southern Evangelical Mind (1972), deals with religion and revivalism but also captures the ambience of life on the Southern frontier.

There has been no good study of environmental decline during the early nineteenth century, but the American treatment of Indians has received careful examination. Bernard W. Sheehan, *Seeds of Extinction: Jeffersonian Philanthropy and the American Indian* (1973); Reginald Horsman, *Expansion and American Indian Policy, 1783–1812* (1967); and Francis P. Prucha, *American Indian Policy in the Formative Years* (1962), are all good studies, as are Wilcomb E. Washburn, *The Indian in America* (1975), and Ronald N. Satz, *American Indian Policy in the Jacksonian Era* (1975).

CHAPTER 4. W. Elliot Brownlee, *Dynamics of Ascent: A History of the American Economy* (1974), is the best general history of American economic growth. It provides both factual detail and a persuasive interpretive synthesis. The economic development of the young republic is ably examined in Curtis Nettels, *The Emergence of a National Economy, 1775–1815* (1962); Stuart Bruchey, *The Roots of American Economic Growth, 1607–1861: An Essay in Social Causation* (1965); and Douglass C. North, *The Economic Growth of the United States, 1790–1860* (1961), which emphasizes the role of international trade in stimulating economic development. Paul W. Gates, *The Farmer's Age, 1815–1860: An Economic History of the United States* (1960), is a comprehensive study of American agriculture during the period. Population growth is detailed in Ralph Brown's historical geography, previously cited, and in J. Potter, "The Growth of Population in America, 1700–1860," in *Population and History*, edited by D. V. Glass and D. E. C. Eversley (1965), and Richard A. Easterlin, *Population, Labor Force, and Long Swings in Economic Growth: The American Experience* (1968).

Various aspects of the relationship between government and economic development are explored in Joseph Dorfman, *The Economic Mind in American Civilization* (3 vols.; 1946–49); Louis Hartz, *Economic Policy and Democratic Thought: Pennsylvania, 1776–1860* (1948); and in a very good state study by Oscar and Mary Handlin, *Commonwealth: A Study of the Role of Government in the American Economy—Massachusetts, 1774–1861* (rev. ed.; 1969). Robert Kelley's *The Transatlantic Persuasion*, previously cited, contains an excellent chapter on Adam Smith and his influence, which is nicely paired with Kelley's discussion of Jefferson.

The relationship between law and economic development is brilliantly discussed by Morton J. Horwitz, *The Transformation of American Law, 1780–1860* (1977)—a book that should inspire more research into this important field. Horwitz's study is complemented by William E. Nelson, *The Americanization of the Common Law: The Impact of Legal Change on Mas-*

sachusetts Society, 1760–1830 (1975). The section on legal thought in Perry Miller, *The Life of the Mind in America from the Revolution to the Civil War* (1965), is—like most of Miller's work—detailed, perceptive, and challenging.

The standard work on transportation is George Rogers Taylor, *The Transportation Revolution, 1815–1860* (1951). It should be read in conjunction with Carter Goodrich, *Government Promotion of Canals and Railroads, 1800–1900* (1960), and Edward C. Kirkland, *Men, Cities, and Transportation: A Study in New England History, 1820–1900* (1948). Although the railroad boom began in the period following that covered in this volume, a good introduction to that subject is John Stover, *American Railroads* (1961). Robert G. Albion, *The Rise of New York Port* (1939), is a well-written, interesting study of the growth of the Atlantic and coastal trade. See also Harry Scheiber, *The Ohio Canal Era* (1969).

The growth of cities, industries, and immigration are closely entwined. In addition to the work by Richard C. Wade on Western cities, previously cited, see Sam Bass Warner, Jr., *The Urban Wilderness: A History of the American City* (1972), and two books by Constance McL. Green, *American Cities in the Growth of the Nation* (1957) and *The Rise of Urban America* (1965). Marcus L. Hansen, *The Atlantic Migration, 1607–1860* (1940), and Maldwyn A. Jones, *American Immigration* (1960), are two good surveys of the topic; Oscar Handlin, *The Uprooted* (1951) and *Boston's Immigrants* (1959), are outstanding. Two older works on the growth of factories are quite good: Caroline F. Ware, *The Early New England Cotton Manufacture: A Study in Industrial Beginnings* (1931), and Victor S. Clark, *History of Manufacturers in the United States, 1607–1860* (1929). Studies on the workers include Joseph G. Rayback, *A History of American Labor* (1959); Foster Rhea Dulles, *Labor in America* (3rd ed.; 1966); and John R. Commons's impressive *History of Labor in the United States* (4 vols.; 1918–35). Equally impressive is Philip S. Foner, *History of the Labor Movement in the United States* (3 vols.; 1947–64). See also Norman Ware, *The Industrial Worker, 1840–1860* (1924); Hannah Josephson, *The Golden Threads: New England's Mill Girls and Magnates* (1949); and William A. Sullivan, *The Industrial Worker in Pennsylvania, 1800–1840* (1955). Howard M. Gitelman, *Workingmen of Waltham* (1974), is a recent and very good study.

The tariff is the subject of two old and reliable books: Frank Taussig, *The Tariff History of the United States* (rev. ed.; 1931), and Edward Stanwood, *American Tariff Controversies of the Nineteenth Century* (1903). The Panic of 1819 is covered by Murray N. Rothbard, *The Panic of 1819* (1962), and by Walter B. Smith and Arthur M. Cole, *Fluctuations in American Business, 1790–1860* (1935). Marshall's decision in *McCulloch* v. *Maryland* is detailed in Beveridge's biography, cited above, and in Robert K. Faulkner, *The Juris-*

prudence of John Marshall (1966). Studies of the Second Bank of the United States are covered below.

CHAPTERS 5 AND 6. Political development between 1819 and 1820 should be studied as a unit; hence, the bibliographies for these two chapters are combined. Anyone who is attracted to this field runs the risk of becoming ensnared in almost forty years of infighting among historians concerning what to call it. Labels such as the "Age of Jackson," the "Age of Egalitarianism," the "Age of Innovation," etc., abound. The best way to avoid the trap is to begin with a few works that offer solid research and more modest interpretations. George Dangerfield's two studies, *The Era of Good Feelings* (1963) and *The Awakening of American Nationalism, 1815–1828* (1965), offer a balanced perspective up to the election of Andrew Jackson. Dangerfield wisely distinguishes between institutional and ideological expressions of nationalism and also provides a good synopsis of diplomatic events. Glyndon G. Van Deusen, *The Jacksonian Era, 1828–1848* (1959), does a comparable job for the later period, as does Charles G. Sellers, Jr., *Jacksonian Democracy* (1958). Douglas T. Miller, *The Birth of Modern America, 1820–1850* (1970), is a broad, brief work that does not go deeply into political development but does offer useful and exciting interpretations of the changing social order. Miller's book uses the concept of modernization as a theoretical tool, and it is he who calls the period the "Age of Innovation."

From this base, one can turn to the study of politics and political parties. Works that treat politics as a process of ideological, institutional, and social change (rather than as a clash of personalities) include Richard Hofstadter, *The Idea of a Party System: The Rise of Legitimate Opposition in the United States, 1740–1840* (1969), and Richard McCormick's very important study, *The Second American Party System: Party Formation in the Jacksonian Era* (1966). One of the most important and suggestive pieces on the changing political culture is Michael Wallace, "Changing Concepts of Party in the United States: New York, 1815–1829," *American Historical Review*, 74 (1968–69): 453–91. See also Ronald P. Formisano, "Deferential-Participant Politics: The Early Republic's Political Culture, 1789–1840," *American Political Science Review*, 68 (1974): 473–87. Another suggestive study that goes beyond its title is Bertram Wyatt-Brown, "Prelude to Abolitionism: Sabbatarian Politics and the Rise of the Second Party System," *Journal of American History*, 58 (1971): 316–41. Chilton Williamson, *American Suffrage from Property to Democracy, 1760–1860* (1960), describes the changing composition of the electorate, and James Sterling Young, *The Washington Community, 1800–1828* (1966), not only gives a superb analysis of institutional relations within the nation's capital but sheds new light on why congressmen were so fearful of concentrated power during the period.

Surprisingly little has been written on the decline of Federalism after 1815, or on the Administration of John Quincy Adams. Shaw Livermore, Jr., *The Twilight of Federalism: The Federalist Party, 1815–1830* (1962), is the standard work on the former subject, and Samuel Flagg Bemis, *John Quincy Adams and the Union* (1956), covers the latter. A forthcoming biography of Adams by Mary Wilma Hargreaves should greatly expand our knowledge of Adams's disastrous Presidency. The tangled election of 1824 is reviewed by James F. Hopkins, "Election of 1824," in Schlesinger and Israel's *History of American Presidential Elections*, previously cited.

The rise of Jackson and his party, on the other hand, have been exhaustively studied and debated. An excellent place to begin is Marquis James's thorough and gracefully written biography, *Andrew Jackson* (2 vol.; 1933–37), or the second volume of Robert V. Remini's more scholarly study, *Andrew Jackson and the Course of American Freedom, 1822–1832* (1981). Remini produced two other worthwhile studies that are essential: *The Election of Andrew Jackson* (1963) and *Martin Van Buren and the Democratic Party* (1959). It was Arthur M. Schlesinger, Jr.'s *The Age of Jackson* (1945), however, that sparked the post-World War II fascination with Jackson. Schlesinger's book is comprehensive, scholarly, and unabashedly pro-Jackson, whose rise he identifies with the growing political power of the "common man." Lee Benson, *The Concept of Jacksonian Democracy: New York as a Test Case* (1961), attempted to place the common man in better perspective using statistical methods. Benson found that the rise of egalitarian politics was not confined to the Democratic Party, and his book, while not completely successful in its use of statistics, generated other, better studies. Edward Pessen, *Riches, Class, and Power before the Civil War* (1973), for example, suggests that birth and wealth still counted in the political process no matter which party one joined.

Works that forego statistics to examine Jackson's ideological impact include Marvin Meyers, *The Jacksonian Persuasion: Politics and Beliefs* (1957), which suggests that the common man of the Jacksonian period was a "venturous conservative" caught up in, and enchanted by, rapid change, yet longing for the stability of the past. John William Ward, *Andrew Jackson: Symbol for an Age* (1962), explores the hero worship that grew around Jackson's military exploits, his identification with nature, his iron will, etc. Both these works are exemplary in their treatment of popular ideology. Less successful is Michael P. Rogin, *Fathers and Children: Andrew Jackson and the Subjugation of the American Indian* (1975), which is a strained and tenuous attempt to link Jackson's aggressions against the Indians with paternalism, liberalism, and capitalism.

As one moves away from the towering presence of Jackson, the complex and pluralistic nature of American politics begins to emerge. Ronald P.

Formisano, *The Birth of Mass Political Parties: Michigan, 1827–1861* (1971), is a superb state study that exposes the interplay of religious and ethnic subcultures in the formation of the second party system. William G. Shade, *Banks or No Banks: The Money Issue in Western Politics, 1832–1865* (1972), is even better—showing that early party formation was not a clash of haves and have-nots. Both Shade and James Roger Sharp, *The Jacksonians versus the Banks: Politics in the United States after the Panic of 1837* (1970), agree that the Bank issue assumed critical influence later, after the party outlines had basically formed. These works represent the best of the recent, statistically oriented studies of the period, as does Donald B. Cole's analysis of social and economic patterns in New Hampshire, *Jacksonian Democracy in New Hampshire, 1800–1851* (1970), which demonstrates deep cleavages in party preference within—and not simply between—classes. Douglas T. Miller, *Jacksonian Aristocracy: Class and Democracy in New York, 1830–1860* (1967), explores the increasing—not decreasing—social stratification in that city during the period.

As innovative as these works are, they do not specifically address the emergence of third parties—whose histories can be very useful in understanding the larger political process. Walter E. Hugins, *Jacksonian Democracy and the Working Class: The New York Workingmen's Movement, 1829–1837* (1960), is a first-rate local study, but no such examination, either national or local, exists for the Antimasonic Party. Ronald P. Formisano and Kathleen S. Kutolowski, "Antimasonry and Masonry: The Genesis of Protest, 1826–1827," *American Quarterly*, 29 (1977): 135–69, is a useful introduction, and Michael F. Holt, "The Antimasonic and Know-Nothing Parties," in Schlesinger's *History of United States Political Parties* (cited above), is a good short survey. David Brion Davis, "Some Themes of Counter-Subversion: An Analysis of Anti-Masonic, Anti-Catholic, and Anti-Mormon Literature," *Mississippi Valley Historical Review*, 47 (1960): 205–24, is a worthwhile article that links Antimasonry to other manifestations of the "paranoid style" in American politics.

There is unfortunately no comprehensive survey of the Whig Party, which must be studied piecemeal through the works of Formisano and others listed above and in several other works. Lynn L. Marshall, "The Strange Stillbirth of the Whig Party," *American Historical Review*, 72 (1967): 445–68, is an imaginative piece that suggests that the party was initially handicapped by its failure to come to grips with the new style of party organization and recruitment. Arthur C. Cole, *The Whig Party in the South* (1913), and Charles G. Sellers, Jr., "Who Were the Southern Whigs?," *American Historical Review*, 59 (1954): 335–46, examine the development of the party in the South. Biographies are also useful. George R. Poage, *Henry Clay and the Whig Party* (1936), is solid, if a little dated. Richard N. Current, *Daniel Webster and the Rise of*

National Conservatism (1955), and Sidney Nathans, *Daniel Webster and Jacksonian Democracy* (1973), offer more recent perspectives. The most interesting study on the Whigs is Daniel Walker Howe's well-crafted intellectual and cultural profile, *The Political Culture of the American Whigs* (1979).

The works by Schlesinger, Van Deusen, and Sellers cited above provide thorough, readable accounts of Jackson's Presidency. Charles M. Wiltse, *John C. Calhoun: Nullifier, 1829–1839* (1949), is indispensable. Leonard D. White continues his administrative history of the Presidency with *The Jacksonians: Administrative History, 1829–1861* (1954). Sidney H. Aronson, *Status and Kinship in the Higher Civil Service: Standards of Selection in the Administrations of John Adams, Thomas Jefferson, and Andrew Jackson* (1964), explores the patronage issue.

The Bank War has naturally received minute scrutiny from historians. The best general history is Robert V. Remini, *Andrew Jackson and the Bank War: A Study in the Growth of Presidential Power* (1967). Bray Hammond's excellent *Banks and Politics in America from the Revolution to the Civil War* (1957) is critical of the attack on the Bank. Hammond argues that Jacksonians were not hostile to banks in general but only to the Second Bank and its circle of supporters. Thomas P. Govan, *Nicholas Biddle: Nationalist and Public Banker, 1786–1844* (1959), is even more critical of Jackson's motives and policies. Jean A. Wilburn, *Biddle's Bank: The Crucial Years* (1967), finds widespread support among the public for the Bank, while John M. McFaul, *The Politics of Jacksonian Finance* (1972), suggests that the general trend among Jacksonians—especially in the Treasury Department—was toward some kind of central control of the money supply independent of private interests. This contradicts the notion that Jacksonians were *laissez-faire* ideologues. Peter Temin's excellent *The Jacksonian Economy* (1969) is somewhat easier on the President. The United States, Temin argues, would have entered a chaotic period of inflation and readjustment, no matter what Jackson did, because of pressures from the world market.

The man who attempted to untangle it all, Martin Van Buren, still awaits a modern biographer. The best study is James C. Curtis, *The Fox at Bay: Martin Van Buren and the Presidency, 1837–1841* (1970), which should be read alongside the studies by Sharp and Shade cited above.

CHAPTER 7.   The best place to begin studying the artistic and intellectual life of the new nation is in the works of the artists and writers themselves. Competition among museums for paintings by American masters has put worthwhile collections within the reach of most of us. Reprints of Irving, Cooper, Hawthorne, and others are easily available. Given this abundance of materials, the number of Americans who have never seen a painting by Thomas Cole or who have never read *The Scarlet Letter* is appalling.

There are several good works on intellectual history for the period. Perry Miller's *The Life of the Mind,* cited above, is part of a projected multi-volumed work that was sadly never completed because of the author's death. The book he did finish deals with religion, law, and science. The works by Parrington and Curti, also cited above, are broad, sweeping studies that touch almost every area of intellectual expression. Parrington is especially ambitious, although his economic determinism is overstated. Rush Welter, *The Mind of America, 1820–1860* (1975), is a useful survey of ideas, and Russel B. Nye, *The Cultural Life of the New Nation, 1776–1830* (1960), provides context.

Books on select topics offer perspectives that enhance our understanding of intellectual trends during the period. Ekirch's study of the idea of progress and Wyllie's and Cawelti's examinations of the self-made man, all cited above, are far-reaching and suggestive. So is Ekirch's *Man and Nature in America* (1963), which argues—among other things—that the American romance with nature was partly a means of easing the guilt over capitalistic expansion. Leo Marx, *The Machine in the Garden*, cited above, and John F. Kasson, *Civilizing the Machine: Technology and Republican Values in America, 1776–1900* (1976), are first-rate studies that deal with the American ambivalence toward technological change. Henry Nash Smith, *Virgin Land,* also cited above, remains the best single work on the role of the West in literature. Van Wyck Brooks, *The Flowering of New England, 1815–1865* (1936), is an ageless, beautifully written account of the intellectual milieu of that section, and Daniel Walker Howe's *The Unitarian Conscience: Harvard Moral Philosophy, 1805–1861* (1970) is, despite its ostensibly narrow focus, a stunningly well-conceived and provocative examination of the New England mind. William R. Taylor, *Cavalier and Yankee: The Old South and American National Character* (1957, 1961), uses both Northern and Southern writers and intellectuals to explore the romantic myth of the South and the "natural aristocrat." The book is outstanding. The isolation and frustration of the Southern intellectual is ably studied in Drew Gilpin Faust, *A Sacred Circle: The Dilemma of the Intellectual in the Old South, 1840–1860* (1977). On a far larger scale, the frustration of the intellectual has nowhere received better examination than in Richard Hofstadter, *Anti-Intellectualism in American Life* (1963).

The best survey of American art is Oliver W. Larkin, *Art and Life in America* (rev. ed.; 1960). Two books by James T. Flexner—*American Painting: The Light of Distant Skies, 1760–1835* (1954) and *That Wilder Image: The Painting of America's Native School from Thomas Cole to Winslow Homer* (1962)—provide a scholarly, insightful portrayal of the growth of the native school. Clive Bush, *The Dream of Reason: American Consciousness and Cultural Achievement from Independence to the Civil War* (1977), is an ambitious and sometimes erratic attempt to place the development of American art in the context of broader cultural changes. At times it is brilliant. Neil Harris,

The Artist in American Society, 1790–1860 (1966), is an acute interpretation of the profession of art. Good biographies include Charles C. Sellers, *Charles Willson Peale* (1947); Alice Ford, *Edward Hicks, Painter* (1952); and Charles M. Mount, *Gilbert Stuart* (1964).

The literature of the period has been studied so thoroughly and in so many ways that only a sampling of the good books available can be attempted here. Robert E. Spiller et al., *The Literary History of the United States* (2 vols., 3rd ed.; 1963), and Spiller, *The American Literary Revolution, 1783–1837* (1967), are excellent surveys. See also Joel Porte, *The Romance in America: Studies in Cooper, Poe, Hawthorne, Melville, and James* (1969), and R. W. B. Lewis, *The American Adam: Innocence, Tragedy, and Tradition in the Nineteenth Century* (1955). The best study of Cooper is Robert E. Spiller, *Fenimore Cooper* (1931), while the sections on Cooper in William R. Taylor and Henry Nash Smith are sensitive and concise. Washington Irving has been ably studied in Edward Wagenknecht, *Washington Irving* (1962), and Stanley T. Williams, *The Life of Washington Irving* (2 vols.; 1935). Nathaniel Hawthorne has been the subject of several good works; among the best are Mark Van Doren, *Nathaniel Hawthorne* (1949); Lawrence Sargeant Hall, *Hawthorne: Critic of Society* (1941); and Edward Wagenknecht, *Nathaniel Hawthorne* (1961). Both Hawthorne and Emerson receive outstanding examination in F. O. Matthiessen, *American Renaissance* (1941)—a book that also includes chapters on Whitman, Thoreau, and Melville. The two best studies on Emerson are Ralph L. Lusk, *The Life of Ralph Waldo Emerson* (1949), and Stephen Whicher, *Freedom and Fate: An Inner Life of Ralph Waldo Emerson* (1953).

European visitors to the United States left a large body of published observations, many of which worked their way into American thought as classics. The undisputed best is Alexis de Tocqueville's *Democracy in America* (2 vols. 1835). The best recent edition of this work was published in 1969, with George Lawrence as translator and J. P. Mayer as editor. Other editions, some abridged, are available. Frances Wright, *Views of Society and Manners in America* (1821; new edition by Paul R. Baker, 1963), is generally sympathetic to Americans, as is Harriet Martineau, *Society in America* (3 vols.; 1837; abridged edition by S. M. Lipset, 1962). Often overlooked is Alexander McKay, *The Western World: Or, Travels in the United States, 1846–1847* (2 vols.; 1849), which contains the observations of a shrewd, acute Scottish journalist. Many observers lacked McKay's or Tocqueville's balance and wrote devastatingly harsh indictments of American manners and taste. The most caustic are Frances Trollope, *Domestic Manners of the Americans* (2 vols.; 1832, 1960), and Frederick Marryat, *A Diary in America, with Remarks on Its Institutions* (6 vols.; 1839). Charles Dickens, *American Notes* (1842), is as critical of Americans as his novels are of the English. Francis J. Grund's *Aristocracy in America* (2 vols.; 1839) is a sprightly, occasionally hilarious, reply to Tocqueville written by a man who decided to remain here.

The growth of American journalism is covered in Frank L. Mott, *American Journalism: A History, 1690–1860* (3rd ed.; 1962), which should be supplemented by Oliver Carson, *The Man Who Made the News: The Life of James Gordon Bennett* (1942). Horace Greeley's *Recollections of a Busy Life* (1868) contains the reminiscences of a man who was journalist, politician, reformer, and gadfly.

CHAPTER 8. For decades Alice Felt Tyler, *Freedom's Ferment: Phases of American Social History to 1860* (1944), has stood as the best, most sweeping general history of antebellum reform. In many respects it still is, but the publication of Ronald Walters's *American Reformers, 1815–1860* (1978) has at last made available a modern survey by an author of impressive analytical and stylistic skills. Walters's book is both sympathetic and objective, and offers also a fine bibliographic survey. John L. Thomas, "Romantic Reform in America, 1815–1865," *American Quarterly*, 17 (1965): 656–81, is an excellent interpretive essay.

The first section of Perry Miller's *Life of the Mind*, cited above, is a masterful analysis of the evangelical mind that stresses the revivalists' desire to preserve social order. Timothy L. Smith, *Revivalism and Social Reform: American Protestantism on the Eve of the Civil War* (1957), is a good overview. Books that examine various aspects of social change and the emergence of revivalism are John B. Boles, *The Great Revival, 1787–1805: The Origins of the Southern Evangelical Mind* (1972); Whitney R. Cross, *The Burned-Over District: The Social and Intellectual History of Enthusiastic Religion in Western New York, 1800–1850* (1950); Charles A. Johnson, *The Frontier Camp Meeting* (1955); and Paul E. Johnson, *A Shopkeeper's Millennium: Society and Revivals in Rochester, New York, 1815–1837* (1978). Other useful studies include William W. Sweet, *Religion in the Development of American Culture, 1765–1840* (1952); Edwin S. Gaustad, *The Rise of Adventism: Religion and Society in Mid-Nineteenth Century America* (1974); and Clifford S. Griffin, *Their Brothers' Keepers: Moral Stewardship in the United States, 1800–1865* (1960).

Griffin's book is one of several that suggest the motives of the religious reformers were largely occasioned by their desire to arrest their declining status and reassert their authority in the expanding republic. Others that pursue the same theme include John R. Bodo, *The Protestant Clergy and Public Issues, 1812–1848* (1954); Charles C. Cole, Jr., *The Social Ideas of the Northern Evangelists, 1820–1860* (1954); and Charles I. Foster, *An Errand of Mercy: The Evangelical United Front, 1790–1837* (1960). Lois W. Banner takes issue with this interpretation in a lively and persuasive article, "Religious Benevolence as Social Control: A Critique of an Interpretation," *Journal of American History*, 60 (1973): 23–41, which notes that millennialism, institutional needs of particular denominations, and the ideology of republicanism also played important roles. See also Ernest L. Tuveson, *Redeemer Nation: The Idea of America's Millennial Role* (1968), and Sidney E. Mead, *The Lively Experiment: The Shaping of Christianity in America* (1963). Gregory H. Singleton, "Protestant Voluntary Organizations and the Shaping of Victorian America," *American Quarterly,* 27 (1975): 549–60, explains motivation in much the same way as Griffin and others. Singleton's main concern, however, is to show how the benevolent societies presaged the institutional and bureaucratic development of later, corporate structures.

The development of the prison system has received superb examination in David Rothman, *The Discovery of the Asylum: Social Order and Disorder in the New Republic* (1971), which also deals with the growth of mental institutions. See also Blake McKelvey, *American Prisons: A History of Good Intentions* (1977); W. David Lewis, *From Newgate to Dannemora: The Rise of the Penitentiary in New York* (1965); and Gerald N. Grob, *Mental Institutions in America: Social Policy to 1875* (1973). There is unfortunately no biography available of Louis Dwight, but Samuel Gridley Howe—who was a leader in prison reform as well as in his more notable role in education for the blind —is ably portrayed in Harold Schwartz, *Samuel Gridley Howe, Social Reformer* (1956).

There are several good histories of educational reform. One of the best is Michael Katz, *The Irony of Early School Reform: Education and Innovation in Mid-Nineteenth Century Massachusetts* (1968), which—as its title suggests —indicates that the motives behind educational reform were varied and not always altruistic. Also critical are Carl F. Kaestle, *The Evolution of an Urban School System: New York City, 1750–1850* (1973), and Stanley K. Schultz, *The Culture Factory: Boston Public Schools, 1789–1860* (1973). Ruth Miller Elson, *Guardians of Tradition: American Schoolbooks of the Nineteenth Century* (1964), shows how moral values and "traditional" standards were served up alongside grammar and math. Timothy L. Smith, "Protestant Schooling and American Nationality, 1800–1850," *Journal of American History,* 53 (1967): 679–95, argues that the involvement of church and lay leaders in educational reform helped break down denominational rivalries and encouraged the creation of a "Protestant consensus." Jonathan Messerli's *Horace Mann* (1972) is the best biography of that famed educator.

Frederick Rudolph, *The American College and University* (1962), is a good survey of higher education. Useful studies on select topics include Howard Miller, *The Revolutionary College: American Presbyterian Higher Education, 1707–1837* (1976); Burton O. Bledstein, *The Culture of Professionalism: The Middle Class and the Development of Higher Education in America* (1977); and a first-rate article by Ronald Story, "Harvard and the Boston Brahmins: A Study in Institutional and Class Development, 1800–1865," *Journal of Social History,* 8 (1975): 94–121. The essays in Alexandra Olson and Sanborn C. Brown, eds., *The Pursuit of Knowledge in the Early American Republic:*

American Scientific and Learned Societies from Colonial Times to the Civil War (1976), provide a good survey of the attempt to make scientific education available to the common man.

Communitarian and utopian experiments have received closer examination in recent years. Useful works are Michael Fellman, *The Unbounded Frame: Freedom and Community in Nineteenth-Century American Utopianism* (1973), and Mark Holloway, *Heavens on Earth: Utopian Communities in America, 1660–1880* (1951). The Oneida experience has been ably described in Maren L. Carden, *Oneida: Utopian Community to Modern Corporation* (1969). Robert Owen and the New Harmony community are examined in Arthur Bestor, Jr., *Backwoods Utopias: Sectarian and Owenite Phases of Communitarian Socialism in America, 1663–1829* (1950), and J. F. C. Harrison, *The Quest for the New Moral World: Robert Owen and the Owenites in Britain and America* (1969).

Tyler's *Freedom's Ferment* contains a brief, lively account of the rise of Mormonism, and Cross's *Burned-Over District* provides the social and cultural background in which Joseph Smith was raised. Fuller studies include Thomas F. O'Dea, *The Mormons* (1957); Fawn M. Brodie, *No Man Knows My History: The Life of Joseph Smith* (1945); and Robert B. Flanders, *Nauvoo: Kingdom on the Mississippi* (1965).

CHAPTER 9.   The South has received such close scrutiny by historians that one might conclude that little is left to discover. Each year, however, brings new books and articles, and innovations in methodology—especially that using statistical sources—generate new debates and fresh perspectives. Francis B. Simkins and Charles P. Roland, *A History of the South* (4th ed.; 1975), is a fine general history, as are the period studies by Thomas P. Abernethy, *The South in the New Nation, 1789–1819* (1961), and Charles S. Sydnor, *The Development of Southern Sectionalism, 1819–1848* (1948). Also good is Clement Eaton, *The Growth of Southern Civilization, 1790–1860* (1961).

Life in the South has received no better description than in Frederick Law Olmsted, *The Cotton Kingdom: A Traveller's Observations* (1861; new edition edited by Arthur M. Schlesinger, Jr., 1953). Frances Butler Kemble's *Journal of a Residence on a Georgia Plantation in 1838 and 1839* (1863) contains the sensitive and critical observations of an English actress, while Joseph G. Baldwin, *The Flush Times of Alabama and Mississippi: A Series of Sketches* (1853), provides humor. The nonslaveholding, poor white is studied in Frank L. Owsley, *Plain Folk of the Old South* (1949), and in Roger W. Shugg, *Origins of the Class Struggle in Louisiana: A Social History of White Farmers and Laborers during Slavery and After, 1840–1875* (1939). The free black in the South is examined in Ira Berlin, *Slaves without Masters: The Free Negro in the Antebellum South* (1975).

The plantation system and slave culture have naturally attracted deep interest. Ulrich B. Phillips's *American Negro Slavery* (1918) was the first really good attempt at exploring the subject and stood as the standard work for almost forty years. Kenneth M. Stampp, *The Peculiar Institution: Slavery in the Ante-Bellum South* (1956), corrected many of Phillips's biases—especially concerning the treatment of slaves, which was not as humane as Phillips had argued. Stampp's work is still the best general study of slavery available. Less successful is Robert W. Fogel and Stanley L. Engerman, *Time on the Cross: The Economics of American Negro Slavery* (1974), and its companion volume, *Time on the Cross: Evidence and Methods, A Supplement* (1974). Fogel and Engerman's assertion that slavery was profitable and that the slave himself received generally adequate care prompted responses, notably Herbert G. Gutman, *Slavery and the Numbers Game* (1975). The most outstanding recent book on slavery, however, is Eugene D. Genovese, *Roll Jordan, Roll: The World the Slaves Made* (1974)—a stunningly good study by a Marxist historian that explores the paternalistic nature of slavery and the means, chief among them religion, that slaves used to manipulate it. Genovese's other works include *The World the Slaveholders Made: Two Essays in Interpretation* (1969) and *The Political Economy of Slavery: Studies in the Economy and Society of the Slave South* (1965). Other good books on slavery are John W. Blassingame, *The Slave Community: Plantation Life in the Ante-Bellum South* (1972), and William K. Scarborough, *The Overseer: Plantation Management in the Old South* (1966). See also Robert S. Starobin, *Industrial Slavery in the Old South* (1970), and Richard C. Wade, *Slavery in the Cities: The South, 1820–1860* (1964), for analyses of slavery outside the plantation. Stanley M. Elkins, *Slavery: A Problem in American Institutional and Intellectual Life* (2nd ed.; 1968), contains a controversial section on the psychological effects of slavery upon the black. All these works should be accompanied by John Hope Franklin's *From Slavery to Freedom: A History of Negro Americans* (3rd ed.; 1967), a monumental study of the black experience in America.

How Southerners rationalized the existence of slavery in the republic has also attracted extensive and capable study. The pioneering work is William S. Jenkins, *Pro-Slavery Thought in the Old South* (1935), followed by Clement Eaton, *Freedom of Thought Struggle in the Old South* (rev. ed.; 1964). Wilbur J. Cash, *The Mind of the Old South* (1941), is a fascinating study, beautifully written, that probes the ironies of the Southern mind. Taylor's *Cavalier and Yankee*, cited above, is also superb. Harvey Wish, *George Fitzhugh* (1943), is an illuminating account of an eccentric genius, and the selection of Southerners' writings in Eric L. McKitrick, ed., *Slavery Defended: The Views of the Old South* (1963), provides a good sampling of the various approaches to proslavery thought. Three excellent works on white attitudes toward blacks are Winthrop D. Jordan, *White over Black: American Attitudes toward the Negro, 1550–1812* (1968); George M. Fredrickson, *The Black Image in the*

White Mind: The Debate over Afro-American Character and Destiny, 1817–1914 (1971); and William R. Stanton, *The Leopard's Spots: Scientific Attitudes toward Race in America, 1815–1859* (1960).

Genovese presents an interesting perspective on slave resistance in *Roll, Jordan, Roll,* but the most complete study of slave revolts is Herbert Aptheker, *American Negro Slave Revolts* (1943). John Lofton covers the Vesey affair with skill in *Insurrection in South Carolina: The Turbulent World of Denmark Vesey* (1964). Nat Turner's rebellion, discussed in chapter 10, is detailed in Aptheker, *Nat Turner's Slave Rebellion* (1966).

Donald Robinson, *Slavery in the Structure of American Politics, 1765–1820* (1971), chronicles the political problem of slavery up to the Missouri Compromise, and Glover Moore, *The Missouri Controversy* (1953), is the fullest history of that conflict.

CHAPTER 10. The nullification controversy is examined in Charles S. Sydnor's *Development of Southern Sectionalism* and in Charles M. Wiltse's *John C. Calhoun: Nullifier*—both cited above. The most complete and interesting analysis is William W. Freehling, *Prelude to Civil War: The Nullification Controversy in South Carolina, 1816–1836* (1965), a fine study that contains a penetrating examination of the social and economic forces that encouraged unrest and the intellectual rationale. Richard Hofstadter's chapter on Calhoun in *The American Political Tradition,* previously cited, offers an unorthodox, and provocative, view of Calhoun.

Northern attitudes toward the blacks are included in the works by Jordan, Fredrickson, and Stanton cited in chapter 9. Although Eugene Berwanger, *The Frontier against Slavery: Western Anti-Negro Prejudice and the Slavery Extension Controversy* (1967), is a largely political study of the sectional controversy after 1845, the book contains many illuminating insights concerning race prejudice in the Western free states. Leon Litwack, *North of Slavery: The Negro in the Free States, 1790–1860* (1961), is the best study of the plight of Northern blacks.

The literature on abolitionism is a rich and controversial field. The best place to begin is James B. Stewart, *Holy Warriors: The Abolitionists and American Slavery* (1976)—a concise, modern study with a first-rate bibliography. Stewart's book along with Walters's *American Reformers* introduce the reader to issues of motivation, tactics, and personality in the antislavery movement. Other good general works include Gilbert H. Barnes, *The Antislavery Impulse, 1830–1844* (1933); Louis Filler, *The Crusade against Slavery, 1830–1860* (1960); and Merton Dillon, *The Abolitionists: The Growth of a Dissenting Minority* (1973), a somewhat polemical book that dwells on the abolitionists' failure to change white racial prejudice.

The background to the antislavery movement is brilliantly examined in two books by David Brion Davis, *The Problem of Slavery in Western Culture* (1966) and *The Problem of Slavery in the Age of Revolution, 1770–1823* (1975). These works address the question of why—after centuries of unchallenged existence—slavery became a "problem" in Western society. Alice B. Adams, *The Neglected Period of American Antislavery, 1808–1831* (1908), is an old and unsatisfying chronicle of a period that deserves more attention. P. J. Staudenraus, *The African Colonization Movement* (1961), is the best account of the fruitless attempt to settle the slavery issue through deportation.

The sudden appearance of radical abolitionism around 1830 has provoked much debate. Barnes's volume stresses the influence of Theodore Dwight Weld, while Filler's book emphasizes Garrison. Again, Stewart's volume is the most balanced. Ronald Walters, *The Antislavery Appeal: American Abolitionism after 1830* (1976), is an incisive analysis, topically structured, that explores the relationship between cultural conditions and ideological development. So does Lewis Perry's excellent *Radical Abolitionism: Anarchy and the Government of God in Antislavery Thought* (1973). David Brion Davis, "The Emergence of Immediatism in British and American Antislavery Thought," *Mississippi Valley Historical Review,* 49 (1962): 209–30, is a suggestive comparative study. Staughton Lynd, *Intellectual Origins of American Radicalism* (1969), explores the background of nonviolent resistance to unjust laws, with very good chapters on the Revolutionary heritage and the concept of "world citizenship." The tensions that immediatism sparked within the abolitionist movement have been thoughtfully examined in Aileen S. Kraditor, *Means and Ends in American Abolitionism: Garrison and His Critics on Strategy and Tactics, 1834–1850* (1969).

Psychohistory has assumed increasing importance in recent years. When applied to the abolitionists, the results have been controversial. David Herbert Donald's "Toward a Reconsideration of Abolitionists"—a chapter in *Lincoln Reconsidered: Essays on the Civil War Era* (1956)—helped spark the debate by suggesting that abolitionists used reform to offset their own declining status in antebellum society. Certain essays in Martin Duberman, ed., *The Antislavery Vanguard: New Essays on the Abolitionists* (1965), are generally so preoccupied with demonstrating the obvious nobility of the antislavery cause —and linking it to the modern civil-rights struggle—that the reader may become suspicious. This is too bad, for the articles by David Brion Davis, Donald G. Mathews, Benjamin Quarles, and Leon Litwack in the volume are quite good. Bertram Wyatt-Brown does an excellent job of studying the roots of alienation among reformers in "Prelude to Abolitionism: Sabbatarian Politics and the Rise of the Second Party System," *Journal of American History,* 58 (1971): 316–41. Leonard Richards, *"Gentlemen of Property and Standing": Anti-Abolition Mobs in Jacksonian America* (1970), uses statistical methods to argue that Donald looked for status anxieties among the wrong group. Those who were really threatened, Richards concludes, were elite classes that led or participated in violent actions against abolition. Although justly criticized for its analysis of the slave personality, Stanley Elkins's *Slavery: A Problem in American Institutional and Intellectual Life* (2nd ed.; 1968) contains a very interesting section on the role of guilt in the shaping of the abolitionist crusade.

Russel B. Nye, *Fettered Freedom: Civil Liberties and the Slavery Controversy, 1830–1860* (1949), is a very good study of the abolitionists' involvement in politics, including the problems raised by the petition campaign and the gag rule. Robert M. Cover, *Justice Accused: Antislavery and the Judicial Process* (1975), is highly critical of the courts' resistance to all efforts to question the legitimacy of the slave system. Richard H. Sewell, *Ballots for Freedom: Antislavery Politics in the United States, 1837–1861* (1976), is the best, most comprehensive account of political antislavery, with superb chapters on the Liberty Party and its successor, the Free Soil Party.

Black abolitionism has not received the attention it deserves. The best survey is Jane H. and William H. Pease, *They Who Would Be Free: Blacks' Search for Freedom, 1831–1861* (1974), closely followed by Benjamin Quarles, *Black Abolitionists* (1969). See also Quarles's outstanding *Frederick Douglass* (1948).

Abolitionists have attracted a number of capable biographers. William Lloyd Garrison is the subject of two very good recent works: John L. Thomas, *The Liberator, William Lloyd Garrison: A Biography* (1963), and Walter M. Merrill, *Against Wind and Tide: The Life of William Lloyd Garrison* (1963). Benjamin P. Thomas, *Theodore Weld, Crusader for Freedom* (1950), is the only complete study of Weld, although much useful information is presented in Katherine Lumpkin, *The Emancipation of Angelina Grimké* (1974)—a biography of Weld's gifted wife. A better account of the Grimké sisters is Gerda Lerner, *The Grimké Sisters from South Carolina: Rebels against Slavery* (1967). Bertram Wyatt-Brown, *Lewis Tappan and the Evangelical War against Slavery* (1969), is an illuminating and sensitive study of an influential, rich, and complex abolitionist leader. Gerrit Smith, who was equally complex and even richer, has not received modern treatment. Ralph V. Harlow, *Gerrit Smith, Philanthropist and Reformer* (1939), is a comprehensive but dated study. Betty Fladeland's *James Gillespie Birney: Slaveholder to Abolitionist* (1955) is the only recent study—and a very good one—of the man who was twice the Presidential candidate of the Liberty Party. An excellent collective profile is Jane H. and William H. Pease, *Bound with Them in Chains: A Biographical History of the Antislavery Movement* (1972).

CHAPTER 11.   Ray A. Billington, *Westward Expansion,* cited above, contains a good short account of the annexation of Texas. William C. Binkley, *The*

Expansionist Movement in Texas, 1836–1850 (1925) and *The Texas Revolution* (1952), are more comprehensive. The inner workings of the Texas Republic are covered in Stanley Siegel, *A Political History of the Texas Republic* (1956). See also Marquis James's *The Raven: A Biography of Sam Houston* (1929), which remains the best—and certainly most readable—chronicle of Houston's busy life. Martin Van Buren's attempts to postpone the Texas issue are sensitively analyzed in James C. Curtis, *The Fox at Bay,* cited above.

R. G. Gunderson, *The Log-Cabin Campaign* (1957), is an excellent account of the election of 1840, but to understand what really produced that curious contest one should read Richard McCormick's *Second American Party System,* previously cited. Tyler's ill-fated Administration is the subject of Oliver P. Chitwood, *John Tyler* (1939), and Robert J. Morgan, *A Whig Embattled: The Presidency under John Tyler* (1954). The best biography of Tyler is Robert Seager II, *And Tyler Too* (1963). Tyler's relationship with Calhoun—and vice versa—is ably analyzed in Charles M. Wiltse, *John C. Calhoun: Sectionalist, 1840–1850* (1951). These works collectively present a thorough perspective of political and diplomatic maneuverings in Washington during the Tyler years.

Westward expansion was the primary issue confronting the nation and the President. The ideological impulses receive incisive—albeit somewhat cynical —analysis in Weinberg's *Manifest Destiny.* Frederick Merk has produced several works that correct some of Weinberg's biases yet still offer a critical evaluation of expansionist motives—particularly Tyler's. *Manifest Destiny and Mission in American History* (with Lois B. Merk, 1963) is not as sweeping as its title implies; nonetheless, it is an important book that contributes greatly to our understanding of the concept of "mission" in American expansionism. In *The Monroe Doctrine and American Expansionism, 1843–1849* (1966), *Fruits of Propaganda in the Tyler Administration* (1971), and *Slavery and the Annexation of Texas* (1972), Merk exposes the skillful—but sometimes erratic —use expansionists made of anti-British and antiblack prejudice in cultivating support for the acquisition of Oregon and Texas. The importance of Oregon and the territories along the Pacific Coast is stressed in Norman Graebner's excellent *Empire on the Pacific: A Study in American Continental Expansion* (1955). Major L. Wilson, *Space, Time, and Freedom,* cited earlier, is an outstanding study that deals with some of the more intangible—if no less real—desires in the American mind.

The sectional tensions occasioned by expansionism inevitably lead the serious reader to consider the Mexican War and the coming of the Civil War —topics that are covered in the companion volume in this series by Roy F. Nichols and Eugene Berwanger. Several good books provide background for the period before 1846. Richard H. Sewell, *Ballots for Freedom,* previously mentioned, is the best general account of the development of political antislavery, while the first three chapters of John Mayfield, *Rehearsal for Republi-*

canism: Free Soil and the Politics of Antislavery (1980), outline the ideological and political hostilities annexation sparked in the North. Kinley J. Brauer, *Cotton versus Conscience: Massachusetts Whig Politics and Southwestern Expansion, 1843–1848* (1967) is a first-rate state study, which can be supplemented by the first chapters in Robert F. Dalzell, Jr., *Daniel Webster and the Trial of American Nationalism, 1843–1852* (1973). Charles G. Sellers, Jr., *James K. Polk: Continentalist, 1843–1846* (1966), is both superb biography and a sensitive discussion of the aspirations and dilemmas confronting Polk. Polk's successes only hastened the impending crisis by reinforcing the grim specter of a "slave power" conspiracy directed against the North. To begin to understand this all-important concept, one must examine David Brion Davis's brilliant *The Slave Power Conspiracy and the Paranoid Style* (1969).

Index